ATTRACTING, EDUCATING, AND SERVING REMOTE USERS THROUGH THE WEB

D0470479

A How-To-Do-It Manual for Librarians

Edited by
Donnelyn Curtis

*HOW-TO-DO-IT MANUALS
FOR LIBRARIANS*

NUMBER 114

NEAL-SCHUMAN PUBLISHERS, INC.
New York, London

Published by Neal-Schuman Publishers, Inc.
100 Varick Street
New York, NY 10013

Don't miss the companion Web site that accompanies this book at:
www.library.unr.edu/subject/guides/remoteusers.html

CONTENTS

LIST OF FIGURES

PREFACE

Remote library users aren't new. For decades, academic libraries have supported correspondence courses through various means, and remote users frequented bookmobiles, received books by mail, phoned and mailed their reference questions, and used interlibrary loan. But until very recently, remote users have not been numerous. Now, librarians are experiencing a time of great change in this area. The proportion of onsite to remote library users is shifting dramatically. The Web is rapidly changing educational institutions and information-seeking behavior, providing opportunities as well as challenges for libraries. Nevertheless, most libraries still treat remote users as peripheral users. They give preferential service to their walk-in users. Libraries are still organizationally structured to support onsite users of onsite materials, managing electronic resources and remote users with add-on processes and services.

Attracting, Educating, and Serving Remote Users through the Web: A How-To-Do-It Manual for Librarians is designed to help libraries effectively help these users. Librarians often realize that remote users pose special challenges. Because librarians don't regularly see remote users, we usually don't know them very well. Sometimes we are not sure just how many of them exist. If we talk to people in our communities or our universities outside the library, we find that many of them do not know that their library offers superior and otherwise expensive electronic resources. It is not intuitive to information seekers that the library Web space is "special" and that they will have to go through an authentication process to use the proprietary resources listed there.

NEW EXPECTATIONS, NEW CHALLENGES

A new group of information seekers clearly populates the world. The Web may be a big, messy place, but simple-to-use search engines give the appearance of covering it all. On the Web, people seldom have a problem finding acceptable information of some kind. The expectations of these information seekers are much different than the expectations of library users in the very recent past.

Now, especially, people want their information quest to be both convenient and easy. In the recent past, coming to the library to track down information using print indexes and the card catalog and then electronic databases and the online catalog was not easy, but users came to expect some complexity, and there were always librarians to help. It is easy to be seduced by the Web into leaving all that behind, even if it means trading quality for ease. Information seekers of today do not always know how to differentiate between high– and low–quality electronic resources, and they often do not know about library-provided information on the Web. But even when they do, many users will not accept any difficulty in using these resources. The same person who might have used a magnifying glass to use the arcane print version of *Science Citation Index* might not have the patience to have to learn how to use the Web version.

User expectations have recently changed in other ways, too. Waiting three weeks for a book to arrive through interlibrary loan is much less acceptable now that so many retailers take advantage of rapid-delivery options. Someone who can order a book through Amazon.com and have it delivered within two or three days will not accept a library's "rush order" process that takes six weeks. Local users may continue to visit the library just as they will continue to patronize a local bookstore, but for different reasons than they visited in the past. Many of them will expect the same kind of conveniences from their Web-accessible library that are afforded them by Web-accessible businesses.

Attracting, Educating, and Serving Remote Users through the Web is designed to help libraries meet the urgent challenges posed by the expectations of today's information seekers. User demands usually drive the development of the library's electronic presence. But in our rush to stay relevant to the remote users who make up an ever-increasing proportion of our patrons, libraries for the most part have not taken a systematic or innovative approach to the demands of the new information environment. We have not thought enough about the fundamental changes we must make to provide good service to remote users. How do we attract them? How do we communicate with them? How can we try to keep up with the new demands at the same time we are doing the library work we have always done, sometimes with diminishing resources?

RE-THINKING PRIORITIES

Many librarians rightfully complain of feeling frazzled, frustrated, burned out, and inadequate. Librarians frequently say that their plates are already too full, that if they are to accept any more responsibilities, something must be removed. There seems to be little evidence of any significant plate clearing. Outsourcing has made some room in some cases and in other cases certain tasks or duties have fallen off plates and nobody has noticed. In this environment many librarians have been able to make only minimal efforts to serve their remote users.

The authors of *Attracting, Educating, and Serving Remote Users through the Web* work together in the University of Nevada, Reno, Libraries. Ours is a medium-sized academic library system, and we share many of the concerns of most libraries these days. We have been fortunate to have a prudently managed materials budget that has allowed us to invest heavily in electronic resources, but unfortunate in our level of staffing. (Is there a library anywhere that considers itself well staffed for the electronic age?) Faculty in our university are actively developing Web-based courses, not just for distance education. Our library dean is a strong leader in the development of a campus information infrastructure.

We still select, acquire, and catalog books, journals, and AV materials, staff service points, conduct orientations, and attend meetings, but now we also create and maintain Web pages, negotiate license agreements, and select and acquire and catalog electronic books and journals. We provide electronic reserves and a reference chat room, deliver materials to faculty offices, and authenticate users and help solve their access problems and answer dozens of e-mail messages a day. It is not surprising that like most librarians, we have not spent enough time on outreach activities to get to know our remote users or to publicize electronic services and attract more remote users, despite the fact that we are spending over a million dollars per year on electronic resources. Things are changing. Our numbers are getting smaller for most of what we have traditionally measured. Our gate count is going up, but we know that is because the main library is a social hangout and it has a large computer lab. The decreasing numbers include reference and interlibrary loan transactions, circulation, and in-house use of periodicals. Other numbers are getting proportionately larger: hits on our Web pages, usage of our electronic journals, books, databases and reserves, and calls to the help desk. We have come to realize only very recently that our remote users are becoming our primary users. We have known that we needed to change our priorities, and that we couldn't expect ourselves to be able to "do it all." Still, we knew that we needed and wanted to do a better job of connecting with the Web-based information seekers in our university community and designing satisfactory services for them. If we did not make a shift, we would become increasingly marginalized as they bypass us for commercial services or settle for low quality sources that they can find easily on the Web.

FACING THE FUTURE

At the University of Nevada, Reno, library faculty and staff have been collectively engaged in a major rethinking process. Ironically, it is not a typical strategic planning process that has inspired us to think about our remote users (though since we started writing *Attracting, Educating, and Serving Remote Users through the Web*, our university has begun a major planning process, and remote services figure prominently in our part of it). Our initial impetus to think about remote users was a planning process for a new library *building* to be completed in five years. As we determine the scope of the user services and staff processes we will need to accommodate in our new library, it is challenging to keep in mind that most of our future users, like many of our current users, will prefer to use their own computers, in their own homes and offices, to gather and process information. The library building must be designed primarily for those activities not conducive to the Web environment: a face-to-face meeting place, a cultural center, a place to collaborate on the development of educational technology, and a place to use the resources that must stay in the library (as well as providing computers for those who need them). Our new library will be our high-touch complement for high-tech services, most of which will be designed for use primarily outside the building. As the library is being built to satisfy certain campus needs, our library staff resources increasingly will be devoted to the satisfaction of the needs of our remote users—to the development of new services that will not be waiting for the new building. *Attracting, Educating, and Serving Remote Users through the Web: A How-To-Do-It Manual for Librarians* is an outcome of the future-oriented thinking that has been taking place in our library. We know how hard it is for librarians to take the time from day-to-day demands in order to read, think, and plan for the future. We haven't had a choice. To plan a library that won't be finished for at least five years requires thinking in fundamental terms about the library's role in a very different future. We know that we can't actually predict the future of information technology, but there are some very strong indicators that can't be overlooked. The library as we have known it is rapidly becoming obsolete, and if we can't start turning it around NOW, we will see its painful contraction.

ORGANIZATION OF THE BOOK

Rick Anderson sums up our collective out-of-the-box thinking in terms of our very function and operation in Chapter 1, "Reaching Out—the Library's New Role." A by-product of that thinking has been the application of our shared vision of the future to the services we provide today. To get from there to here it has helped us to write the chapters of *Attracting, Educating, and Serving Remote Users through the Web*. There are many ways to define a "cutting edge" library, and we like to think our library has met one key requirement. During the last few years we have been consistent and successful in breaking from tradition to use technology for innovative, user-oriented purposes. Designing user-centered services can be difficult when users are not physically present. In Chapter 2, "Getting to Know Remote Users," Donnelyn Curtis provides current demographic information, introduces relevant research on the behavior of Web users, and advises librarians on methods for knowing their own remote users. Another major challenge is to get these users to the library's Web gateway and make them comfortable and successful there. Chapter 3, "Presenting the Virtual Library," by Donnelyn Curtis and Araby Greene, offers principles of Web design for the presentation and integration of information resources, and guidelines for serving diverse users through one site. The next four chapters guide readers through the transformation of traditional library services—reference, document delivery, and library instruction—to serve the needs of remote users. In Chapter 4, "Providing Electronic Reference Services," Araby Greene walks us through helping and communicating, directly and indirectly, with our unseen users. Chapter 5, "Maximizing Current Awareness and Document Delivery Services," by Margret Ressel and Millie Syring, is a look at the tools and practices libraries can use to help remote researchers keep up with publication in their disciplines. "Providing Library Instruction for Remote Users," Chapter 6, by Amy Shannon and Terry Henner, is a guide to teaching how to use electronic resources outside the library, through the Web and on the road. Chapter 7, "Integrating Library Resources into Online Instruction," by Amy Shannon, focuses on providing resources and services to the teachers and students of Web-based courses.

There is more to providing Web-based resources than providing links on Web pages. Carol Parkhurst shares her technical expertise on "Supporting the Remote User of Licensed Resources" in Chapter 8. She explores issues of access control and management. Finally, we all know that quality Web-based resources and services are an increasing financial burden for libraries to bear. Community support is no less important in these times, but it is more of a challenge to maintain friends and donors who may not be as library-oriented once they are online, and to turn remote users into supporters. In Chapter 9, Betty Glass and Vicki Toy Smith cover the essential concerns of "Fundraising and Public Relations in the Electronic Environment."

WORKING IN UNISON

Attracting, Educating, and Serving Remote Users through the Web is our opportunity to articulate our new vision and share it with other librarians who may or may not have begun to think about the future relevance of their libraries. It is very clear to us that libraries must adapt to these changing times, quickly, and that change of this urgency and magnitude is extremely difficult without a shared vision within the library. The cooperative spirit that allowed ten librarians to write nine chapters for a unified book is the type of cooperation that is required for a library to reach out and successfully begin to serve its remote users. We were able to write cohesive chapters because we understood and believed in a united purpose. Most of the chapters can stand alone, to help individuals within a library redesign the services for which they are responsible. For a library to get the most from this book, we suggest that those who selectively read the chapters that are relevant for their services also read the first two chapters. The first chapter will give the participants a common starting point, and help them work together to re-orient the library's priorities. The second chapter will focus attention on the recipients of these transformations in services, the remote users themselves.

Although our experience is with an academic library, the concepts and examples presented here are applicable to every type of library. Some of these services for remote users are already well developed in our library, and we bring our experience into the chapters about those services. For other services that are less developed at UNR, we highlight the experiences of other libraries. In some cases, we have developed new services during the time it has taken to produce the book. All of the chapters reflect our collective thinking about the best ways to connect with remote users in providing various services. The authors of *Attracting, Educating, and Serving Remote Users through the Web* provide an overview of a range of services, and a context within which to think about them. We have challenged some accepted and basic principles of librarianship. At the same time, this is a how-to book that provides step-by-step instructions, Web scripts, and very specific guidelines for developing new services or improving existing services. We present carefully-chosen, high-quality sources for further information, most of which are on the Web.

For this reason, we have developed a companion Web site with links to all the Web sites that we have recommended for further information. It is organized to correspond to sections of chapters in this book. Access this site at **www.library.unr.edu/subjects/ guides/remoteusers.html**. These are truly exciting times to be a librarian. *Attracting, Educating, and Serving Remote Users through the Web* explores a fascinating and ever-changing area. For those involved in the everyday challenge and those who greet the ongoing opportunity to transform services to their libraries, we hope our enthusiasm for the experiment is one catalyst to effective action.

ACKNOWLEDGMENTS

We, the contributors, would all like to thank our families, friends, and colleagues for giving us the time, the space, and the indulgence needed to complete our individual chapters.

I, the editor, would especially like to thank the wonderful folks at Neal-Schuman: Charles Harmon for his encouragement, Kevin Allison for his technical help, Michael Kelley, our editor, for his great advice and constant support, and Gary Albert, our production editor, for being exceptionally responsive. I would also like to thank Michele Basta for being there when I needed her editorial involvement and advice, Araby Greene for helping all of us with technical matters throughout the project, Maggie Ressel for the indexing, and Steve Zink, our Library Dean and the Vice President for Information Technology at UNR for his vision and leadership.

Thanks to all the contributors for their commitment to quality, and for following through and helping each other over rough spots. Thanks to my husband, Charles, for his patience, and to my sons, Bowen and William, for putting up with a mother who would take an unfinished manuscript on a family vacation.

1 REACHING OUT— THE LIBRARY'S NEW ROLE

by Rick Anderson

CHAPTER OVERVIEW

- The Library Is Dead; Long Live the Library
- Ownership "vs." Access
- A Menu or a Bowl of Noodles?
- The Hubris of Collection Development
- Challenges for Libraries
- Challenges for Patrons
- Ramifications for Library Organization
- Off the Road and Into the Woods
- Measurement Without Gate Counts
- A Rich New Area for Librarians

THE LIBRARY IS DEAD; LONG LIVE THE LIBRARY

For over a hundred years, the library has been understood as a place where books, magazines, and other publications are purchased, housed, and organized for use by members of a sponsoring community (usually a town, school, or university). The very word "library" implies the centrality of printed books.

Traditionally, library patrons have come to the library somewhat like supplicants to a temple, seeking the knowledge (or at least the information) contained therein, guided in their search by priests and priestesses who were party to the complex gnosis of traditional knowledge organization—Dewey and LC schedules, the anatomy of subject headings, the organization schemes of citation indexes, and especially, in recent years, the mystic runes of Boolean logic. In the library a seeker could encounter a wealth of information, most of it in a physical format of one kind or another and all of it mediated by this priesthood of knowledge experts.

EVERYTHING IS DIFFERENT NOW

Two fundamental things about the traditional library model have changed, and they've changed quite recently.

Fundamental Shift #1

First of all, while the print collection still remains the core of most public libraries (where the majority of patrons are looking for reading materials and ready-reference information), print is increasingly vestigial in research libraries.

Print has never been a very good medium for publishing research, but until the advent of the Internet (and, in particular, the popular embrace of its graphical interface, the World Wide Web), print resources were essentially the only option available to researchers. This is no longer so. In 2002, information seekers are able to gain access to an enormous amount of research material via the World Wide Web, and, not surprisingly, they show a marked preference for this mode of access over the use of print materials. In fact, while many librarians still think of electronic resources as complements to the print collection, their patrons tend to see things the other way around.

Are students and researchers better served by online content than by print sources? Are they getting the same quality of information that they used to? As far as the position and perceived necessity of libraries are concerned, it may not matter. Whether the migration of scholarly information from print to online formats is a good thing or a bad thing may be an interesting philosophical question, but it is increasingly irrelevant. The simple fact is that very few patrons are using print indexes and bound journal volumes now, and in the very near future most of those materials will probably not be used at all.

Fundamental Shift #2

What all of this means is that there is no longer any really compelling reason for patrons to visit the library in person, and that's the second fundamental change that is affecting the traditional model of library service. Gate counts for research libraries are dropping everywhere, and even public libraries are seeing more and more patrons who use the Internet to determine the availability of desired books and only come to the library itself to pick them up.

THE LIBRARY AS PORTAL

None of this is to say that people don't need the library or that they don't use it—on the contrary, library resources are getting more use than ever. But gate count and physical circulation statistics are decreasingly relevant ways of measuring library use. Indeed, the library's role as a temple filled with knowledge, to which patrons come in order to fill their minds, index cards, and tote bags, is being replaced by a new role: the library is now, and will increasingly be in the future, a portal through which authenticated users gain access to information that is held and administered elsewhere. Their status as patrons of the library gives them access to more and higher-quality information than they could get otherwise, but the library itself now tends to offer guidance and navigation help rather than a careful selection of materials from that universe.

While patrons will still come to the library in the future (in large part because the library, if designed and programmed correctly, can be a wonderful social and academic center), they will no longer have to do so in order to benefit from its core services.

This is not, at base, a new idea. In fact, libraries have been serving users from a distance for many years. The old model of remote service, however, was based on a concept of the library as a repository for physical items; items that were sent to outlying neighborhoods in a bookmobile, or sent to homebound patrons by mail or fax. Relatively few took advantage of such services, either because they preferred to go to the library themselves or because the services were restricted to a certain class of patron. The primary access point for services and materials was still within the confines of the library building.

The emerging model for libraries, however, is one of distributed access points and sharply decreasing centralization. The library now provides a pathway to information that is housed and maintained elsewhere, rather than copies of publications that the library "owns." By doing so the library functions more as a broker, and less as a physical distributor and central access point. Many patrons now take advantage of remote access, and for some it is the only contact they have with the library.

Online services are not "virtual" either in the sense of being not-quite-complete or in the sense of being ephemeral and illusory—they are both complete and concrete. A patron who downloads and prints (or simply bookmarks) a journal article from an online database ends up with a document that is generally just as complete and useful as one photocopied or read from a print issue—and sometimes more complete and more useful. The more it serves as an electronic portal rather than a physical collection, the more a library could conceivably exist and function without any of the usual physical trappings—a building, bookshelves, loading dock, etc. There is little reason, however, to expect that personnel needs will diminish, as we shall see below.

OWNERSHIP "VS." ACCESS

It's understandable that librarians should be concerned about a decline in gate counts. If people aren't physically coming to the library, how can we justify our existence? There's a good answer to that question, but in order to get there it will be necessary to leave some cherished fictions behind. One of these is the mistaken idea that libraries own the information in their print collections. They don't, of course. What they own are *copies*—physical representations—of that information. To the degree that the content itself can be owned, it is owned by whoever holds the copyright.

This means that a library doesn't distribute information to its community in the same way that, say, a food pantry distributes food—instead, it acts as an access broker, using the community's money to buy access to information on the community's behalf. In the past, the library typically purchased print access, leading to the optical illusion of ownership. Increasingly, now, the library purchases online access, an arrangement that breaks down the illusion and leaves those previously fooled by it feeling uneasy about an apparent lack of "ownership" (more practical concerns about permanence of access are justified, of course, and require careful attention).

INFORMATION DOESN'T ACTUALLY WANT TO BE FREE

There is no reason to believe that the library's broker function is going to become less necessary simply because of a shift from print ownership to online access. The 1990s saw a brief flirtation with the idea that information could, or ought to, be "free." But with the collapse of the dot-com market in 2001, the inherent silliness of that idea has become clear. Information is a commodity, and little of it will get produced unless it's possible to make a living at it; as long as it takes work to create information, people will expect to be paid to do so. Like all commodities, information—and especially high-quality information—costs money, and every community has members that cannot afford to buy access to all of the information they need (Anderson, 1999).

This is what makes libraries so important: a library is the means by which a community purchases and distributes access to information so that its members can get what they need without having to buy it as individuals. What's changing is not the necessity of this function, but the methods by which librarians discharge their duties.

A MENU OR A BOWL OF NOODLES?

When the library's primary mode of operation was to gather materials into a discrete physical collection, it made sense to offer a catalog of those materials. Having the stuff on hand was only half of the service—patrons needed help locating and pulling particular pieces of the collection from within the stacks. But a catalog that tells patrons where to find materials physically within the library is less useful in a library that increasingly provides access to patrons who are not physically present.

More and more, libraries must provide direct links to the information itself rather than a set of directions to a physical item in a physical location. And we need to illustrate the relationships between different pieces of information, rather than merely marking commonalities with similar or identical subject designators. It may be that for electronic resources we need to stop thinking in terms of a "catalog" at all, and instead build something that looks (conceptually, anyway) less like a restaurant menu and more like a bowl of noodles—a complex and multidimensional structure that describes linkages and pathways rather than externally-imposed categories. And which, also like a bowl of noodles, is "edible" in and of itself.

GUIDES NO MORE?

In fact, it's possible that librarians need to let go of one of their most cherished historical functions. They have always been known for their ability to help patrons locate obscure facts, gather relevant articles, or just find another book you'll enjoy if you liked the last one by Anne Rivers Siddons. Given the enormity and disorganization of the World Wide Web and the low quality of so much that it offers, librarians have tended to see that part of their jobs as becoming increasingly, not decreasingly, important.

The problem, as many librarians have found, is that patrons will often settle for mediocre or marginally relevant information that can be found in a quick and intuitive way (and without asking a librarian) rather than go to the effort that may be required to sift high-quality information from the chaff. The answer to this dilemma is probably not to be found in educating patrons—trying to get people to change their behavior is increasingly a losing proposition. Instead, libraries will do best to make finding high-quality information an easier and more intuitive process.

In fact, as central as the guide function has always been in the past, it's important to remember that our ultimate goal as librarians is to abdicate that role. We want our patrons to be able to find the information they need without our help. As it turns out, the tools for easing that process are more advanced than most librarians know; it's just that they aren't yet to be found in libraries. A number of software companies have already developed what is known as "agentware"—neural networks of "self-learning agents" that sense the context of specific words in a search query and return increasingly relevant search results (Feldman and Yu, 1999). Such products are miles beyond traditional search engines (and light years beyond the library catalog) in terms of efficacy and sophistication, and they are already being used in the industrial and intelligence communities—though not all are convinced that these tools will live up to current expectations (Allen 2000).

Why not in libraries? Our goal, after all, is to make ourselves obsolete, at least as guides and helpers. Ultimately, isn't the perfect library one that gives its patrons access to highly relevant information that they would not be able to afford on their own, and then makes that information so easy to get that no further assistance is needed? As long as information costs money, the broker function will be one that no software can replace. But if we think that nothing can beat a librarian at helping patrons find good, relevant information, we are almost certainly wrong—and if we aren't wrong today, we will be tomorrow.

THE HUBRIS OF COLLECTION DEVELOPMENT

As we provide more and more service to patrons from a distance, we will need to rethink traditional attitudes towards selection of materials. In the past we have chosen items for our collections based on three primary criteria: relevance (does this book or journal support the institutional mission?), quality (does it provide accurate and useful information?), and cost (can we afford it? do we have the space?). When choosing materials for remote patrons, some of these criteria—in fact, all of them—need to change.

Why is this so? Don't we need to be as concerned about relevance, quality, and cost in the electronic realm as we were with print? Surprisingly perhaps, the answer may be "no." This is a controversial issue, of course. With a number of publishers offering to sell online access to their entire journal catalogs at bargain-basement per-title prices, there is much discussion about the wisdom of taking them up on the offer (Frazier, 2001; see also the letters published in response). Some librarians feel that to do so will only save low-quality journals from a well-deserved death in the marketplace; others point out that what looks like a bargain price is still too much to pay for a journal that you wouldn't have chosen to purchase in the first place. Some see this as yet one more way that librarians can abdicate a central part of their institutional mission—the selection of content.

All of these arguments have their attractions, but they don't carry the logical weight in the current information environment that they did in a primarily print world. First of all, the ability of librarians to select what patrons really need may have been exaggerated from the beginning—libraries that have taken advantage of the online package deals offered by such journal publishers as Springer, Elsevier, and Wiley often report that journal titles to which the libraries did not previously subscribe get levels of patron use comparable to those journals that had been actively chosen for the collection by librarians. Second, whether we approve of it or not, it is now true that patrons can choose between print and online formats for their research, and that they will generally choose what is available online—not necessarily because it's better, but because it's easier to get. Are they always better served by what they find online? Not always, no. If we point that fact out to them in convincing ways, will they change their behavior? In most cases, probably not.

WHITHER—OR WHETHER—COLLECTION DEVELOPMENT?

In general, should we be selective (to facilitate access to specific information for our specific communities) or broadly acquisitive (casting as wide a net as possible to increase the likelihood of access to what's needed)? In the past, when each journal and monograph was purchased as a separate item, and when those items had to be stored physically, economics forced us to be selective; today, many libraries could, at least theoretically, double the amount of information offered to their patrons without any impact on library shelf space, and the cost of adding new journal titles has dropped precipitously with the advent of all-or-nothing online access packages. Could it be that the era of collection development is over? Given that our ability to accurately predict what library patrons will want to use is imperfect at best, there is at least a rational argument to be made for simply providing access to as much information as possible.

CHALLENGES FOR LIBRARIES

Offering patrons access to information at a distance has meant entering a whole new universe of technical, legal, and even philosophical issues for libraries.

AUTHENTICATION, THE LAW AND FIRST PRINCIPLES

From a technical standpoint, libraries now have to worry about issues of patron identity and authentication that, in the past, were solved with the issuance of a library card. Remote authentication requires both skills and equipment that were unheard of in libraries until just a few years ago. Then there are issues of Web design, server maintenance and administration, and link maintenance. All of these duties draw on skills that have not traditionally been taught in library school.

Legally, the illusion of information ownership in libraries (fostered by the relative permanence of print formats) has finally been shattered by online access. In the print world, acceptable uses of copyrighted information was governed almost exclusively by copyright law. But copyright law is difficult to enforce at best, and, when it can be enforced, is relatively toothless. What protected the rights of copyright holders wasn't so much the law as it was the manifest difficulty of committing profitable acts of piracy in the print realm.

In the electronic realm, where a document can be copied and distributed to thousands of recipients with a couple of mouse clicks, copyright holders are understandably skittish. This skittishness expresses itself in the terms of license agreements that may significantly restrict the downloading and redistribution of online information. Libraries, whose primary interest is the distribution of information, are often at odds with publishers over the acceptability of license terms, and the repeated negotiation of those terms has turned many a librarian into a sort of *ad hoc* expert in contract law.

The philosophical implications of selling and redistributing online access are closely tied to the legal ones, and provide some of the most interesting questions for publishers and librarians alike: in a transaction that by its very nature involves caches, temp files, hyperlinks, and screen views, what exactly constitutes a copy of a document? How has the meaning of the word "permanent" changed? Is the library a repository of information, or a portal to a virtual universe through which one is authorized to pass by virtue of one's institutional affiliation? In the past, a library exchanged money for physical documents; in the present, a library purchases the limited right to provide temporary access—what does this mean for the nature and purposes of the institution itself?

PERMANENCE AND PRESENTATION

Other challenges for libraries are less abstract:

- Given the relative transcience of online resources, how will we provide access in perpetuity to our patrons? Is that something we should worry about, or does our mission need to change in such a drastic way that we no longer see the library as a place that holds a more or less permanent "collection"?
- If we do decide that a permanent archive of library materials is necessary, who will create and administer it where online content is concerned? Libraries, or publishers, or some third party as yet undefined? (The October 2000 issue of *Serials Review* offers a number of perspectives on this topic.)

Another very practical problem comes from traditional cataloging practices. Electronic information is not bound to physical formats, and thus can be acquired at such a rate that current methods of organization/presentation/cataloging are almost impossible.

- How will we adapt to this?
- How does one represent the sudden acquisition of 4,000 e-books to patrons in a timely, meaningful, and helpful way?
- Will we have to gradually stop thinking in terms of discrete physical items (books, journal issues) and start thinking in terms of interlocked webs of information (such as the World Wide Web) and amorphous masses of unrelated information (online databases)?

CHALLENGES FOR PATRONS

THE DIGITAL DIVIDE

Remote access to library materials offers certain drawbacks. For one thing, some members of every library community have no easy access to computers or the Internet. It's tempting to think that this is a problem that will solve itself—that just as televisions and telephones have become essentially universal, so will Internet-ready computers. The problem is that even in the twenty-first century, televisions and telephones are not actually universal. Those without them may be in the minority, but under-served minorities are an important part of the mission of most libraries.

Of those who do have access technically speaking, there will always be some who have difficulty acquiring the skills needed to use the technology well. The Internet offers many natural-language search interfaces, but few of them make truly targeted searching possible; for that, one needs at least a basic understanding of Boolean logic, and it's difficult to see that requirement disappearing anytime soon—the Internet is simply too vast and the logic of term inclusion and exclusion is simply too basic. Then there are issues of browser configuration, troubleshooting, and so forth, some of which may not require particular expertise to solve in the future, but most of which do for now. To some degree the "digital divide," like the economic divide, is probably permanent.

RAMIFICATIONS FOR LIBRARY ORGANIZATION

For librarians, one of the most disturbing aspects of the migration from centralized to distributed access is its potential for serious organizational upheaval in the library. If library patrons don't need to be in the library in order to take advantage of its services, are there services—or entire departments—that cease to be necessary? Do some librarians need to worry that they are becoming obsolete in the new information economy?

YES, YOU SHOULD WORRY

In a word, yes. But not because all the traditional duties of librarianship themselves are necessarily going to go away. The library will still be providing access to more information than most people will be able to comprehend and navigate without help (though, as now, they will not always realize that this is the case); the library will still be paying invoices and will still need to verify that what was paid for has been received or access established; the library will still need to find a way to represent those resources to its patrons.

The skills needed to perform such tasks, however, may change significantly in a library that is primarily devoted to providing access through the Web. Reference librarians will do less and less of their work in a face-to-face situation with patrons; most of their service interactions may take place on the telephone, or via e-mail or real-time chat. In such a context it will be much more difficult to know when a patron is comprehending, or is frustrated, or is ready to move on to another issue. Writing ability will become at least as important as interpersonal skills—in an e-mail or real-time chat situation, the most empathetic and skilled reference librarian could fail utterly if he lacks the ability to write clearly and concisely. In the area of acquisitions and serials work, license negotiation has already become an integral duty, one that can be highly intellectually and emotionally demanding. And the question of "receiving" is complicated to the degree that physical items no longer arrive in the library—instead of verifying an item's physical arrival, "receiving" is increasingly coming to mean "confirming access."

DOWN WITH COMPLETENESS AND ACCURACY

Some of the most drastic changes will be visited upon catalogers. The traditional library catalog has been a representation of a physical collection; however, a library that focuses on serving users at a distance must rethink the function and presentation of its catalog. What purpose does a call number serve in this context? Are Library of Congress subject headings helpful anymore? Is the MARC record the best underlying architecture for an online catalog? Here is a particularly controversial question: Are patrons better served by one complete and accurate record, or by the ten less complete (and perhaps even less-than-perfectly accurate) records that can be created in the same amount of time? It's possible that the values of completeness and accuracy that have informed cataloging work for so long are becoming obsolete. Could it be that in an environment in which information resources change, come into existence and disappear with frightening velocity, library patrons are better served by a quick and dirty process than by a slow and thoughtful one?

DOWN WITH TRADITIONAL BOUNDARIES

What all of this may mean for library organizations is a blurring of traditional boundaries. Perhaps the line between copy cataloging and original cataloging needs to be breached. Perhaps the Serials staff needs to interact directly with the public in ways it has not done before. What is clear is that libraries need to respect boundaries less than they have in the past. We no longer have the luxury of doing what we were hired to do.

BREAKING DOWN THE BARRIERS WITHIN—OR HELPING LIBRARIANS CLIMB OVER THEM

When Librarians Resist Change

Not all resistance to change in libraries comes from those who fear for their jobs. Some of it comes from library workers who:

- feel that libraries need to make demands on patrons in order to train them for the future
- harbor genuine philosophical objections to the idea that a library ought to make life easier for its users
- fear the breakdown of traditional boundaries within the organization
- see the library collection as a cultural monument of which the catalog is a semi-sacred artifact
- are simply uncomfortable with change itself
- may have come to the library profession precisely because it seemed to offer a place where time-tested standards apply, guiding principles remain constant, and life proceeds in a predictable manner

Resistance is Futile

Those in the latter category have either been rudely awakened already, or soon will be. Resisting the massive and ongoing shift of research publication from print to online formats used to be merely unwise; now it is patently impossible. That shift has taken place not because librarians wanted it to, but because our patrons did, whether we knew it or not. The shift to online resources has succeeded because it meets our patrons' needs—the need to get relevant information quickly and easily, to transport and store it conveniently, to transmit it to others cheaply and quickly.

While online resources offer some drawbacks (dependence on a complex and fragile infrastructure, occasional incompleteness, volatility, less human oversight), the fact that the benefits heavily outweigh those drawbacks could not be clearer. Our patrons have voted with feet and fingers, and the referendum is over. Any librarian who ever talks with patrons on this topic, or has compared his institution's gate count and circulation statistics with online usage patterns, has seen the writing on the wall. We simply do not have the option of deciding which direction scholarly research is going to go; we only get to choose how we will deal with the direction in which it has already gone. As harsh as it may sound to say so, those who object in principle to change are going to become increasingly unhappy in library work.

Philosophy and Practicality

Philosophical objections are knottier, and must be treated carefully and with respect. However, a library administrator charged with implementing fundamental change will have to be firm as well as respectful. Most libraries are not, in fact, charged so much with preserving a cultural heritage as they are with serving the needs of a fairly well-defined constituency; a research library whose host institution offers no degree in architecture may have very few books on architecture in its collection, and that is as it should be.

Similarly, it is true that many online resources do not offer the same permanence as that offered by a print collection. The relevant question is "Does it matter?" Perhaps permanence is of less value than it once was (except in a few very large libraries), and immediacy and wide distribution are of greater importance. Appropriate courses of action will vary from institution to institution, but the relevant question must be asked everywhere.

Knottiest of all, philosophically speaking, is the question of the library's role in the educational process. It's the old "give a man a fish/teach a man to fish" argument—isn't it our job to ensure that our patrons gain skills rather than just obtain information? This is a question each library will have to answer for itself. However, it's worth pointing out that every library has a number of different constituencies, and that its responsibilities vary somewhat by constituency. A college freshman needs to learn certain research and information-gathering skills in order to succeed in and beyond the academy, and one could argue that the library has an important role in helping her acquire those skills. The library's responsibility towards faculty, however, is somewhat different. In general, we will probably serve all of our users best if our primary goal is to help, rather than to teach. Library users will have more than enough character-building experiences in their lives; perhaps the library should be an oasis where they find relief rather than a wilderness that toughens them up for future trials.

THE THRILL OF RISK, THE BEAUTY OF FAILURE: MANAGING THOSE WHO ARE MANAGING CHANGE

There's a story about a CEO who discovered a hugely expensive mistake that had been made by someone in his company. In the course of fixing the problem, another manager asked him whether the offending employee should be fired. "Fire him?" responded the CEO. "Are you crazy? I just invested half a million dollars in his education!"

Libraries are not corporations, of course, and historically librarians have not generally been rewarded for coming up with and implementing crazy new ideas. This will need to change. For libraries to become more, rather than less, relevant and indispensable to their users in the future, they will have to actively encourage risk-taking and iconoclastic thinking. This is not to say that a library's goal should be innovation for its own sake—doing new things is not always better than doing old things. But the library's goal *should* be giving patrons the best possible access to the largest possible amount of high-quality, high-relevance information. If the best way to do that is to completely turn our backs on some of the things we've done in the past, so be it.

We need to be prepared to depart from professional norms when doing so will benefit our patrons. And we need to encourage those who have crazy ideas to implement them and to run the risk of making mistakes, even big ones. A historical unwillingness to take such risks is part of the reason libraries are now being ignored by so many of the people they were established to serve.

OFF THE ROAD AND INTO THE WOODS

Some of the most exciting opportunities for librarians are in areas that have not been within our purview in the past, sometimes because other people did those jobs, and sometimes because the jobs simply didn't exist before. Some in our profession worry that the library is going to become obsolete, but new opportunities open up around us constantly. For example, many research libraries are establishing electronic reserves systems and helping the teaching faculty learn how to manage them—but how many librarians are working with faculty to create sophisticated Web-based multimedia learning modules? Librarians are acquiring online access to financial, demographic, and sociological data at an unprecedented rate, but how many are working with faculty to create and organize data sets of specific relevance to their departments and projects?

UNBURDENING OURSELVES

Instead of being a reflection or microcosm of the information world, libraries are now in a position to help shape it. But there's an obvious problem: our plates are full already. How can we do all these new things when we're going full-tilt with the things we've always done in the past?

The answer is fairly obvious, and has been hinted at already: we need to stop doing some of those things. Perhaps, as suggested above, we need to spend less time (maybe even *much* less time) on traditional cataloging. Perhaps we need to reexamine the necessity of journal check-in. Perhaps it's time to finally bite the bullet and receive all of our books shelf-ready. It's not that traditional tasks like check-in and copy cataloging have no value; it's just that we need to weigh the benefits they provide against the cost of lost opportunities—in other words, the benefits that we could be realizing by doing *other things instead*. Our opportunities are almost literally limitless, but only if we are willing to swallow hard and plunge off the paved road and into the underbrush, leaving some of our traditional burdens behind us.

OUT OF OUR OFFICES AND INTO THEIRS

Let's face it. There are some patrons who take secret pleasure in no longer needing to come to the library. For them, the institution was ruined decades ago when they were grade-school students baffled by the logic of the Dewey Decimal System or the *Readers' Guide to Periodical Literature*. Others love the library and would enjoy doing their research there, but are simply too busy to make the necessary trip across town or across campus.

Whatever their reasons, it is clear that fewer and fewer people are physically crossing the thresholds of research libraries. The forward-thinking librarian sees this as an opportunity, not a crisis—a chance to make online resources as complete and easy to use as possible, and to expand the number of people who actually make use of the library's services. Offering remote access is a chance to make libraries as essential in the electronic era as they were in the print era, only richer, more complete, and more fun.

But we don't have to stop there. Remote access offers us not only the opportunity to provide research services at a distance, but also the opportunity to do so at an unprecedented level of interpersonal closeness. If our users aren't coming to us, why don't we go to them? Outreach isn't a new idea, but in the past it has frequently been offered in an "eat your peas" spirit—traditional programs of bibliographic instruction often send the message "Let us help you become better library users." Training can be helpful, and sometimes faculty specifically request it. But what we should probably offer more frequently than we do is our physical presence in the patron's domain—a chance, for example, for individual faculty members to ask us in person, in their work environment, why they can't get access to a particular article they need and for us to help them resolve the problem; or a chance to sit down with someone who needs help designing a Web page that lists library resources for her students; or simply a chance to spend some time talking with a department about the coming materials budget scenario.

Our users are no longer coming to us. But that doesn't necessarily mean that they don't want to see us—it may simply mean that we need to go to them.

MEASUREMENT WITHOUT GATE COUNTS

If fewer and fewer people are walking through the doors of your library and checking out books, how do you represent the fact that your resources are still being used? Ultimately, it's not our dependence on gate counts that really needs to change, but our definition of a "gate." We do need to know how many people are taking advantage of the services we offer, whether or not those people are ever physically present.

The good news is that by offering online access to information resources, we also increase our ability to demonstrate not only how much use our resources are getting, but which ones are getting the most use and even what kinds of use they're getting. Although the availability and utility of usage statistics varies from publisher to publisher and vendor to vendor, most are hearing the voices of librarians when they insist on the development and improvement of those functions and services.

It remains for administrators, of course, to recognize that the digital library is not merely a "virtual" one, and that services provided to users from a distance are every bit as real and valuable as those provided within the library's walls. Sometimes, however, it is the patrons themselves who need to be convinced of the usefulness of these services—or simply informed that they exist.

A RICH NEW AREA FOR LIBRARIANS

Service to remote users constitutes a rich new area of exploration for libraries and offers the potential to serve users in ways that neither they nor we have ever thought possible. It is neither the end of libraries nor a new beginning; librarians are still needed to do most of the things they have always done, and the underlying functions they serve—as information brokers acting on behalf of sponsoring communities to serve those who can't afford broad access for themselves—will remain essential as long as it costs money to create information. What is changing, and changing quickly, are the methods by which they perform those functions. Instead of reaching out to invite people through the doors of our buildings so that they can help them find books and articles, librarians now increasingly reach out to help people find their way through doors that exist in Webspace, doors to which they have a key by virtue of their membership in the library's sponsoring community. Once patrons are through those doors, it's the librarian's job to help them find and select from the various pieces of information on offer. Increasing gate counts would be the wrong goal; instead, librarians need to increase their ability to solve research problems for patrons in the way that makes life easiest for them.

REFERENCES

Allen, Maryellen Mott. 2000. "The Myth of Intelligent Agents." *Online* 24 no. 6 (November/December): 45–51.

Anderson, Rick. 1999. "The Debate over Service Fees: What Was the Question, Again?" *Library Collections, Acquisitions and Technical Services* 23 no. 2 (Summer): 183–190.

Feldman, Susan E., and Edmund Yu. 1999. "Intelligent Agents: A Primer." *Searcher* 7 no. 9 (October): 42–55.

Frazier, Kenneth. 2001. "The Librarians' Dilemma: Contemplating the Costs of the 'Big Deal.'" *D-Lib Magazine: The Magazine of Digital Library Research* 7 no. 3 (March) [Online]. Available: www.dlib.org/dlib/march01/frazier/03frazier.html [2001, November 10].

Serials Review. 2000. 26, no. 3 (October): 50–88.

"To the Editor: Letters." 2001. *D-Lib Magazine: The Magazine of Digital Library Research* 7 no. 4 (April) [Online]. Available: www.dlib.org/dlib/march01/frazier/03frazier.html [2001, November 10].

2 GETTING TO KNOW REMOTE USERS

by Donnelyn Curtis

CHAPTER OVERVIEW

- What We Mean by Remote
- Demographics
- Research on Users
- Cultural and Historical Context
- Understanding Your Own Remote Users

WHAT WE MEAN BY REMOTE

Remote users could be anywhere, thousands of miles away or in the building next door. They might even be using a computer in the library building for a reference chat session with a librarian who is at home. What makes users "remote," for the purposes of some parts of this book, is the fact that they are using a computer (any computer, anywhere, any time) to interact with library-provided resources or services (which may or may not be based in the library building). If we can observe them using computers in the library, they are less remote than those who are dialing in from their homes, dorms, offices, or their labs or hotel rooms on other continents, but unless they engage us or we engage them in a face-to-face interaction, they are functionally remote. There are degrees of remoteness, of course. For the rest of this section, and most of the book, remote implies outside the library.

You will never see most of your remote users. Some libraries even register their patrons through the Web, so they don't ever have to come in to get a library card for authentication purposes. Most libraries require one initial visit from those who are allowed to access licensed products according to the terms of the license agreements. But we can hardly get to know them while they're signing up for their library card the way we can get to know them when we are working with them at the reference desk or helping them find materials.

Some might argue that we don't generally know our on-site users that well, either, but seeing them repeatedly or for a prolonged period in our building makes them much more real to us, even if our knowledge is superficial. We talk to them. Some of them will thank us for our help, or complain about our policies. If they can't find something they are looking for, we might notice them wandering in the stacks, even if they don't ask for help. We can usually tell whether their information quest was successful. Within the library we can witness and correct navigational difficulties by providing better signage or rearranging furniture. But if someone at home is lost in our Web site or unsuccessful in a database, we don't know about that. When we are sitting in a library office designing services for in-house users, we can step through the doorway and see some of them. When we are designing services for remote users, we have to conjure up a picture, which may or may not be accurate.

There are more differences than similarities among remote library users. All they have in common is that they have access to a computer and the Internet and a library that uses the Web to provide materials and services to them, as members of a campus community, citizens of a county or city, or employees of a company. There are many people who fit that description who have not visited their library's site, but who have used other Web-based information resources. In generalizing about remote library users, we will sometimes include prospective users, calling this larger group "Web users."

DEMOGRAPHICS

Web users are on the "right" side of the digital divide. The data from the Fall 2000 "Falling Through the Net" report indicates they are more likely to be from a household headed by someone with "some college experience," under 50 years old (though the over–50 group is experiencing the fastest growth in Internet use), with a household income over $35,000. In fact, they fit the profile of traditional library users.

Those Americans least likely to have Internet connections are those with disabilities and black and Hispanic Americans (even with adjustments for income and education). While a third of the U.S. population used the Internet at home as of August 2000, only 16.1 percent of Hispanics and 18.9 percent of blacks had done so. Additionally, single-parent households are half as likely to have Internet access as dual-parent households. There is no longer a gender gap (except among single parents) or an urban/ rural gap, but urban users are more likely to have broadband access. The statistics show that e-mail is by far the most popular application for home Internet users (U.S. Department of Commerce . . . , 2000).

Demographics of another kind are generated by the company comScore, which maintains a large database comprised of Internet usage data from 1.5 million PCs used by volunteers at home, at work, and at universities. A recent article based on comScore data indicates a significant difference in Web site preferences corresponding to differences in ethnic background, educational level, and income level. When the most popular 5,000 Web domains are sorted by the educational level of American visitors, "It appears that the less-educated use the Web to amuse themselves and their friends. In contrast, the well-educated use the Web as part of their careers . . . as an economic tool, the Web most helps those who could already intellectually help themselves" (Sailer, 2001). The comScore database is designed to help client advertisers and is not available to the public, but occasional news stories reveal bits of analysis based on their data. Other companies also analyze Web traffic and user actions, usually in terms of e-commerce.

RESEARCH ON USERS

The characteristics and online behavior of Web users is of interest to Web designers and Web-based businesses and service organizations everywhere. Considering the amount of investment in e-business and the amount of data generated by Internet use, the lack of user analysis is surprising. Some usage research is really market research and is closely guarded as such. The field of Human Computer Interaction (HCI) has been around for years, but research agendas have not kept pace with the development of the Internet. Many of the published generalizations about remote library users and Web users in general are based on anecdotal evidence and limited observation or local samples.

SURVEYS

Some libraries have conducted surveys and published or made available on the Web their findings about their users:

- Central Michigan University used a click-through Web form; 1004 users responded. *Conclusions:* "Remote access is not restricted to one kind of user, and it is not confined to hours that the library is closed." Respondents used resources within the library as well as from remote locations. They favored online help guides. Traditional services should not be abandoned, but new services should be developed (Graham and Grodzinski, 2001: 303).
- The State University of New York College of Agriculture and Technology at Morrisville, a two-year college with some baccalaureate programs, issued a paper questionnaire to students in Freshman English courses. *Conclusions:* The students had less Internet experience than was anticipated. Overall, the students perceived information on the Web to be accurate. The college needs an information literacy program (Weiler, 2001).
- Duke University sent an e-mail questionnaire to randomly selected graduate students; 41 out of 100 responded. *Conclusions*: For these students, the Internet is "pervasive and interwoven into the fabric of student life, a channel for communicating and finding things out, and a way of learning and of living." On a usage scale of 1 ("rarely or hardly ever") to 5 ("very frequently") e-mail was rated 4.8; using search engines to find information and using library-provided Web sources were both rated 4.3. Chatting in chat rooms was rated 1.1. The most requested improvement was for all journals to be online (Lubans, 2000b).
- Duke University sent an e-mail questionnaire to randomly selected juniors; 59 out of 177 responded. *Conclusions:* On the above-mentioned 1–5 scale, e-mail was rated 4.9; using search engines to find information was rated 3.9; using library-provided Web sources was rated 3.1. The library should shift more support to technology (Lubans, 2000a).

Note: John Lubans has conducted several surveys of Web users of different ages. See the details at his Web page: www.lib.duke.edu/lubans/john.html.

PROCESS TRACING

Other studies are based on "process tracing," or the careful observation of everything that transpires between the user and system during an information retrieval session (including thoughts and emotions).

Wang, Hawk, and Tenopir (2000) carried out a "cognitive and holistic" study of the ways novice and advanced students in a library and information science graduate program used the Web to find answers to two questions. The subjects of their study had difficulty developing correct mental models of Web sites and did not bother learning how to use Web search engines effectively. 87.5 percent of the participants found answers to the first question, but 42.7 percent of the answers were incorrect. 77.7 percent of those with incorrect answers were confident their answers were correct. There was not a significant difference between the results of novice and experienced students, except that the experienced students were more confident in their incorrect answers. The researchers concluded that "The current status of Web organization imposes greater difficulties for effective information seeking than do other electronic systems such as CD-ROM and online databases," and that Web content providers need to do a better job of providing users with information about how objects and spaces are organized on the Web. Interface designers need to provide clues that "facilitate correct mental model development" and context-sensitive help. Advanced instruction in Web searching should "bring users to the web behind the screen."

ANALYSIS OF CAPTURED USER QUERIES

Jansen, Spink, and Saracevic (2000) studied the results of "real users" doing real searches using the Excite search engine. They analyzed transaction logs of 51,473 queries by 18,113 users and compared their analysis to earlier studies of online information retrieval (IR). They found that

- the Excite queries were short, averaging 2.21 terms. In the earlier IR studies, the number of terms used in a query ranged from 7 to 15. Only 4 percent of the Excite queries included more than 6 terms
- there were not many queries per search—the mean number was 2.8
- query modification was not typical—67 percent of users did not modify a query or
- 58 percent of users viewed only the first page of results (10 entries per page). The mean number of pages examined was 2.35. 77 percent of viewers did not go beyond two pages
- only 5 percent of queries used the "more like this" relevance feedback feature
- Boolean operators were not used much, and when they were, they were used incorrectly 50 percent of the time

- phrase searching with quotation marks was used in only 6 percent of the queries
- a very large array of unique terms was used for searching. The 63 terms that were used over 100 times represented only one third of one percent of all terms. Half the terms were used only once

Jakob Nielsen (2001b) also studied search behavior on e-commerce sites and found very similar results: the average number of search terms was 2.0, and the subjects of his study also did not use Boolean query syntax. Their first attempts were successful only 51 percent of the time, and subsequent attempts (by the 50 percent who did not just give up after an unsuccessful search) were increasingly less successful (second query, 32 percent; third query, 18 percent). He suggests providing a link to "advanced search" rather than having it on the home page. In another column, "Are Users Stupid?" (2001a), Nielsen comments that Web designers often persist in believing that their own users are smart enough to handle a complex or sophisticated design. But, he says, "it is not a question of whether users are capable of overcoming complexity and learning an advanced user interface. It is a question of whether they are willing to do so."

Nielsen suggests (2001b) that our search interfaces could show easy ways to extend a search, and postulates that a long-term solution might be that school districts would teach children how to formulate search queries. We don't see signs of that happening currently, but academic librarians can play a role by assuring that the education students who will become teachers learn how to formulate search queries. But remember, many education students are remote users, enrolled in distance education programs or taking night classes while they work, often commuting to do so. See Chapter 7 for ways the library's resources and instruction in their use can become part of these classes.

CULTURAL AND HISTORICAL CONTEXT

Librarians have correlated the development of the Web with certain changes of attitudes and research behavior among their users. Some observers blame the Web for the changes in people's behavior, and others believe that the phenomenal popularity of the Web is based on larger cultural conditions. Whether the chicken or the egg came first, we are in a new situation with users and it doesn't do any good to dwell on the past. Understanding the environment within which our users currently function will help us develop successful library services for the future.

INFORMATION OVERLOAD

In a book for librarians we don't need to say too much about the glut of information available to remote users. The amount of scholarly information doubles approximately every seven years, and the number of Web servers almost tripled in one year from 9,950,491 in January 2000 to 27,585,719 in January 2001 (Zakon, 2001). In November 2001 there is an invitation on the Google site (www.google.com) to search 1,610,476,000 Web pages. And that number doesn't include all the pages on the Web. Some, such as the licensed resources libraries provide, are not on the "public access Web" and some are too new to be found. The unsearchable "deep web" gets deeper as an increasing number of Web pages are generated "on the fly" from relational databases. Search engines improve, intelligent agents become available, but the Web just keeps getting bigger, more disorganized, and more impenetrable.

POSTMODERNISM

Remote users, and all of us, in fact, live in a postmodern world, whether we realize it or not. Postmodernism has facets in many disciplines and is hard to define, as is the condition from which it diverges, modernism. Roughly speaking, postmodernism is a cultural condition in which there is perceived to be no central authority or single version of reality. The Web is a perfect example of a postmodern artifact: amorphous, subjectively experienced, decentralized, and nonlinear. In their article about postmodernism and academic library services, Harley, Dreger and Knobloch (2001) describe the postmodern elements that characterize the interactions of students with information:

- consumerism—information is a commodity. Choosing among competing products, students will often sacrifice quality for convenience and low cost (in terms of time and effort)
- superficiality—as long as they can make something work, students don't care about the underlying mechanics or structure of a system, the process of doing research, or the organization of resources
- knowledge fragmentation—the Web, without critical thinking skills, can be a misleading place. A Web search

can land them on a site without context, and opinion often masquerades as fact

The authors of the article believe it is the role of the library to make up for deficiencies within the culture by teaching students some cognitive skills, giving them some intellectual tools. This is in line with the large body of literature on the role of libraries in teaching information literacy and critical thinking. However, we don't always have the opportunity to come into contact with students, especially if they are remote. And even when we do, our impact may be minimal, despite our good intentions. The best we can do is to understand where our users are coming from and meet them there, or at least half way, and help them take advantage of our resources and services by making it intuitive to do so.

MY GENERATION

Richard Oliver, in an article in *Management Review* (2000) christened the first generation of the new millennium the "My Generation." "While earlier generations have been influenced by technology, the MyGens are the first to be wholly shaped by it" (2000: 12), and they are accustomed to the personal touch, to customized products, and to e-commerce systems with embedded intelligence that can remember their likes and dislikes and configure themselves for individual customers. MyGens download selected MP3 files for their own players and personalize their PDAs for their own needs. "As this generation moves through higher education and into the work environment, libraries clearly need to personalize their products, offering differentiated levels of service that focus on the user point of view" further observes Debra Ketchell (2000: 175).

UNDERSTANDING YOUR OWN REMOTE USERS

In order to provide relevant service, what you really need to know about your own particular remote users is their information needs, their level of information literacy and whether

- their equipment and technical abilities allow them to use your resources

- they are finding their way to the quality resources you have provided
- you are providing the best resources for their needs
- they are learning anything from the way you have organized access to information
- they have expectations that are not being met
- your navigational and organizational schemes make sense to them
- your instructions or online help are effective

There are several ways to approach the challenge of understanding unseen users and their needs. You can collect information directly from them, using registration forms and surveys, follow their tracks with usage data, infer from what you know about certain people you know (including yourself) who use remote services, and extrapolate from local demographic information. Each of these methods is flawed and incomplete, but together they will give you information you can use. Asking users questions is the most direct way to get information about them. The challenges are 1) asking the right questions and 2) getting them to respond. Forms and questionnaires will not always provide straightforward answers to most of the questions on the above list, but some of the information they elicit will be useful.

REGISTRATION DATA

If you have a special registration process for remote users of your electronic resources (or services such as document delivery), you could have them answer some questions on the registration form. A library that offers customization options (see the portals section in Chapter 3) has a further opportunity to ask users some questions when they set up their profiles. Commercial sites frequently ask for personal information such as gender, age, income level, education level, and buying habits when someone registers for a customized service. As long as they are getting something in return for divulging personal information, and as long as they feel the information will be used only for marketing or product improvement purposes, most people don't seem to mind divulging it (Oliver, 2000).

The main advantage to collecting information through online or paper registration forms is that every person who registers is required to fill them out. The drawbacks are that

- the questions need to be short, simple, and few in number

- the data won't help you understand the ways that your users interact with your resources
- online forms may not elicit truthful answers from users accustomed to assuming alternate Web identities
- you will need to safeguard information that is associated with individuals to protect their privacy

SURVEYS

Surveys allow you to ask targeted users the questions that are important to you. They can be structured, consisting of simple yes/no questions or Likert scale questions (statements that can be rated on a disagree/agree response scale) to provide quantifiable data, or they can be unstructured, asking open-ended questions that will help you determine users' feelings and preferences. They can be administered by phone, by mail, or electronically by e-mail or through the Web. The challenge in managing a survey is to get a high response rate or at least a representative response rate. One of the advantages of using a survey to collect information about prospective users is that the survey itself may alert them to resources and services they did not know about. Weingart and Anderson reported that when conducting a survey on electronic database awareness at Utah State University, "the investigators did not anticipate in advance that the survey and the accompanying documentation would go a long way toward meeting the needs the survey itself identified" (2000: 132).

Web-Based Surveys

To collect information about how remote users interact with your Web site, Web-based surveys are certainly applicable. You can craft something elaborate or just ask a few questions with a pop-up window. You can buy off-the-shelf survey software or you can script your own. The advantages are that you can

- get feedback from users at the time they are using your site
- ask for input on alternate interfaces by showing the alternatives
- collect data in electronic form for electronic analysis, eliminating error and saving time
- revise the survey easily
- allow respondents to skip questions based on answers to other questions
- provide respondents with appropriate questions based on the information about themselves that they declare

- randomize answer choice order
- randomize question order
- require answers to some or all questions
- identify and remove duplicate responses
- offer incentives for completing a survey (but really good incentives might encourage duplication from a different address)
- program the survey to appear on Web pages a certain percentage of time, creating a more diverse sample

Disadvantages are that

- the response rate may be low
- the self-selection of respondents may result in responses that are not representative of typical users
- you won't be able to survey non-users of your site

Jakob Nielsen (2001c) suggests that Web surveyors who want users' feedback on their interface draw on other methods as well. Although it might be tempting to simply post a survey online asking for opinions on a new site design, you may not get reliable input. Users who see the survey and fill it out before they've used the site will offer irrelevant answers. Users who see the survey after they've used the site will most likely leave without answering the questions. Nielsen recommends that you

- watch what people actually do
- not believe what people say they do
- definitely not believe what people predict they may do in the future
- collect preference data from users only after they have used a design and have a real feeling for how well it supports them

One question that does work well in a Web site survey is "Why are you visiting our site today?" This question investigates users' motivation and they can answer it as soon as they arrive. It is difficult to craft a survey that will provide meaningful input, so you should consider adapting a standard survey form.

E-Mail Surveys

If you can obtain the e-mail addresses for representative members of your remote user community, you can ask them some questions by e-mail about their use or non-use of your library's Web site or licensed resources. You will need to let recipients know that their responses will be kept confidential and that identifying information will be stripped from their messages and they will be cumulated with other responses. Advantages of e-mail questionnaires are that

- personalization may result in a better response rate
- respondents will feel less constrained by the e-mail format than they would if they were using a form; e-mail encourages informal communication
- you can communicate with nonusers and discern some of the reasons they have not been using the library's resources
- you can either target a certain population or you can randomize the recipients
- the survey itself may alert potential users to resources they were unaware of

Disadvantages are that

- you will need to preserve the privacy of the respondents and convince them you are doing so
- it may be hard to standardize the results
- you may not get the candid responses that a more anonymous format will elicit
- some users will consider it to be "junk mail" and will not respond

Phone Surveys

Telephone surveys are similar to e-mail surveys in that you are not limited only to those people who are using your site, and you can target users or nonusers or a subgroup. Advantages are that

- the response rate will be very good
- the interactivity will allow you to ask follow-up questions and probe for more in-depth responses
- the interviewer has a great deal of control and involvement

Disadvantages are

- possible interviewer bias that might affect responses or the interpretation of responses
- a large amount of work in recording and compiling results

OPPORTUNITIES TO COMMENT

If you provide opportunities for feedback on your Web pages, some of your users will take advantage of them. See Chapter 4 for instructions on how to enable "mailto" links and how to set up form handlers for processing messages originating from your Web pages. If you have a comments forum where you post real questions from patrons and your answers to their questions, and if the interaction that is made public shows that you take the comments seriously, others will be encouraged to participate, and you will find out what at least some of your remote users think about your library services.

FOCUS GROUPS AND INTERVIEWS

Libraries often use focus groups to give them a rich understanding of user perspectives. The focus group format works well to ascertain user needs and expectations and to provide some insights on why people use or don't use services. However, librarians tend to invite people they know to be participants in focus groups, and those who accept the invitation may do so because they consider themselves to be library "friends," or else they may have an axe to grind. Finding neutral participants who are willing to spend the time is sometimes difficult. Finding remote users who do not come to the physical library is even more difficult. Issuing a blanket invitation on library Web pages and offering some kind of incentive for participation (food is good) may or may not work. The moderator should be someone who does not represent the library, preferably someone skilled and experienced with focus groups. Electronic focus groups on the Web are a convenient way to convene off-site users. Advantages of focus groups are that they

- provide results quickly
- are low cost
- give you the opportunity to really get to know the participants

Disadvantages are that

- the results may be "messy" or inconclusive, and difficult to classify, compile, and communicate to others
- the small number of participants may not represent all user groups
- managing the group and keeping the participants on track is not easy

LOCAL DEMOGRAPHICS

Depending on where you live, someone may have localized the digital divide statistics. If not, local census information will provide clues about the possible connectivity saturation or lack of saturation in your area. Knowing your local ethnic, age, and gender mix as well as family demographics will help public libraries design more relevant services. Public libraries can use census information to tell them which languages are spoken in the community and to what extent, how many home-based businesses are in the area, how many children are home-schooled, and other such facts (Maxymuk, 2001). The Chamber of Commerce often compiles a community economic profile that should be of use in scoping out the potential users of library resources. University data books or Web sites maintained by offices of institutional research can provide similar information about the university population.

USAGE DATA

Some people who work with the Web already have some experience with server logs and other ways to collect statistics about Web sites. Statistics can be gathered from server logs, proxy servers, and authentication systems.

Analysis of Web Logs

A number of software tools are available to help you gather and analyze data about the use of your Web site, in addition to the tools that might be built into your system. Their cost ranges from free to $20,000 or more. You can probably get by with free and low-cost software to document the volume of your traffic. But for helping you really understand your users, they do not have a tremendous amount of value. Some examples of the types of information they can provide about your site for a designated period of time (often displayed in graphic format) are

- the number of visits to your site, broken out by day or hour
- specific IP addresses for visitors
- which domains they represent (countries, .com, .edu, .org, etc.)
- referring sites (search engines, other Web pages visited just before your site)
- what browsers and platforms were used
- the average number of your pages they visited; how much information was served

- which specific pages were accessed
- the number of unique and repeat visitors
- entry pages, exit pages
- search terms used to find the site

You won't get perfectly accurate data, for several reasons:

- Your visitors may have dynamic rather than static IP addresses, which are assigned from a pool as they are needed
- They may be going through proxy servers so you won't know their actual IP address
- Web pages can be cached on the proxy server, meaning that after the first time, they will be accessed from another computer besides your server
- Some of the use of your Web site will be from within the library
- Some of the use of your Web site will be by staff

You won't be able to track the usage of resources that are not on your library's server. In other words, if a user visits a page that lists your databases and chooses one, you won't know which database was chosen. You will need to get usage statistics for off-site resources from your vendors (be prepared for a lack of standardization). On some library Web sites there are intermediate pages for each database that will help track comparative usage. Such pages can provide instructions to help users make better use of the database, but it does require an extra click. Those who have bookmarked the database URL won't be counted, and those who do not have authorized access to the database will be counted, even if their attempt to connect is unsuccessful.

Spending some time analyzing server logs can be interesting, but like most quantitative information, it can't really tell you the important things about your remote users. Some examples of Web analysis tools are

- AccessWatch (accesswatch.com/)—Shareware, $30. Platform: Windows, Macintosh, UNIX, and others
- Analog (www.analog.cx/)—Free
- WebTrends Log Analyzer (www.webtrends.com/)—around $200/year

Search Log Analysis

To get a glimpse into your users' minds, look at actual searches as recorded in the search logs of your online catalog, Web site search, and/or any local databases. This will help you see (in excruciating detail) the kinds of problems they might be having with searching in general and with your systems in particular. It will also give you a sense of locally popular subjects (if you monitor subject searches in an ongoing way) and may show you where you have gaps in your resources.

USABILITY TESTING

Usability testing requires the close, on-site observation of real users using your system. Remote users will benefit from any modifications you make to the presentation of your resources and services as the result of usability tests you might perform, and what you learn about the users under observation will generally apply to both remote and on-site users. Some general principles for usability testing (Battleson, Booth, and Weintrop, 2001; Talin, 1998; Dickstein and Mills, 2000) are to

- test no more than five users and run as many small tests as you can afford
- videotape the subjects if possible
- script your questions carefully
- design realistic tasks for the users; avoid recruiting users who are familiar with your system
- test the test beforehand; practice conducting the test with in-house volunteers
- conduct the test in a quiet place
- provide incentives or compensation for participation
- describe to the users the purpose of the observation; let them know you are not testing them and that difficulties they have will help you identify problems
- ask the users to verbalize their thoughts; remind them if they forget
- decline to provide help during the process
- record the results as soon as possible after the test is completed
- consider usability testing as an iterative process; as you make changes in your system, test it again

Some recommended Web sites for information about usability testing are

- *useit.com: Jakob Nielsen's Website* (www.useit.com)
- James Hom's *The Usability Methods Toolbox* (www.best.com/~jthom/usability)
- Keith Instone's *Usable Web* (www.usableWeb.com)
- Talin's *A Summary of Principles for User-Interface Design* (www.sylvantech.com/~talin/projects/ui_design.html)

There are several good books on the subject as well. Battleson, Booth, and Weintrop recommend

- *Usability Testing* by Jakob Nielsen (Boston: Academic Press, 1993)
- *The Handbook of Usability Testing: How to Plan, Design, and Conduct Effective Tests* by Jeffrey Rubin (New York: Wiley, 1994)
- *A Practical Guide to Usability Testing* by Joseph C. Dumas and Janice C. Reddish (2nd ed., Exeter: Intellect, 1999)

WHAT YOU ALREADY KNOW

As librarians we usually try not to generalize our own information retrieval behavior to help us understand our users, since we have training, knowledge, and experience that they lack. However, it might be useful to observe your own off-duty self as a Web consumer. If you are using the Web to pursue a personal interest, do you always use your library's gateway? When you use a new search engine, do you learn how it operates first? If you catch yourself being unlibrarian-like in your recreational use of the Web, you will be catching a glimpse of typical user behavior. Perhaps more useful is to watch family members or friends using the Web, or to ask them questions about their search habits. You will feel freer to probe than you would with strangers.

REFERENCES

Battleson, Brenda, Austin Booth, and Jane Weintrop. 2001. "Usability Testing of an Academic Library Web Site: A Case Study." *The Journal of Academic Librarianship* 27 no.3 (May): 188–198.

Dickstein, Ruth, and Vicki Mills. 2000. "Usability Testing at the University of Arizona Library: How to Let the Users in on the Design." *Information Technology and Libraries* 19 no.3 (September) [Online]. Available: www.lita.org/ital/1903_mills.html [2001, July 15].

Graham, Krista, and Alison Grodzinski. 2001. "Defining the Remote Library User: An Online Survey." *portal: Libraries and the Academy* 1 no.3 (July): 289–308.

Harley, Bruce, Megan Dreger, and Patricia Knobloch. 2001. "The Postmodern Condition: Students, the Web, and Academic Library Services." *Reference Services Review* 29 no.1: 23–32.

Jansen, Bernard J., Amanda Spink, and Tefko Saracevic. 2000. "Real Life, Real Users, and Real Needs: A Study and Analysis of User Queries on the Web." *Information Processing & Management* 36 no.2 (March): 207–227.

Ketchell, Debra S. 2000. "Too Many Channels: Making Sense out of Portals and Personalization." *Information Technology and Libraries* 19 no. 4 (December): 175–179.

Lubans, John. 2000a. *Study 4: Internet Use (February, 2000) among 3rd Year Students at Duke University Durham, North Carolina, USA. Draft, Initial Findings* [Online]. Available: www.lib.duke.edu/lubans/study4b.html [2001, July 29].

———. 2000b. *Study 5: Graduate Student Internet Use* [Online]. Available: www.lib.duke.edu/lubans/study5.html [2001, July 29].

Maxymuk, John. 2001. "Figuring it Out on the Internet: Statistics You Will Love." (Internet Column). *The Bottom Line* 14 no.1:1.

Nielsen, Jakob. 2001a. "Are Users Stupid?" *Jakob Nielsen's Alertbox* (February 4) [Online]. Available: www.useit.com/alertbox/20010204.html [2001, August 13].

———. 2001b. "Search: Visible and Simple." *Jakob Nielsen's Alertbox* (May 13) [Online]. Available: www.useit.com/alertbox/20010513.html [2001, August 4].

———. 2001c. "First Rule of Usability? Don't Listen to Users." *Jakob Nielsen's Alertbox* (August 5) [Online]. Available: www.useit.com/alertbox/20010805.html [2001, August 5].

Oliver, Richard W. 2000. "'My' Generation." *Management Review* (89 no.1 January): 12–13.

Ray, Randy. 2000. "Focus Groups make Foray into Cyberspace." *Toronto Globe and Mail* (September 26) [Online]. Available: www.globetechnology.com/archive/gam/Specials/20000926/ECFOCU.html [2001, July 29].

Sailer, Steve. 2001. "Analysis: The Web's True Digital Divide." *Virtual New York* (July 17) [Online]. Available: www.vny.com/cf/news/upidetail.cfm?QID=203267%3C/A [2001, July 20].

Talin. 1998. "A Summary of Principles for User-Interface Design" [Online]. Available: www.sylvantech.com/~talin/projects/ui_design.html [2001, November 10].

U.S. Department of Commerce. National Telecommunications and Information Administration. 2000. *Falling Through the Net: Toward Digital Inclusion* [Online]. Available: www.ntia.doc.gov/ntiahome/fttn00/contents00.html [2001, August 15].

Wang, Peiling, William B. Hawk, and Carol Tenopir. 2000. "Users' Interaction with World Wide Web Resources: An Exploratory Study Using a Holistic Approach." *Information Processing & Management* 36 no.2 (March): 229–251.

"Web-Based Surveys: Just Ask Them." 2001. *PC Magazine* (January 12). ZDNet Reviews [Online]. Available: www.zdnet.com/products/stories/reviews/0,4161,2665963,00.html [2001, August 13].

Weiler, Angela. 2001. "Two-Year College Freshmen and the Internet: Do They Really 'Know All That Stuff?'" *portal: Libraries and the Academy* 1 no.2 (April): 161–167.

Weingart, Sandra J., and Janet A. Anderson. 2000. "When Questions are Answers." *College and Research Libraries* 61, no.2 (March): 127–134.

Zakon, Robert Hobbes. 2001. *Hobbes' Internet Timeline* vol. 5:3. [Online]. Available: www.zakon.org/robert/internet/timeline/ [2001, July 27].

3 PRESENTING THE VIRTUAL LIBRARY

by Donnelyn Curtis and Araby Y. Greene

CHAPTER OVERVIEW

- Getting Users to the Virtual Library
- The Virtual Library Entrance
- Inside the Virtual Library
- Web Portals
- A Few Words About Usability

GETTING USERS TO THE VIRTUAL LIBRARY

How do prospective users discover that there is a library Web site and what is there? They may hear about one or more of the library's Web-based services through word of mouth, or see promotions for Web-based library resources. They may be students whose teachers have told them to use something specific, such as electronic reserves, at the library's Web site or (most likely) they assume that the library has a Web page, since just about every organization does.

If prospective users guess that the library has a Web presence, 1) what prompted them to think of checking out the library's Web site—what do they assume is there? and 2) how do they go about trying to find it?

THINKING OF THE LIBRARY

We would like to believe that members of our community think of checking our library Web site when they need information, as readily as they used to stop by the library in pre-Internet days. But chances are, nowadays they would first think of using "the Web" to satisfy an information need. If they are specifically looking for a library site, it will probably be for something related to their prior experience with the physical library, and not to find electronic resources. For example, they might be looking for information about an event that will be held in the library, library hours, or the location of branch libraries. If they are already accustomed to using the online catalog for finding library materials, they might suppose that the catalog would be available on the Web, especially if they have some kind of experience searching other Web-based catalogs or databases at places like amazon.com or reel.com.

Libraries can engage the first-time visitor who initially seeks information about the physical library and its print offerings with an entrance page that is interesting and informative. We will discuss ways to optimize the design of the home page later in the chapter. First, though, we need to think about ways to get potential users to the site.

FINDING THE LIBRARY ON THE WEB

There are several ways someone can find a Web site:

- Following links from likely places
- Guessing the URL
- Using a gateway site
- Using a search engine
- Heeding advertisements

Links From Likely Places

Most libraries are units of a larger organization that has a Web presence. You should lobby for a strategic link from the site of your governing body, if there isn't one already.

More than 25 percent of ARL libraries are part of universities that do not have an "immediately visible active link to the library" on their home page, according to a recent study (Astroff, 2001: 98). University politics will sometimes prevent the library from doing anything about the difficulty visitors might have in finding the library site on the university's site, but it may be worth reminding administrators of the amount of money the library now spends to provide access to electronic resources. Astroff observes that "A university interested in its presence in cyberspace should be celebrating its cyber libraries" (2001: 98).

Public libraries, as well, may not be listed in places where townspeople would expect them to be. For example, some Reno residents might expect to find a link to the public library at the Reno City Government Web site, www.cityofreno.com/. But they would find nothing there about the library. That's because the public library in Reno is operated by the county. Does everyone who lives in Reno know that? Couldn't the city government Web site point confused folks in the right direction? It isn't likely that the city Webmaster would have thought of doing something like that, because the main mission of the Web site is to deliver information about city services. But if asked, the city might be willing to add a link to some county services such as the library (or not, depending on the political climate at the time, but there is no harm in asking).

There could be links to the library's main page or to certain internal pages from relevant pages on a university site or a city or county government site. For example, there might be a link from the Health Department page to a public library's compilation of health-related information resources. Links to subject pages on academic library Web sites would be appropriate on university department Web pages, and from course syllabi (see Chapter 7 for more discussion). The school district pages might link to all libraries in the area that are open to students.

Another place for any library that serves the public to be listed would be on local Web sites that provide information about community events, arts or cultural organizations, or community resources in general. For some places it is difficult to identify Web pages that are designed for residents instead of tourists, but most towns have them. It's worth spending some time surfing. If your library Web provides links to pages that provide community information, you can check those pages for links to the library, and contact the owners if there are none. Think symbiotically!

To find out which Web sites DO link to your library, you can use the Alta Vista search engine (www.altavista.com) or the Google search engine (www.google.com) with the syntax link:http:// yourlibrary'sURL. Try www.linkpopularity.com for a combined search of AltaVista, Google, and HotBot for sites that link to your URL. You might be surprised, or even puzzled about some of the links to your site.

Guessing the Library's Domain Name

Studies and anecdotal evidence indicate that if they are looking for a particular site, experienced Web users will often try to guess its URL, or domain name. More than 50 percent of Web users will first try going directly to a site by guessing its URL, while only 22 percent say they use a search engine, according to the *Cyberbranding 2000* study of 1,548 consumers by BrandForward Inc. (Bronstad, 2000).

It is easier to find Nike (www.nike.com), The Olympic Committee (www.olympic.org), or Harvard University (www.harvard.edu) than it is to guess the URL for most libraries. To make it easier for those who would guess, a library can set up alias URLs (like nicknames) that would seamlessly redirect users to the real URL. For example, the Harvard Library URL is lib.harvard.edu, but library.harvard.edu will also work. Check with your server host for their policies and prices for alias domain name registration.

Academic libraries' URLs that are constructed logically (with "lib" or "library" and the university's acronym and "edu" at the end, with or without "www") are guessable. Public libraries' URLs are generally not as intuitive for users. Can you guess the locations of the libraries that are represented by the following URLs?

1. www.cpl.org
2. www.clpgh.org/
3. www.mdpls.org
4. www.imcpl.lib.in.us/

1. Cleveland 2. Pittsburgh 3. Miami/Dade County 4. Indianapolis

If you were to see the following domain names you could probably guess which libraries they belong to, but if you were trying to guess the URLs for the Tucson, Phoenix, Chicago, and Missoula public libraries, you would probably not have thought of these:

- www.lib.ci.tucson.az.us
- pac.lib.ci.phoenix.az.us/web/
- www.chipublib.org/
- www.missoula.lib.mt.us

The following domain names are ones that experienced Web users might try if they are guessing the URLs for these libraries:

- www.fayettevillelibrary.org/
- www.toledolibrary.org/
- www.bozemanlibrary.org/

You can find out which names are available by entering your proposed domain name or alias in the search box at any of the domain registration sites listed by the Internet Corporation for Assigned Names and Numbers (www.icann.org/registrars/accredited-list.html). Any of these accredited registrars can register a domain name or alias name for you.

Gateway Sites or Web Directories

Yahoo! (www.yahoo.com) is by far the most popular gateway site. It does a very thorough job of providing organized access to all kinds of libraries by location. If that's the way you try to find your public library's Web page if you live in Houston, you would first have to notice the small word "libraries" under "Reference" on the busy Yahoo! page, and then find "Public Libraries" on the long list of types of libraries, and then on the next page choose "By Region" under "Categories" and then "By States," and then perhaps "Cities," and you will get to a page that has all the libraries in Houston, including the Houston Public Library. If you click on the name, you will be there—after six mouse clicks. You would be better off typing "Houston Public Library" in the Yahoo! search box. Your results would be a somewhat confusing list, but "Houston Public Library" is on the list, in bold type. One click and you're there.

Because many people use hierarchical directories to find Web sites, your traffic will increase if you register with Yahoo! and its most popular competitors. For a price, you can have someone register your library's site with hundreds of Web directories and search engines (for example, Microsoft offers this service at www.submit-it.com/), or you can find instructions for site registration at the major directories, which are listed, with links to them, at allsearchengines.com/directories.html.

Web Search Engines

There are numerous popular search engines on the Web: Lycos, WebCrawler, AltaVista, HotBot, Excite, Infoseek, Netscape, Google, and others. You can register your main page with each of these to maximize your presence in search results. A directory at html.about.com/cs/addurlpages/index.htm provides links to the submission forms for the major search engines. Note: There is often a cost associated with registration. Search engines also find unregistered sites.

Another way to optimize your "retrieval" status in a Web search is through your Web site's metadata in the hidden <head> section of an HTML document. To a search engine, the most important header element (or tag) is <title>. The name of your library should be there, and the city, university, or agency to which your library belongs. The actual name of your library, if it is named after a person, may not be known to your user community. This tag: <title>Fogelson Library—Home Page</title> will not help someone who is looking for The College of Santa Fe Library if they do not know its formal name. You can provide more information that might help people find your library using the meta tags "description" and "keywords." Your content in the description tag will be used in place of the summary the search engine would ordinarily create. The keywords tag provides more fodder for search engines.

The Denver Public Library has made good use of meta tags to increase its chances of being retrieved by search engines and to control what is displayed on results lists:

<META NAME="description" CONTENT="Welcome! The Denver Public Library (DPL) is the largest urban library system between Chicago and Los Angeles. We serve as the primary information resource for the City and County of Denver, the State of Colorado and the Rocky Mountain West.">
<META NAME="keywords" CONTENT="denver public library, dpl, rick ashton, denver, information, books, resources, public, library, colorado, bibliographic, western history, western history photos">
<TITLE>Welcome to the Denver Public Library</TITLE>

The above metadata will result in the following display on a list of search engine results:

Welcome to the Denver Public Library
Welcome! The Denver Public Library (DPL) is the largest urban library system between Chicago and Los Angeles. We serve as the primary information resource for the City and County of Denver, the Sta . . .

The above entry shows up at the top of the results list using Excite (www.excite.com) to search for "Denver Public Library." If there were no <title> tag, the heading for the entry would read "No Title" or "Untitled" (depending on the search engine), and someone scanning quickly through the list might miss it, or dismiss it. The title is also used to populate your browser's history list, and to create names for bookmark entries.

Any of the search terms "dpl, rick ashton, denver, information, books, resources, public, library, colorado, bibliographic, western history, western history photos" will also retrieve the Denver Public Library entry. Some Web authors try to trick search engines by using keywords such as "sex, nude models, hot, MP3," etc. in the keywords tag, even though their sites are not that titillating. If the name of your library is commonly misspelled, consider including the misspelled version among the keywords.

Constructing meta tags is simple. You can write your own code or fill in the blanks at one of the meta tag generators on the Web, such as Meta Tag Builder (vancouver-webpages.com/META/mkmetas.html). Meta tags are especially valuable for retrieval purposes on pages that are mostly graphics or that begin with scripts instead of textual content.

Most search engines also search the <body> section of Web pages, the content that users see. In fact, search engines give more relevance to words in the text of Web pages than to those in the <head> section, with the frequency and location of words on the page helping to determine where the site will rank in a search results list. Think about the words that might be used by those trying to find your library, and make sure those words are in the content of your Web page, or in a meta tag, preferably both. If you have special Web pages that deserve national attention, be sure that all the words that would describe those pages are present in the <head> or <body> of the page.

Marketing Your Library's Web Site

Promoting a library Web site isn't as difficult as you might think. Your audience will be easy to target. Your strategies will be determined by the size and character of the community your library serves.

Your local newspaper might run articles if you write press releases. The Web phenomenon is still newsworthy, if there is a human interest angle (long-lost relatives finding each other, a specialized local business now selling to worldwide customers, homebound people doing things they were never able to do before, someone becoming the world's expert on the rare disease of a spouse). The common element in stories about the Web is "connection." If your library has helped someone connect to Web-based life-changing information, you should toot your own horn in a way that will attract other users to your resources. Public librarians should get to know the Technology reporter at their local newspaper.

The campus newspaper is an ideal vehicle for informing college students about what is available through their library Web. If the editor does not want to do that story, an option is to buy advertising space. At the University of Nevada, Reno, we were able to get a public relations class to take on the library as a project. The students came up with a brochure, a newspaper article, and some great ideas for expanding our public relations efforts. Some minor inaccuracies were promulgated in their publicity campaign, but it was useful for us to see the library through their eyes.

You can target faculty at universities as individuals or members of a department to receive customized e-mail messages luring them to the library's Web site (with a link embedded in the message). Short demonstrations at meetings can work well. Visits to individual offices on campus allow librarians to bookmark the library page on faculty computers and ensure that necessary plug-ins such as Adobe Acrobat Reader are installed. Public librarians can also do this kind of outreach by inviting themselves to meetings of groups that would benefit from their online resources: genealogy groups, business organizations, hobbyists of any type.

The Web is still new territory for many people, and new users will continue to sign on. The October 2000 report *Falling Through the Net: Toward Digital Inclusion* showed that "the overall level of U.S. digital inclusion is rapidly increasing." In August 2000, 51 percent of households had computers, and 41.5 percent had Internet access, up from 26.2 percent in December 1998. Many libraries teach new Internet users to navigate the Web, a role that gives them an opportunity to promote their own offerings. If the library provides space or computers to other groups teaching about the Web, their promotion of the library's Web site could be a condition for using the facilities.

The University of Nevada, Reno Library allows users with university PPP accounts to check out an installation CD-ROM that includes localized Internet tools such as a Web browser configured for proxy authentication (see Chapter 8) and with the library's Web site as the "Home" URL. If your library successfully provides easy access to the resources your users most want to use, they may voluntarily choose it as their home page. The Palo Alto Public Library provides instructions on "How To Make The Palo Alto Library Your Home Page" at www.city.palo-alto.ca.us/library/myhome.html.

If the library has done a good job with its Web design, publicity can be simple. Your community needs to know that the library offers important, useful, and high quality information and services through its Web site, and how to get there. Don't expect them to remember the URL, though, even if it is straightforward. Good marketing strategists know that it takes repetition to market your product—you don't know when the consumer will be receptive, but when they are, you want to be there. Putting the library's URL on something they will see regularly is a good idea. Bookmarks (the paper kind) are more enduring than handouts, especially if printed on heavy stock. Inserting it into a book that is being checked out might cause the bookmark to be kept and used, and perhaps even noticed. Flyers and posters can be posted in strategic places such as computer labs on campus. The library might give away "Do Not Disturb" doorknob signs for dorm residents with the library URL printed on them.

A public library might be able to send brochures or bookmarks through utility companies along with bills. A public service announcement on late-night television might catch the attention of some viewers. A library booth at the state fair, street fair, health fair, or job fair might be appropriate, especially if you can afford to give away promotional items such as pens, key chains, refrigerator magnets, or book bags. Post-it notes printed with the library's URL could end up anywhere and everywhere.

Several public and academic librarians shared their strategies for publicizing library Web sites in a recent listserv discussion (web4lib archives, 2001).

- Hanging a professionally printed ten-foot banner sporting the library's URL on the front of the library building (Stephanie Spearman of the Northwest Georgia Regional Library System).
- Printing the library's URL at the bottom of the "date due" slips for borrowed items, and "Basically, include the Web address everywhere library contact information is published" (Robert Tiess of the Middletown Thrall Library in Middletown, NY).
- Giving away coffee mugs with the library logo and OPAC URL during student orientations; this also encourages the use of covered containers for beverages (Shawn Ammon of the Creighton University Health Sciences Library).

Of course, these methods will only work with users who come to the physical library. You can use virtual banners in the form of banner ads at appropriate sites. During the school year, Web visitors to the heavily used Gettysburg College site can see a banner advertising library services, randomly alternating with other campus ads (Katherine Furlong).

THE VIRTUAL LIBRARY ENTRANCE

So, diverse visitors will arrive at your library's Web site through many means. Their expectations will vary from none to extremely high. They may be passing through, beginning a research project, or urgently looking for something specific. Your library's home page must satisfy as many needs as possible. It must

- intrigue and hold the attention of the casual visitor
- provide instant gratification to the focused information seeker

- lead the inexperienced researcher through the first steps of doing research
- convey a promise of depth to those with complex information needs while at the same time promising ease of use to those with simpler needs

Attracting users to your site is only the first, tenuous step. No matter how wonderful your resources may be, users will not try very hard to find hidden treasures, nor will they want to jump through technical hoops for uncertain gain. Visitors to a library Web site are different from visitors to a library building. They have not invested much effort in getting there, and they can easily leave. And they will, if they feel frustrated in any way, and they may never come back. Downtime should be kept at an absolute minimum, and if backup services can't be arranged, server maintenance should be scheduled during low-traffic times. A community or university library may not have any direct competition, but its Web site is just one of thousands vying for attention. Web designers will tell you that users form their first (and lasting) impression of a Web site within 5–20 seconds. Slow-loading graphics will not be tolerated during a first visit. But a too-plain, especially a too-text-heavy site will also make a poor impression on users who are accustomed to commercial attention-grabbing sites.

COGNITIVE ASSISTANCE

It is not possible for a library's home page to represent all things to all users. That doesn't mean you shouldn't try to satisfy diverse users, but you need to do so without offering too many choices. Research shows that users will abandon a site with an overabundance of links. "They decide to quit not because the information isn't there, but because the amount of cognition it would take is so high," reports Ed Chi, a researcher at Xerox PARC ("Web Surfers Hunt Like Animals, Researchers Find," 2001). Library Web designers must lay some of the cognitive groundwork in the way they organize the initial access points.

Usability expert Jakob Nielsen cautions that "If everything is equally prominent, then nothing is prominent. It is the job of the designer to advise the user and guide them to the most important or most promising choices (while ensuring their freedom to go anywhere they please)" (1999). Server traffic statistics will tell you which are the most popular parts of your Web site, which may or may not be the ones you want to emphasize. Although your Web visitors will be diverse, there are some things you can expect them to have in common. They will prefer the "edible" content, the "bowl of noodles" mentioned in Chapter 1, to a mere menu. That means emphasizing the full-text content your library provides.

PRIMARY USERS

Sometimes you have to choose to focus on the needs of one type of user over the needs of others. An upper division, undergraduate journalism class at the University of Nevada, Reno invited librarians to their critique of the library's entry page. Their insights prompted us to redesign the page. Whereas we had thought our design to be simple, intuitive, and functional enough for freshmen, some seniors were complaining that it was intimidating, that they didn't understand most of our terminology, and that they couldn't find some of the services that seemed to us to be the most prominently displayed. At the risk of alienating some of the faculty and other sophisticated users, we took the students' advice and

- removed all but the most essential words
- used the very simplest words possible
- added goofy little cartoon graphics
- increased the use of (tasteful, we hope) animation
- changed some colors to add emphasis to the navigation bar, which they hadn't recognized as such

At the same time, we felt we should provide a way for faculty and graduate students to go directly to a menu of resources and services of importance to them, allowing them to bypass the central, simplified paths developed for inexperienced undergraduates (see www.library.unr.edu).

GUIDELINES FOR ENTRANCE PAGE DESIGN

There is no formula for an entrance page that will work for every library. But following these guidelines will help you make a good first impression:

- Make sure it loads quickly (test it at the Web Site Garage; websitegarage.netscape.com/O=wsg/index.html)
- Use no more than two fonts
- Use a moderate number of harmonious colors
- Keep the layout balanced and uncluttered
- Focus attention on the most important content
- Make the page short enough that your users will not need to scroll (at least to see the most important parts) at the most common resolution (600×800)

- Design simple-to-use navigation that is clearly recognizable as navigation
- Test to make sure the site is functional with the most common versions of both Internet Explorer and Netscape, using both Macintosh or Windows operating systems

The library's home page presents the library to the world, so you want to put some thought into the image it conveys. It is a lucky library that has a Webmaster who is passionate about usability, has a good sense of design, and technical expertise. Without such a person (even with such a person), library Web design is a challenge. Most often, successful Web design involves the combined talents of several participants. You might be tempted to hire a professional designer; just be sure that your designer understands your priorities. It is much easier to design a pretty site than a usable site, so don't let yourself be seduced by razzle-dazzle.

One last thing to keep in mind about first impressions—through a search engine or a link from a site you do not control, a user might land on a library page that is not the home page. The library identity must be clear on each page, and there should be an obvious way to get to the home page. Users who drill down into a site tend to use the "Back" button to backtrack through familiar territory. But someone who lands on an internal page will appreciate a menu bar or some kind of navigational links to the featured areas of your site.

INSIDE THE VIRTUAL LIBRARY

Assuming that you've succeeded in attracting users to your Web site and made an excellent first impression, your next challenge is to make certain they will stay and take advantage of all the wonderful resources and services your library provides. Web users are fickle, and they will stay with a site only as long as it continues to satisfy their needs and comply with their expectations. Considering the complexity of library-sponsored resources, it is very difficult for libraries to make their sites user friendly throughout.

This is not a book about Web design. Yet we don't want to minimize the importance of paying a great deal of attention to this key aspect of providing services to remote users. Although we can provide only a cursory summary of the issues of presenting library resources, we urge you to investigate them further.

AUTHENTICATION AND AUTHORIZATION

One of the most difficult issues facing librarians trying to provide access to quality resources that are licensed only for their users is to let those users in and keep others out, without creating obstacles that will frustrate their legitimate users. Most of Chapter 8 deals with this issue.

THE ROLE OF YOUR ONLINE CATALOG

If you are hoping that your remote user community will come to your library site first to satisfy their information needs, you will need to come to grips with the role of your online catalog. "Integrated system" has a new meaning in the Internet era. You will need to seamlessly integrate your library catalog with full-text Web-based resources into a rich and user-friendly system if you want to satisfy your users. How to do that is the big issue. Using your catalog as the only or the primary gateway to your online resources has a great deal of appeal to librarians, but it is not the best way to serve users.

The Catalog as Gateway

Your integrated library system (ILS) is undoubtedly the most expensive online resource your library provides, in terms of your initial investment, maintenance, and the amount of staff time that has been and continues to be devoted to its local maintenance. The ILS has evolved into a truly remarkable centerpiece of most library processes: acquisitions, serials management, circulation, reserves, access to the library's holdings, and in some cases resource sharing and interlibrary loan. Web-based catalogs provide the opportunity to link to Web-based resources including photographs and other images in the library's collection as well as licensed and free full-text resources. It can play a role in the authentication of remote users. And it is a powerful search tool for those who know how to use it.

Because the catalog has always been the key to accessing the library's resources, ostensibly it seems logical to expand its role in the Web environment. Many libraries, with the best of intentions, present their catalogs as the gateway to all their resources. They catalog databases, electronic journals, electronic books, government documents, Web pages, local images, and full-text resources with the belief that they are integrating access to all materials, regardless of format. Users of such an enhanced catalog will encounter a wealth of resources, but it will not serve all of their information needs, and there is another problem: unless

- the cataloging staff is greatly increased
- the amount of print items being cataloged is greatly reduced, or
- the cataloging processes have been rigorously simplified

the attempt will prove to be an exercise in frustration. If the library broadens its concept of the "holdings" that should be made available to its users through the catalog (and for remote users, that would be as many full-text sources and quality Web pages as the library can acquire or identify), then the catalogers will be overwhelmed by the magnitude of their new cataloging responsibilities.

Maintenance of catalog records becomes a daunting task as Web-based resources come and go, URLs change, and servers crash. A book is cataloged one time and unless the library changes its classification system, the record doesn't need to be altered until the book is withdrawn. Serials records have always required more upkeep, but the maintenance of serials records that now include links to online journals the library has acquired from publishers or through subscriptions to databases can overwhelm those who are responsible for them. The content of full-text databases is especially unstable lately. Beautiful MARC records for journals that are no longer part of a full-text database are worse than useless in your catalog. To catalog Web pages in a significant way requires an ongoing effort throughout the library.

If your staff can meet the challenge of cataloging and maintaining the records for your online resources, you will be providing a wonderful service to the users of the catalog. But don't be fooled into thinking that cataloging your online resources will provide meaningful access to everything your users seek. Don't let the magnitude of this project divert your attention from the parallel task of providing easy and granular access to full-text resources, and don't let your commitment to your catalog blind you into thinking that its maintenance should be your highest priority. We are not trying to discourage you from making the best use of your catalog. But we believe that the added challenges require a new approach, using different standards and much more flexibility than in the past, and that catalogers should also be very much involved in providing access to materials through other channels besides the catalog.

The major problems with the library catalog as the gateway to online resources in the world occupied by remote users are that it

- is designed to describe known physical items in the library, and that's what it does best

- doesn't look and act like a familiar Web-based resource; it is hard to use
- does not provide article-level access to full-text materials in databases

Online Catalogs are Hard to Use

We sometimes lose sight of this, but in the context of the studies on Web searching, the library catalog interface is beyond the comprehension of many Web users. More experience online does not translate into better searching abilities. The opposite appears to be the case: users now expect search interfaces to be simple and intuitive. The fact that library catalogs have for the most part migrated to the Web does not make them automatically easy to use. A 1996 article by Christine L. Borgman, "Why Are Online Catalogs *Still* Hard to Use?" presents an excellent analysis of the problem: "that most current online catalogs are based on card catalog design models, that this model does not map well onto online systems, and that the model is not based on information-seeking behavior" (494). Searchers are required to structure a query in terms of the content of information entities that are generally unknown to them. Most users don't have the conceptual framework for understanding the structure of bibliographic records or the use of Boolean logic to retrieve them. As functionality is added to online systems, so is complexity. If you think your online catalog is easy to use, take a look at a recent transaction log. If you are a reference librarian, you probably don't need a transaction log to tell you what kinds of difficulties are encountered in using the catalog.

ACCESS TO ARTICLES

Most casual users who have not been through a library instruction session (and even some who have) do not understand the distinction between the library catalog and library databases.

Remote users want to get directly to quality full-text resources as easily as possible. Your Web design should not lead them to believe that the library catalog is the place to start their search. If they conduct a subject or keyword search in most catalogs they will retrieve a high proportion of records for print materials. If they are able (if the system allows it, and if they figure out the procedure) to limit their catalog search to online resources, they will still not find articles in journals.

Undergraduates and the non-specialized public will be best served by a Web page with prominent links to multi-disciplinary databases containing the full text of current articles in magazines and journals. Their quest may well end there, assuming the interface is navigable and the formats are manageable. You can improve their rate of success by offering online reference assistance (see Chapter 4) and instruction geared towards remote users (see Chapter 6).

Remote researchers, faculty and graduate students, and other specialized users usually require access to journal literature, and will be well-served by leads to the full-text databases in their disciplines. Most of them will need to use specialized bibliographic databases as well, requiring a second step that could take them to your catalog, through a function in the database or as a separate process they will initiate. Depending on their level of motivation, they may or may not be able to successfully negotiate all the steps.

The gateway that would most benefit these users is a cross-domain search engine, if you can provide one. For them, a system of deep links within electronic resources, such as SFX, is also valuable. Providing an infrastructure for deep linking is probably the best reason to catalog individual electronic journals.

RESOURCE INTEGRATION

Although we can't recommend your ILS as the gateway to all your electronic resources, we do encourage you to provide an integrated gateway to your Web-based databases, including your ILS. Several software options are becoming available for libraries that want to offer their patrons the ability to search multiple databases, including OPACs and the Web simultaneously. Various terms for this capability are "broadcast searching," "cross-domain searching" and "information portal" (not to be confused with other kinds of portals such as the one discussed later in the chapter). Some products are based on the Z39.50 ANSI/ISO Standard (see the NISO Z39.50 at www.niso.org/standards/resources/Z39-2.pdf), whereas others use the Open URL approach (Van de Sompel and Beit-Arie, 2001). Both approaches require content-producers to adhere to emerging standards to ensure the interoperability of databases. An ARL Scholars Portal Working Group (2001) is working on a project to develop a "single search" tool for academic libraries, possibly with a commercial partner. The marketplace is filling rapidly as vendors, including most major ILS vendors, recognize how much it is worth to libraries to be able to provide a way to make searching their resources easier for their users. Some of the currently available products are

- WebFeat (www.paratext.com/webfeat/)
- Metalib by Ex-Libris (www.exlibris.co.il/metalib/)

- ZPortal by Fretwell Downing (www.fdgroup.com/fdi/zportal/about.html)
- MuseSearch by MuseGlobal (www.museglobal.com/try/)
- OCLC WebExpress (www.oclc.org/webexpress/)
- InfoTrac Total Access (www.galegroup.com/servlet/ItemDetailServlet?region=9&imprint=000&titleCode=INFO26&type=4&id=172049)

The implementation of cross-domain searching software requires a time commitment on the part of the library. The software must be customized for each library, and there is a certain amount of ongoing maintenance involved. Some of the companies will take care of the configuration and maintenance for an additional fee. For any of these products you are considering, ask for an estimate of the amount of time required to support it. Ask for the names of other libraries using the software, and contact librarians who have been involved with its implementation. Some of the products come to market before all the bugs are worked out. You may wish to be an "early adopter" of one of these, to get a substantial discount and more options for customization and even interface design. But stay flexible. You should avoid a commitment to a long-term license, because you may later prefer another product that comes along. Consider working within a consortium for added support and a lower price.

Integration of proprietary resources, as well as just about all the services discussed in this book can be outsourced. One new entrepreneur in the field is the Jones e-global library™, "the only virtual library designed specifically for online students to support your web-based educational programs" (www.e-globallibrary.com/). This company will provide reference service, an instruction tutorial, Web pathfinders, and a package of full-text resources, and/or it will work with the library to customize the resources.

LINKS

The integration of resources is also enriched by an increasing amount of linking between them. Your users will appreciate your activation and provision of links.

Links from Databases to Articles

Unfortunately for remote users, not all databases provide the full text of journal articles, especially specialized databases. We are seeing efforts by most major database providers to link to journal articles or other full-text documents at publisher sites and other locations. But this doesn't usually happen automatically;

you will need to let the database provider know about the packages of electronic journals to which your library subscribes.

- Cambridge Scientific Abstracts and ISI databases provide a linking service as part of the subscription to their databases
- SilverPlatter and Ovid provide add-on linking services: SilverLinker and OpenLinks
- Bibliographic records in OCLC FirstSearch databases are linked to full text in other FirstSearch databases
- EBSCOhost records link to full text through their EBSCO Online service
- PubMed has links to journals at publishers' sites

Links between Articles

If your library subscribes to a large number of electronic journals from major scientific, medical, and technology (STM) journal publishers, your users will be able to leap from one journal to another through articles' reference lists (a very attractive feature for scholars), thanks to CrossRef (www.crossref.org/), a cooperative initiative among publishers, based on the Digital Object Identifier System (www.doi.org/). The library doesn't need to do anything to enable CrossRef linking, but you may want to demonstrate and promote this feature as a way to attract and retain users. You will need to know and let your users know that a CrossRef link will take them to the full text of an article only if the library has a subscription to the online journal at the publishers' site. The same is true for links from the PubMed database. Experiment with reference links in some of your electronic journals to see how many of them provide access to actual full text before promoting the capability. If the results are disappointing, check again in a few months—this is an evolving project.

Library-Initiated Linking

The development of the OpenURL standard (www.library.caltech.edu/openurl/) for electronic resources, as sources and targets, allows libraries to take an active role in enabling links between their resources. SFX is the first OpenURL tool to be made widely available commercially, but we can expect other such products to emerge. The main advantages are stated on the SFX Web site (www.sfxit.com/): "No more 'dead' links whereby the user clicks on a link to navigate to a new information space but finds that they do not have rights of access to the resource to which they have linked and are therefore blocked from access. SFX allows the librarian to define the library's electronic collection, including both licensed and freely available resources; and to determine the manner in which the component resources can be linked to best suit the library's users." See Figure 7–8 in Chapter 7 for an example of an SFX menu of linking choices. The disadvantages are that the way this is done, behind-the-scenes tables of sources and targets must be updated and maintained on a library server. Furthermore, the interoperability protocols are still emerging and not all database providers have enabled OpenURL linking.

Libraries can make other kinds of links using product-specific software tools that are less sophisticated. SiteBuilder from ProQuest allows the library to establish links to individual journals, individual articles, or to canned searches of ProQuest databases. The search results will include articles as they are added to the database. Links to similar live search scripts can also be constructed in many online catalogs, and in some cases you will be able to script a search that will limit the results to online full-text resources such as electronic books.

TRACKING DOWN A KNOWN ARTICLE

Sometimes remote users, like all users, do not need to search a database or group of databases because they are looking for specific articles they have already identified. Faculty, graduate students, and other researchers tend to find out about the relevant literature in their field through a network of colleagues, or they work from lists of references in articles.

You might think that the integration of access to serials through a gateway catalog would be an advantage for these users; however, once they have discovered electronic journals, or a citation database that provides links to the full text of articles, they tend to lose any interest they might have formerly had in the library's print holdings. They will track down and use print resources as a last resort if they can't find the full text of what they need online. And, like undergraduates, some of them will adjust their needs to suit the online availability of sources. Users who are strictly remote may not have a choice. The catalog is generally not the place for them to start.

The idea that someone with a citation to an article will want to see a complete serial record that provides access to the library's holdings in all formats (print and microform holdings, links to online issues) in one integrated display, is unrealistic in today's environment. The problems are that

- it is counterintuitive for experienced OPAC users to use the library's catalog for something that is on the Web, be-

cause they have been trained to see the catalog as an access tool for resources in the library; and it makes more sense to them to look "on the Web" for a Web-based resource
- the intricacy of combined holdings information on one OPAC screen can confound novice users, despite our best efforts at straightforward presentation; they will learn to scan the record for a link to full text, but they will feel that they are having to wade through irrelevant information

Debate continues about providing catalog access to serials through the single-record, integrated approach vs. the separate-record approach. To provide access through the catalog to all their electronic journals, some libraries use a hybrid approach.

It is our opinion, based on personal observation (of librarians and users), that most users with a citation in hand would prefer to check a simple Web list of electronic journals in hopes that their target journal will be listed; then afterwards they will check the catalog (or not) for a journal that is apparently not online. Some libraries use their ILS as a database for generating Web lists of electronic journals so that users looking for titles in either place will find them, with only one database to be maintained. Very brief records will suffice for the purpose of generating Web lists and providing title access, and shortcuts and tools will allow you to batch load hundreds at a time if you have a list of journals with their URLs. MARCMaker and MARCBreaker, downloadable free of charge from the Library of Congress (lcweb.loc.gov/marc/makrbrkr.html), can be used with word-processing software and Excel to transform lists into simple records you can import into the catalog and export en masse for revision.

BROWSING

It's not easy to engineer a virtual library that will satisfy the diverse needs of a variety of users. In our efforts to make searching easy, we can easily forget that many people keep up to date in their academic disciplines or personal pursuits by browsing issues of magazines and journals. In the library, they might take a stack of journals or the recent issues of several journals to a table and peruse the tables of contents or flip through the issues. The virtual library should offer a similar opportunity. In fact, the virtual library can provide better browsing access to periodical literature.

Alerts services (see Chapter 5) can notify users when a new issue of a favorite journal becomes available (usually earlier than the print version will be in the library) and provide a table of contents for the issue. In the library, current periodicals can be shelved only one way—either alphabetically or by subject (in call number order). Either way inconveniences some users. In the virtual library, electronic journals can be listed both ways on library Web pages.

You will greatly expand your users' browsing options (as well as the success of those looking for a known article) if you include journals from aggregator databases, especially in databases that allow direct links to the tables of contents for individual journals. We don't want to mislead you into thinking that managing Web lists of electronic journals is an easy job and that it won't eat up someone's time, but we believe the effort is worth it. Find something less important that you can stop doing in order to make the time. If that isn't possible, consider a commercial service such as

- Serials Solutions (www.serialssolutions.com)
- TDNet (www.tdnet.com)
- Journal WebCite (www.JournalWebCite.com)

to produce Web lists for you. They may not be able to produce subject lists, but alphabetical lists are better than no lists. Electronic journal management companies are springing up like mushrooms. To find out about others, and to read about ways that other libraries handle this big job that keeps getting bigger, consult recent articles or postings in

- the archives of the SERIALST: Serials in Libraries Discussion Forum at http://list.uvm.edu/archives/serialst.html
- *Serials Review*
- *The Serials Librarian*

SITE SEARCH

Some library Web sites do not have a site search function because they have found that users can't differentiate between what is on the site and what is not, and will try to conduct catalog or database searches in the site search box. Nevertheless, site search is such a standard feature of Web sites that some of your users would note (and miss) its absence. We recommend having it, but not in a prominent location. On our own Web site (www.library.unr.edu) our catalog, databases, electronic journals, electronic books, and selected Web resources are prominently listed, while a "search" button on our menu bar has a mouse-over menu with options to search the "Library Web," "World

Wide Web," several local databases, "Site Index," and "Site Tree." It isn't a perfect solution, but for us it works.

SITE MAPS AND INDEXES

Site maps and indexes can be quite helpful to users who can't find what they are looking for or who want to see an overview of the site organization. Users can link from listings to the page or item they want. They don't have to know an exact term or name for something, since they can scroll and browse through the lists. Each has its advantages and disadvantages; if you can manage to provide both, you will provide a good service to your remote users.

Site Maps

A simplified graphical map (with links) can be designed manually, or a complete map (that looks like a hierarchical list) can be generated by your server software. The usefulness of an automatically generated site map will depend on the logic of your directory structures and how descriptive your header titles are for each page. There will be one listing for each unique page. The advantages of an automatically generated site map are that it

- doesn't require any staff time
- is always accurate and up-to-date
- can help orient users to the structure of your site

Site Index

A site index is usually created manually and is more conceptual. Its usefulness will depend on the amount of time someone is willing to spend in creating it and keeping it updated as Web pages change and resources are added. The advantages of a manual index are that

- you can list items that users might be trying to find but that do not have their own pages, such as individual databases
- you can list an item more than one time using synonymous terms or alternate names or acronyms or even common misspellings.

ACCESS ISSUES

Don't forget about your disabled remote users. If your Web design takes their needs into consideration, you will be able to provide much better access to information resources and services than they have ever had before. For a good discussion, see

- "Does Your Library's Web Page Violate the Americans with Disabilities Act?" (www.atnet.org/articles/ADA-library.html) and
- Practical Accessibility: Core Concepts (www.dartmouth.edu/~webteach/articles/access.html)

OVERALL SITE DESIGN

The biggest mistake librarians make in designing their Web sites is to categorize their resources and services in ways that make sense to them, which might reflect an organizational structure or an abstract scheme that doesn't make sense to users. As much as possible we need to see our offerings through users' eyes, which is especially difficult when there are diverse user groups. Involving representative users in usability studies of the site design (see Chapter 2) is essential.

One of the most difficult realizations for library Web designers is that users generally don't want to spend any time "exploring" our sites. They are generally there to conduct what Web designer Roger Black calls an "information transaction," looking for "one thing." Our job is "to open a clear path for people to their objective" (Schlosberg, 2001). What makes that hard is that we are offering "a lot more than one thing," and "then there's also the problem that people don't all behave the same way" (Schlosberg, 2001). So we have to provide a variety of paths and access tools, meanwhile helping our users find what they are looking for amidst the clutter. How to do that is beyond the scope of this chapter, but there is a wealth of information to help you meet the challenge of designing a usable Web site. We recommend the following sources of more information:

- new.architect—www.webtechniques.com
- Usable Web—www.usableweb.com
- WebReview.com—www.webreview.com
- Web Design Group—www.htmlhelp.com
- Web Design—webdesign.about.com/mbody.htm
- Research-Based Web Design & Usability Guidelines (National Cancer Institute)—www.usability.gov/guidelines/

We especially recommend one book, *The Web Style Guide: Basic Principles for Creating Web Sites* by Patrick Lynch and Sarah Horton (New Haven and London: Yale University Press, 1999).

It should be clear by now that the most difficult challenge for library Web designers is to provide a site that will satisfy the needs of a wide range of users. Some libraries meet this challenge by letting users customize their own library Web page, using the MyLibrary or portal approach.

WEB PORTALS

The term "portal" implies "doorway." So, a Web portal would be an entry point that makes sense out of the inherently chaotic World Wide Web. Yahoo! and other portals, such as AltaVista, Excite, Lycos, HotBot, and WebCrawler started out as Web directories, search engines, or a hybrid of both. However, in their efforts to keep visitors coming back, all of these portals added many new features and services, such as e-mail, shopping malls, financial services, instant messaging, and so on (Web Portal, 2001). They wanted to become as "sticky" as possible, like the first online services, Compuserve, Prodigy, and AOL, all of which tried to offer so much there was no need to go anywhere else (Gottesman, 1999).

Yahoo! is still the most popular Web portal, but there are many others, such as MSN, AOL, My Netscape, and ICQ (pronounced "I-seek-you"), which offer Web chat as a primary attraction.

Libraries adopted the word "portal," but have narrowed the scope somewhat to mean a Web site that is customized for a particular audience in order to make sense out of information resources.

CUSTOMIZATION OR PERSONALIZATION?

The terms "customization" and "personalization" are sometimes used interchangeably because most of us aren't clear about the difference, and there do not seem to be any standard accepted definitions. However, several experts, including Jakob Nielsen (1998) and IT World columnist, Michael Rosenberg (2001), agree that the difference is control.

The *user* controls customization, selecting from an array of options. For example, a portal offering customization may allow the user to select stock ticker symbols, newspaper headlines from various sources, a horoscope month, a zip code for weather information, and so on. Most portals use customization.

A *computer* controls personalization. It tracks the paths users take through a site and attempts to construct a model of user preferences. Amazon.com's book recommendations are an example of personalization. If personalization sounds intrusive, it is. Nielsen asserts that personalization is over-rated, and sums up the major difficulties with it:

"Basically, personalization requires that the system know a lot about the user. Also, users don't want to spend time setting up a complex system of personalization. Amazon works because it actually knows what millions of people are buying. If a lot of people who buy a certain book tend to also buy another title, they must be somewhat similar. This kind of analysis takes a lot of computing power, but it's based on spending, which says more for what people like than what they say. On the other hand, personalization is a lot like 'Big Brother is Watching You.' In other situations, it seems distasteful, if not scary" (1998).

Both customized and personalized sites may store user preferences in a database, a cookie, or both, so that when users return, the server will remember them. Chris Hoofnagle, legislative council with the Electronic Privacy Information Center (EPIC) (http://www.epic.org) identifies the problem with personalization as one of privacy. In customization, Hoofnagle said, a customer can "basically tell the business how you want content pushed or how you want to be identified." Personalization, on the other hand, does not give the user control (Hill, 2001).

Now that we have that straight, MyLibrary projects are customization applications. The user chooses from an array of options in several categories, such as subject indexes and databases, electronic journals, selected Web sites, reference tools, new books, and so on.

Portals are intended to gather an individual's chosen research tools into a personal toolbox, where they are always available and up-to-date. They are ideal for people working on specific projects or who want to keep up with a special research interest. They present desired information or information resources, eliminating the need to navigate to it, set bookmarks, or perform other kludges to preserve preferences.

This type of cross-resource access is a boon to patrons and what libraries can do well. However, an underlying assumption here is that libraries cannot design Web pages well enough to facilitate fast access to subject or other resources without supplementing the "regular" Web site with an alternative that is more user-driven. The long-term goal, which is worthy and appropriate, is that libraries will use emerging technologies to create a much more flexible, user-driven Web space than we can now imagine. For now, a customizable portal may be an excellent short-term solution for some libraries.

The obvious question to ask before creating or adapting a MyLibrary application is: Why do we need customization? Why is it so difficult to navigate quickly to desired information? Is there a real need for individualized pages, or is this an excuse for a poorly designed Web site that does not work very well. If the Web site is well designed and easy to navigate, does customization provide added value that makes it worth doing?

At this point, we do not know enough about how researchers actually use customized Web interfaces, nor have we solved the problem of presenting interdisciplinary resources on a menu. In a thoughtful article about MyLibrary@NCState, Tripp Reade examines these issues, new ways to increase user control, utilities that could enhance the usefulness of portals, and the limitations of customization (2001).

There are numerous MyLibrary sites, but the one that started it all was the MyLibrary project at North Carolina State University. Visitors to NCSU's MyLibrary, at my.lib.ncsu.edu/, may login to a guest account, change the guest profile, and see the results. Librarians will be interested in information about the project, available at my.lib.ncsu.edu/?cmd=about&kid=39. The source code and documentation are available for download.

A list of MyLibrary and other customization projects is available at the University of Leicester ELITE Project Web site (www.le.ac.uk/li/distance/eliteproject/elib/mylibrary.html).

Another major project worth examining is the California Digital Library, MyLibrary@CDL project, which was extensively evaluated throughout the University of California University system. A "Statement on Development of MyLibrary@CDL" that includes an evaluation of the project and its future is available at www.cdlib.org/libstaff/system_services/projects/mylibrary/statement.html. The report has an interesting twist, in that users liked the idea of the service, but wanted so many features added to it that giving them what they want would cause development costs and maintenance to be prohibitive. Also, a library Web portal would seem to compete with other campus portals. Since the entire CDL system is to undergo extensive development in the near future, the MyLibrary component was left in place, but not emphasized or upgraded.

Other libraries, as well as the CDL system, will want to take a hard look at how the transformation of library catalogs into inclusive information systems meshes or competes with portal development. The abandonment of MyLibrary at CDL reflects a nascent movement to truly integrate library access to owned and "rented" information. Future integrated library systems may integrate portal functions, but in a new way. Therefore, it may not make sense to invest the kind of staff time and expertise into developing a separate customization module, at least not until the direction catalogs are taking is clear.

HOW A CUSTOMIZED PORTAL WORKS

To come to any informed decision about whether portal development is worthwhile, it is useful to understand how they work. Portals can be simple, with only a few choices for the user, or elaborate, but if you look under the hood, most share certain characteristics and requirements:

- A database is needed to track and store preferences made by users
- Each user must have a unique ID and a password in order to protect privacy and to remember choices in the user's profile
- The user must be able to choose from an array of well-organized options, so that the end result is focused for a particular type of user or a particular discipline. For example, a user should at least be able to choose a set of subject indexes and electronic journals in which he has an interest
- The user must be able to add, change, and delete items from his or her profile. The database itself must be in a secure folder on the Web server, but permissions must be set to allow the IUSR (generic Internet visitor account) to write to it. However, all input goes through Active Server Pages technology (ASP) or whatever secure method is in place; the IUSR never accesses the database directly
- Some content can be constant. It can be updated as needed, but the format and general content has a reassuring consistency. Basic subject guides or resource lists fall into this category
- Some content needs to be fresh, such as news items, or updated frequently, such as a new books list
- Personal contact information is necessary. In libraries, a user should have not only a MyLibrary, but a MyLibrarian!

WHAT TYPE OF USER BENEFITS FROM A WEB PORTAL OR MYLIBRARY?

The user who understands the choices offered and who is capable of making wise decisions may appreciate having a focused and predictable Web page from which to launch research forays. Advanced researchers, faculty, mature upper division and graduate students, and anyone with very specialized interests are obvious potential beneficiaries. But does a portal make sense for lower-division undergraduate students? Do they have enough background knowledge to construct a useful portal? Do they have a need to restrict their view of the world of library resources? It seems logical that there may be a threshold of information literacy beyond which portal construction makes sense, and below which, it may do more harm than good. In other words, if a beginning student limits his view of library resources to a few items, will the end result be a Swiss cheese view of the information universe? Perhaps necessity will drive discovery, and an overly structured, somewhat narrow view of resources will not retard the development of scholarship competency. Nevertheless, it is something to consider.

COMBINING MYLIBRARY WITH MYLIBRARIAN

Every MyLibrary page should have contact information. Better yet, the user should be able to see a list of subject specialists or other experts, and add their e-mail links or other contact information to a personal page. But, just imagine your MyLibrary with a chat icon that buzzes one's personal librarian, or a link that dials their extension or digital phone. Someday, this will not only be feasible, but commonplace.

CUSTOMIZATION TOOLS

A portal, or customized Web interface, is, in the simplest terms, a database queried from a Web form, with results displayed in the user's browser. To accomplish this magic, several tools must work together:

- A relational database, such as Microsoft Access, SQL Server, MySQL, or PostgresSQL. Access can be used as a "front end" for SQL Server, but should not be used for portals unless the user base is very small
- A way to connect to the database from a Web page. A popular standard method is Open DataBase Connectivity (ODBC), an Application Programming Interface (API) that acts as a middleman between Web pages that contain SQL queries and proprietary database software. ODBC translates a query on your Web page into language your Database Management Software (DBMS) understands, using a database-specific ODBC driver. In Windows, you specify a System Data Source Name (DSN) in the ODBC dialog box (found in the Windows control panel) that identifies the location of the database and the proper ODBC driver. There are ODBC drivers for Access, SQLServer,

PostgresSQL, Oracle, and various other DBMS
- A way to query the database from a Web page. SQL is the standard query language used with ODBC and other methods of accessing data, such as ADO (ActiveX Data Objects). SQL is straightforward, easy to understand, and stable
- A scripting language. A Web page must include one or more scripts in order to tell ODBC to open a database connection, process an SQL query, write to the resulting HTML document, or perform other tasks. HTML cannot do this by itself, and SQL queries by themselves are not scripts. The choice of scripting language depends on the technologies used with a particular Web server to achieve interactivity in Web pages. If you have a Windows NT server using ASP technology for interactive pages, the scripting language of choice is usually VBScript. Other languages, such as PERL and JavaScript can also be used with ASP. The University of Washington uses an ASP application for MyGateway (Guest Login is available at www.lib.washington.edu/resource/login.asp). On Unix systems running Apache server, PERL is a standard scripting language. PHP is an open source scripting language that can be used in both Windows and Unix environments. NCSU's MyLibrary application is written in PERL for Unix systems (Morgan, 1999).

Some libraries may use ColdFusion to build database-driven Web sites. While the basic principles are the same, this suite of proprietary software tools uses its own high-level markup language (CFML, or ColdFusion Markup Language) to interact with relational databases and to create Web pages. A discussion of the merits of ColdFusion versus ASP or other technologies is beyond the scope of this chapter.

NEAR-PORTAL EXPERIENCES

Some libraries have developed Web sites that provide customized information for certain types of users, and may even refer to them as "portals." Strictly speaking, they are not portals, since they are written for targeted groups of users, not individuals who customize pages for themselves. However, since they require no effort on the part of the user, these near-portals may serve their audiences even better than portals (if you think about it, a "near-death" experience would probably receive a better rating than a "death" experience from people who have had one).

Lehigh University has created an exemplary near-portal experience for the Lehigh community. The University home page has a top-level menu for Libraries. One of the choices is "Subject Resources," which leads to a page labeled "InfoDome: Scholarly Web Resource Collections" (www.lehigh.edu/~inlib/infodome/).

At first glance you might think that InfoDome is similar to other subject guide pages. However there are some characteristics and features that set it apart:

- InfoDome is a database-driven application designed by a team of librarians and instructional technology specialists
- There is a top-level Web page for each Lehigh college. From there, resources specific to each major are listed separately. This arrangement puts subject resources firmly in context of related disciplines. For example, a student can go to the Humanities page for a list of general resources, and then to Art, Literature, History, and other majors within Humanities
- The subject pages integrate subscription resources and Web sites. Each page has an area for "featured resources"
- The user may search for selected Web sites, which are cataloged and also searchable in the library catalog. In fact, "the system creates a list of Web page catalog descriptions by going out to ASA, Lehigh's Library Catalog, and retrieving all Web page descriptions for that category. The results list is in LIFO (last in, first out) order" (Johnson, 2001)
- The resource descriptions are based on the MARC record, and "evolving metadata standards, including the Dublin Core." For each Web site record, there is metadata for: title, URL, abstract, Library of Congress Subject Headings, and the library's own subject categories (Johnson, 2001)
- Maintenance of resource records is done though the catalog, so all searches retrieve current records

Lehigh's integration of selected Web resources into its library Web site and the library catalog gives users more than one way to find the same information. The innovative use of catalog data for more than one purpose also enforces consistency, which lessens confusion.

Even without creating a portal, there are obvious advantages gained from

- organizing subject resources in parallel with an institution's course catalog to create discipline-specific resource guides

- making selected Web sites available from the same page as subscription resources
- including links to electronic journal lists or search pages from subject research guides
- organizing around users' "purpose"—research, need a few good articles, need facts, want to learn about what the library has to offer, etc.

Many academic libraries, of differing sizes and administrative structure, have followed one or more of these practices on their Web sites. For example, visit the subject resource pages of the University of Southern California Library (www.usc.edu/isd/electresources/) and the University of Nevada, Reno Libraries (www.library.unr.edu/subjects/).

Whether to portal or not to portal matters less than if the solution developed at your library works well for your community. Portal construction is not a trivial commitment in terms of staff time or expertise. It may very well be that the next generation of library catalogs will integrate functions we now associate with portals.

A FEW WORDS ABOUT USABILITY

Each user has his or her own criteria for determining the usability of remote library resources and services. Your library's Web site will benefit from your adherence to universal principles of good design, but it must also reflect the mix of your own users. Above all, you want your electronic resources to be used heavily and successfully, and that will only happen if your users are satisfied. Whether or not users are satisfied may depend less on the quality of your resources and their presentation and more on their expectations. Through promotional outreach and instruction you can influence those expectations, but keep in mind that their other experiences on the Web will have a great deal of influence. You will want to build on their experiences and be in synch with the Web at large. Banish thoughts that begin with

- "they should be able to . . . "
- "it is our responsibility to make sure they learn to . . . "
- "it is good for them to have to . . . "

To satisfy your users' expectations and ensure their success it may seem that you have to "dumb down" your presentation of resources and services for remote users. So be it. The alternative is to not have many users because they are getting their information somewhere else.

One last comment on building a usable virtual library: if you do a good job that doesn't mean you will get to rest! Success breeds higher expectations, and your users will be asking for more.

REFERENCES

ARL Scholars Portal Working Group Report. 2001. [Online]. Available: www.arl.org/access/scholarsportal/ [2001, July 5].

Astroff, Roberta J. 2001. "Searching for the Library: University Home Page Design and Missing Links." *Information Technology and Libraries* 20, no.2 (June): 93–99 [Online] Available: www.lita.org/ital/2002_astroff.html. [2001, July 26].

Borgman, Christine L. 1996. "Why Are Online Catalogs *Still* Hard to Use? *Journal of the American Society for Information Science* 47, no.7 (July): 493–503.

Bronstad, Amanda. 2000. "By Any Other Name." *Austin Business Journal* (July 28) [Online]. Available: austin.bcentral.com/austin/stories/2000/07/31/ focus1.html [2001, July 19].

Gottesman, Ben Z. 1999. "Portals." *PC Magazine* (November 2). ZDNet Reviews [Online] Available: www.zdnet.com/products/stories/reviews/ 0,4161,2354132,00.html [2001, July 11].

Hill, Kimberly. 2001. "Privacy and Personalization—Can't Have One Without the Other?" *NewsFactor Network* (August 29) [Online]. Available: www.newsfactor.com/perl/story/13189.html [2001, November 11].

Horton, Sarah. 2000. "Practical Accessibility: Core Concepts." In *Web Teaching Guide*. [Online]. Available: www.dartmouth.edu/~webteach/articles/ access.html [2001, July 25].

Johnson, Jean. 2001. "Help & Introduction." *Infodome*. Lehigh University. [Online]. Available: www.lehigh.edu/~inlib/infodome/ [2001, July 12].

Morgan, Eric Lease. 1999. "MyLibrary@NCState: The Implementation of a User-centered, Customizable Interface to a Library's Collection of Information Resources." [Online]. Available: hegel.lib.ncsu.edu/development/ mylibrary/sigir–99/ [2001, July 12].

Nielsen, Jakob. 1998. "Personalization is Over-Rated." *Jakob Nielsen's Alertbox* (October 4) [Online]. Available: www.useit.com/alertbox/ 981004.html [2001, July 11].

———. 1999. "Prioritize: Good Content Bubbles to the Top." *Jakob Nielsen's Alertbox* (October 17) [Online]. Available: www.useit.com/alertbox/ 991017.html [2001, July 30].

Reade, Tripp. 2001. "Unpacking the Trunk: Customization and MyLibrary@NCState." *Computers in Libraries* 21, no.2: 30–34.

Rosenberg, Michael. 2001. "The Personalization Story." *ITWorld.com* (May 11) [Online]. Available: www.itworld.com/Man/2676/ITW010511rosenberg/ [2001, July 11].

Schlosberg, Jeremy. 2001. "Roger Black on the Art of Web Design." *Media Life* (February 5). [Online]. Available: www.medialifemagazine.com/news2001/feb01/feb05/1_mon/news3monday.html [2001, August 6].

U.S. Dept. of Commerce. National Telecommunications and Information Administration. 2000. *Falling Through the Net: Toward Digital Inclusion* [Online]. Available: www.ntia.doc.gov/ntiahome/fttn00/contents00.html [2001, July 28].

Van de Sompel, Herbert, and Oren Beit-Arie. 2001. "Open Linking in the Scholarly Information Environment Using the OpenURL Framework." *D-Lib Magazine* 7 no.3 (March) [Online]. Available: www.dlib.org/dlib/march01/vandesompel/03vandesompel.html [2001, August 14].

Web4lib archives. 2001. [Online]. Available: sunsite.berkeley.edu/Web4Lib/archive.htm [5 July 2001].

"Web Portal." 2001. *Webopedia*. INT Media Group, Inc. [Online]. Available: webopedia.internet.com/TERM/W/Web_portal.html [2001, July 11].

"Web Surfers Hunt Like Animals, Researchers Find." 2001. *SiliconValley.com* (May 15) [Online]. Available: www.siliconvalley.com/docs/news/svfront/019243.htm [2001, July 24].

4 PROVIDING ELECTRONIC REFERENCE SERVICES

by Araby Y. Greene

CHAPTER OVERVIEW

- Overview of Electronic and Digital Reference Services
- Telephone Reference—the Original AskA Service
- E-Mail Reference and AskA Services
- Expert Systems
- Real-Time Reference Services
- The Future of Digital Reference
- Appendix: Example of an E-Mail Web Form With an ASP Form Handler

---

OVERVIEW OF ELECTRONIC AND DIGITAL REFERENCE SERVICES

All of the Web-based tools that librarians create to help information seekers find answers, advance research, or satisfy curiosity may be thought of as "electronic reference services." The gateway to this collection of services is usually the library Web site, which organizes and explains information resources by subject, purpose, or audience. Electronic reference tools may include self-help subject guides with annotated collections of hyperlinks, tutorials for new users, customized portals, and human-mediated services such as e-mail and chat.

The term "digital reference services" is quite specific, referring only to electronic reference services that are Web-based and human-mediated. They add a personal touch to high-tech, going far beyond static collections of hyperlinks. The Virtual Reference Desk organization has defined the term:

> Digital reference, or "AskA", services are Internet-based question-and-answer services that connect users with experts and subject expertise. Digital reference services use the Internet to connect *people* with *people* who can an-

swer questions and support the development of skills (Virtual Reference Desk, 2000).

WHO USES ELECTRONIC REFERENCE SERVICES?

Just about everyone. We think of remote users as people working at home, in a dorm room, at work or school, perhaps in a hotel room. In practice, users on campus or at the far end of the top floor of a large library are also remote users. Even people within walking distance can appreciate the timesaving convenience of electronic reference services. Others are more comfortable using a computer to get help than initiating a face-to-face interaction.

It is important to recognize that our remote users are not alike in their learning styles or preferences for finding help:

- Some people want to "AskA" question, and will gravitate towards e-mail reference and chat applications
- Others would rather figure things out for themselves, or interact with computer-assisted search systems
- For the independent-minded, Frequently Asked Question (FAQ) files or databases and expert systems are attractive options
- Some people are specialists. They want to see information that relates to their personal research interests, but have little interest in other resources. This group may prefer a customized portal to the library home page

Ideally, a library will have an array of electronic reference services that appeal to users with different levels of expertise as well as personal preferences. In addition, it should be easy to combine types of service to meet a particular information need. For example, a complex chat question might require an e-mail follow-up. An FAQ archive may partially answer a question, but invite the viewer to initiate a chat session. A portal user may need to consult a subject specialist. Fortunately, the Web makes it easy to jump from one type of service to another by using hyperlinks on selected pages or by creating a directory of interactive services.

AN ARRAY OF SERVICES

Step back for a moment to take a horizon-to-horizon view of the various kinds of electronic reference help that libraries offer remote users. Because the telephone has played such an important role for a very long time, and continues to complement electronic reference, it is included in our overview. Also, the digital telephone is evolving into a hybrid tool combining telephone service, PDA functions, and Web access. Eventually, it will become a realistic option for delivering electronic short-answer reference help.

We can broadly categorize types of electronic reference services for this discussion as mediated help and guided self-help. Mediated help can be:

- Human-mediated
  - Telephone reference service
  - E-mail reference
  - Chat and Instant Messenger services
- Computer-assisted
  - Expert systems that lead the user to appropriate information
  - Portals or customized "MyLibrary" pages

Guided self-help includes:

- Virtual Reference Desks (VRDs)
- Subject guides and pathfinders
- Frequently Asked Question (FAQ) Web pages or searchable databases

This chapter will focus on new techniques that libraries are actively using and developing—namely, mediated AskA services using e-mail and chat, with an excursion into experiments with expert systems. We will also look at forces that are shaping the future of electronic reference, such as the expanding availability of broadband services and new Internet protocols.

TELEPHONE REFERENCE—THE ORIGINAL ASKA SERVICE

The telephone was the instrument of choice for helping remote users until the wide availability of Web access offered new ways to communicate. Numerous articles about improving telephone reference service were still being published in the mid–1990s, with a rapid decline in recent years. Because the telephone continues to be an important adjunct to electronic reference, it is worth reviewing its virtues and limitations for communicating with remote users.

STILL GOOD AFTER ALL THESE YEARS . . . BUT NOT ALWAYS GOOD ENOUGH

Reference librarians honed the short-answer telephone reference interview to a high level of efficiency, and reference desk staffers are very good at projecting their sense of care and concern for each caller. There is no substitute for immediate feedback and the goodwill flowing from a friendly exchange. In some environments, the telephone will remain very important.

Rural library users may not have access to the Internet, slow connections may make online chat an exercise in futility, or an aging population may feel more comfortable with the telephone. In some urban areas, having to drive to the library and spend forty minutes cruising for a place to park is daunting. In these environments, it may be a wise investment to expand and improve telephone reference service.

However useful and necessary, there are obvious challenges in providing really good telephone reference service:

- Conflicting needs of the person standing in front of you at the desk and the person at the other end of a persistently ringing telephone
- Unavailability of telephone service after Reference Desk hours. To help users who work late at night, Enoch Pratt library initiated a "Night Owl" telephone service, described at www.epfl.net/info/nightowl.html. Other libraries use voicemail systems to let people leave reference questions when the library is closed
- Complex questions that are often impossible to answer adequately over the phone. Clarification may also require multiple phone calls. Referrals are time-consuming

On the plus side, a brief telephone call can clear up confusion in a frustrating e-mail exchange. There is also no reason why a telephone question cannot be answered by any appropriate and efficient means, such as e-mail or document delivery. Experience with the benefits and limitations of telephone reference service has taught us effective techniques for efficiently handling short-answer reference questions in *any* environment, including e-mail and real-time Web chat.

E-MAIL REFERENCE AND ASKA SERVICES

Many libraries have e-mail reference services. Several years ago, it felt daring to offer such a service in a public venue such as the World Wide Web. We worried about being overwhelmed with e-mail questions and being overburdened with questions from visitors who were not part of our primary clientele. Now, it's different. Searchers have a multitude of AskA services to query, from the venerable Internet Public Library Reference Center (www.ipl.org/ref/) to "Ask the Makeup Diva" (www.makeupdiva.com/). Educators have been going to AskERIC for answers since 1992 (ericir.syr.edu/About/).

A helpful exercise for libraries planning an e-mail reference service is simply to visit Web sites of other libraries that offer the service. Bernie Sloan, a librarian at the University of Illinois at Urbana-Champaign, has compiled a list of over 90 library "E-Mail Reference Sites" at alexia.lis.uiuc.edu/~b-sloan/e-mail.html. The list was compiled from responses to his queries on library-related discussion lists.

Many of these library sites provide useful examples of Web forms, and policy or procedure statements. Most of them are at U.S. libraries, but the list includes libraries in Canada, Australia, the Netherlands, Singapore, and Estonia.

To create a mental "benchmark" for comparing AskA services, take a close look at the Internet Public Library Reference Center home page, a good example of an AskA service that is feature-rich and not at all intimidating (www.ipl.org/ref/). The site has a retro look that creates a sense of familiarity, much like the portly butler at "Ask Jeeves" (www.askjeeves.com). A large cartoon of a library reference area nearly fills the screen. The Reference Desk is labeled "Ask A Question."

When a visitor clicks the "AskA" link, the browser displays an informational page about e-mail reference that clearly states rules and procedures and leads to a question form. Standard e-mail guidelines are also provided for people with old browsers that do not support forms. Another important function of this page is to inform the visitor about "Frequently Asked Questions" and subject "Pathfinders." Overall, the tone of the site is professional and caring.

TECHNOLOGIES FOR E-MAIL REFERENCE

Technically, setting up e-mail reference service can range from absurdly simple to challenging. The important thing is to start somewhere. It takes only one little "mailto" link to open communications between visitors who need help and reference staff. That first link is *infinitely* better than nothing, so we'll start with it, and work up to more complex solutions.

Mailto Links

The simplest way to enable e-mail reference is to put one or more "mailto" hyperlinks to a person or special reference mail account on your Web site. A "mailto" link requires no software at all on the part of the library, but the user must have access to e-mail in order to send a question.

Adding e-mail reference functionality is as easy as typing HTML code for a mailto link:

<a href="mailto:account@server.ext">Ask a Question!</a>

Notice that the mailto anchor ("a" is for "anchor") tag does not use forward slashes after the colon. Other than that, it is like any other hyperlink. When a Web visitor clicks the link, the browser's default e-mail program opens with a blank message pre-addressed to the location of the "mailto." Of course, the library must have a procedure in place that ensures frequent checking of reference mail and prompt handling of responses.

Forms that Mail Themselves

The next level of sophistication involves adding a form to the e-mail reference Web page. Writing the HTML code for a form is straightforward, and instructions are in any HTML primer or reference book. However, to *do* anything with user input, the <form> tag must specify an "action" that captures the information and sends it to a script or program for processing. Such scripts or programs are called "form handlers." See a sample form and ASP form handler in the appendix at the end of the chapter.

Until recently, form handlers were nearly always Common Gateway Interface (CGI) programs composed as Perl (Practical extraction and report language) scripts or in the C programming language. However, PHP (which started out as "Personal Home Page Tools," and now loosely stands for "PHP: Hypertext Preprocessor") is becoming a popular alternative to Perl for CGI or other server-side scripting (Bakken and Schmid, 2000), particularly on Unix servers.

On Microsoft NT or Windows servers, Active Server Pages Technology (ASP) is often preferred for its built-in support, efficiency, and flexibility.

Server-side scripting with CGI, PHP, or ASP ensures that your e-mail forms will run on any browser, even Lynx! Your choice of

---

Figure 4-1. Script Resources for E-Mail Forms in a Unix Environment

- Perl—Large user-base makes technical support and ready-made scripts easy to find. Download Perl from www.perl.org/
  Script Resources:
  - FormMail, from Matt's Script Archive, is a standard from which many other scripts are derived. (www.worldwidemart.com/scripts/formmail.shtml)
  - ScriptSearch.Com (www.scriptsearch.com/Perl/)
  - CGI Resource Index (cgi.resourceindex.com/)

- PHP—Scripts can be designed to work independently or with CGI. PHP supports database connectivity.
  Download PHP from www.php.net/
  Script Resources:
  - ScriptSearch.com (www.scriptsearch.com/PHP/) has user-rated scripts
  - PHP Resource Index.com (php.resourceindex.com/)

Figure 4-2. Script Resources for E-Mail Forms on Windows NT or Windows 2000 Servers

- PHP—Open-source. Scripts can be standalone and written in HTML pages or used with CGI. Supports database connectivity. Download PHP from www.php.net/
  Script Resources:
  - ScriptSearch.com (www.scriptsearch.com/PHP/) has user-rated scripts
  - PHP Resource Index.com (php.resourceindex.com/)

- ASP—Nearly all ASP scripts are written in VBScript, so it is easy to find script examples and support. ASP scripts can be written in other languages, such as JScript, PerlScript, or Python.
  Script Resources:
  - FormMail for ASP, a well-crafted version by Mike Hall, based on the Perl script from Matt's Script Archive (www.brainjar.com/asp/formmail/)
  - The ASP Web site, 4GuysFromRolla, has scripts with good documentation and a searchable database of articles about ASP (www.4guysfromrolla.com/)
  - ASP 101 offers scripts for all levels of expertise (www.asp101.com/)

scripting language will depend on your Web server, your preferences, and more often than not, what your Systems Administrator can support.

Once user input is captured from your form, the script specified in the form's "action" parameter must reformat it as a proper e-mail message. Then, to actually send the e-mail to a library re-

---

Figure 4-3. For FrontPage Users

The FrontPage form handler can save user-input ("form results") to a file or database as well as send it to an e-mail address. Right-click on the form and select "Form Properties." Click the "Options" button to open a menu of formatting choices for e-mail and file results. To save results in a file, specify a filename and choose "File Format" from eight variations of plain text, delimited text, or HTML.

Use the FrontPage 2000 database wizard to quickly create a "connection" to the database, a search form, and a results page. The wizard is fine for simple search forms and results, but it may not be able to create the exact type of search options or results display that you want.

---

cipient, Simple Mail Transport Protocol (SMTP) server software must also be installed and running on your Web server.

SMTP server software is easy to install and configure, so it should not present a barrier to getting started. A separate e-mail account to receive e-mail reference questions is recommended to facilitate sharing among staff, especially for times when people are on vacation or otherwise unavailable, and for quality control or tracking purposes. The reference e-mail account can be on any convenient server, which might not be the library Web server.

Remember to read the "Terms of Use" before installing any copyrighted script. Most are generous about letting you modify code to meet your needs, but require that the copyright notice remain intact.

E-Mail Forms with Content Stored in a File

A simple archive of reference questions received through the library's AskA service is a reservoir of raw data that can be analyzed to identify user groups and common difficulties, such as missing instructions, problems with access, and needed services. It will also serve as a backup if messages are lost in transit. However, raw data is not very useful as a public Web page because it's unfiltered and could reveal personal information about users.

If you have an AskA Web form, you already have a script or e-mail form handler that processes it, sending the user's question to the reference service e-mail address. With some modifications, the same script can also write the user input to a file.

Writing input to a file gives librarians an opportunity to use the data. However, if you want to make the e-mail question archive available on a public Web, as a browse list or a searchable resource, a Database Management System (DBMS) becomes essential.

Figure 4-4. What is a DBMS?

In simple terms, a DBMS is a collection of programs that enables you to create, change, delete, and otherwise manipulate individual records in a database. Popular DBMS software includes Microsoft Access, Microsoft SQL Server, Sybase, Oracle, Informix, and others. All of these DBMS support the use of Standard Query Language (SQL) to create search statements or "queries" that retrieve records from a database that match certain criteria or that contain specified search terms.

Custom Forms with Content Stored in a Database

Store reference questions and responses in a database to achieve more control over the way your e-mail reference form is processed and to add customized search and display functions. You will find the most resources and user support for DBMS that can be queried using Standard Query Language (SQL).

The database software chosen by Unix and Microsoft Windows 2000 or NT users may differ, but SQL is the same everywhere. It's proven, powerful, and easy to learn.

If you have a database containing reference questions and answers, you can use an SQL query to dynamically retrieve all current records or a set of records that matches specific search criteria. An SQL query statement cannot be placed on a Web page independently. The query is always included within a script that includes other code to open a database connection, execute the SQL statement, format query results as HTML, and close the database connection.

There are many resources for Web developers building database applications for a Unix environment. Examples of Perl or PHP scripts will be available for download from

- ScriptSearch.Com—www.scriptsearch.com/Perl/
- CGI Resource Index—cgi.resourceindex.com/
- PHP Resource Index.com—php.resourceindex.com/

Of these options, PHP is the most attractive. It is an open-source server-side scripting language that can be used with either Unix or Windows servers to access SQL databases. Moreover, you can "embed" (write) PHP code directly in HTML pages, a convenience that can shorten the test and debug phase of development. PHP is often used with MySQL, an extremely popular (free!) open-source SQL database for Unix systems.

MySQL is also available for other operating systems, including Windows NT and Windows 2000. For more information about licensing and support, or to download MySQL, visit the MySQL home page at www.mysql.com/.

Active Server Pages technology is also an option for Unix developers, but ASP support is not a built-in component of Apache or other Unix Web servers as it is with Microsoft Internet Information Server for Windows. Using ASP on Unix machines requires a commercial version of ASP for Unix, such as Chili!Soft ASP (www.chilisoft.com/).

For Windows NT or Windows 2000 servers, a sensible choice is a Microsoft Access or SQL Server database application with Active Server Pages (ASP) technology. PHP is another option for database access. It is open-source, cross-platform, and robust, with a growing PHP developer community.

Examples of Database Applications for E-Mail Reference

Most libraries do not use special software packages for managing e-mail reference service. A homegrown system is hard work, but the added functionality is demonstrated at Grant McEwan College (Edmonton, Alberta, Canada), which has developed an open source-based "Virtual Reference Management" package. Visit the McEwan AskA service at www.lrc.gmcc.ab.ca/research/ask/.

Several features of this service make it an interesting example:

- First, only authenticated users can ask a question. Login is accomplished via a popup window that asks for the user's e-mail address
- Second, it offers a keyword or subject search option to anyone. Since many questions are frequently asked, the search function itself may assist visitors who are not affiliated with Grant McEwan College
- Third, the "Ask A Question" page is shared by fifteen colleges in the Alberta, Canada area. Participating libraries answer their own questions most of the time, but the system has been customized to allow every library to see questions and contribute to the answers. Hours of availability are entered into the system so that questions do not remain unanswered when a particular library is closed

Information about the service on the main page is brief and clear, stating who may use "Ask A Question," how soon to expect an answer (within 24 hours), what kinds of questions may be asked, and what kind of help is available. What the service does not do is also plainly listed. While the screen does not explicitly state that answers are returned via e-mail, patrons enter

Figure 4–5. Grant McEwan College "Ask a Question" Service

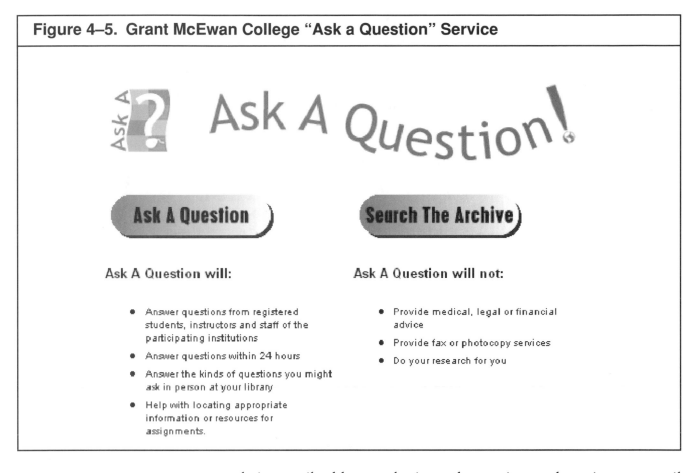

their e-mail address to login to the service, and receive an e-mail response.

The source code of the "Ask A Question" Web page indicates that Perl and CGI drive this application. Even if your library uses other development tools, the concepts of service and collaboration demonstrated here could be used as a model.

This application archives both the questions and the answers, making it possible to display the data as a self-help resource or FAQ file. To bring the parts together requires expertise in database management and script writing to handle form output and database access from the Web.

In some libraries, Unix, Perl, and CGI expertise is hard to find, but Microsoft Access is a familiar database. If the library also runs a Windows NT or Windows 2000 server with FrontPage Extensions, all the tools are in place to start learning how to access data from Web pages with Active Server Technology (ASP). If high-volume usage is a factor, an Access database can be upgraded to SQL Server, with Access as the front end for ease of maintenance.

The University of Nevada, Reno Library has an ASP application for handling both e-mail and archiving of comments sent to the Dean of Libraries at www.library.unr.edu/comments/. E-mail reference may use the same application in the near future. The only adaptation needed to use the application for e-mail reference would be different wording on the input form and the creation of a new database. While an outlet for comments serves a somewhat different purpose than AskA services, namely, venting the spleen versus asking a question, the procedures are nearly identical. Someone must respond, and the writer's privacy must be protected. The major difference is that a comment forum usually has no restrictions on the type of comment that can be made, except for the bounds of decency, and perhaps commercial advertising. E-mail reference questions, on the other hand, are best restricted to short-answer questions that do not require extensive research or reporting.

How It Works

The e-mail function is handled by a Web-form that captures user input and sends it to an ASP script for processing. The user does not have to open an e-mail program or have access to e-mail to send a comment.

When the user clicks the Submit button, the ASP script is activated, and performs the following steps:

1. User input is checked for errors or missing values. If no required field is absent and the user has entered a valid e-mail address, the data is processed. Otherwise, a list of errors is displayed.
2. If form input is valid and processed, a confirmation page is displayed.
3. The script formats an e-mail message that is immediately sent to the Dean of Libraries. The Dean will receive the e-mail with the standard subject line, "NEON Comment" so it is easily identifiable.
4. A connection is opened to the comments database, which is updated with the new comment and associated fields. The new comment is flagged to prevent display in the public Web archive until it has been answered.

So far so good. However, there is a logistical problem in getting the Dean's response written to the database. If he simply replies to the e-mail, there is no way for the response to be written to the database. For this reason, a hyperlink to the application's record edit screen is included in the e-mail message. The Dean,

---

Figure 4–6. Comment Form, University of Nevada, Reno Libraries

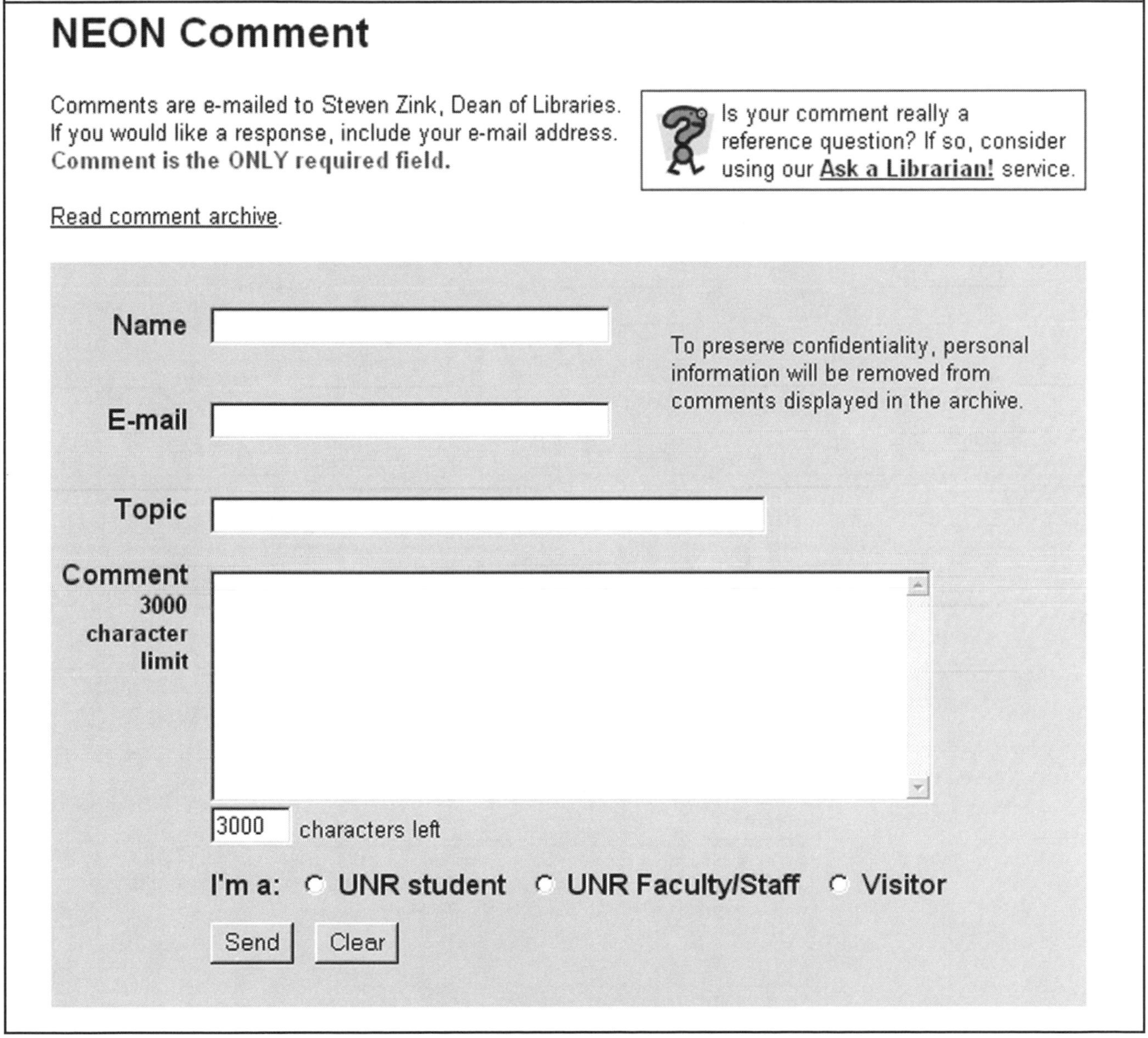

NEON Comment

Comments are e-mailed to Steven Zink, Dean of Libraries.
If you would like a response, include your e-mail address.
Comment is the ONLY required field.

Is your comment really a reference question? If so, consider using our **Ask a Librarian!** service.

Read comment archive.

Name

To preserve confidentiality, personal information will be removed from comments displayed in the archive.

E-mail

Topic

**Comment
3000 character limit**

3000   characters left

I'm a: ⊙ UNR student   ⊙ UNR Faculty/Staff   ⊙ Visitor

Send   Clear

---

or another authorized staff member, can click on the link or go directly to the edit screen URL, which is restricted to account holders and password protected.

The initial record edit screen displays a table of comments written to the database. Each comment and associated information is a database record, which may be edited or deleted. It is also possible to add a "fake" comment and answer that can be anticipated from experience as a Frequently Asked Question.

Figure 4–7. Unanswered Comment from the List of Database Records

Mark ⟋ **Click message number to edit**
☐ 3 Display: Yes

Word Processing in the Library?

Joe Camel

I am writing a research paper and would like to work on it in the library. Does the library have any computers with Microsoft Word?

jcamel@unr.edu

UNR Faculty/Staff

Figure 4–8. Edit Screen for a Single Comment Record

Edit NEON Comment

Fields that display in Web archive are: Subject, Date Submitted, Comment, Response.

Comment ID 3 Date Submitted: 6/19/2001 6:43:25 PM
Display in archive: Yes ⦿ No ○

Subject: Word Processing in the Library?

Commentor: Joe Camel

Comment:
I am writing a research paper and would like to work on it in the library. Does the library have any computers with Microsoft Word?

Response:
Yes, there are PCs and Macintosh computers with word processing software in the E. L. Cord Computer Lab on the first floor of Getchell Library. Be sure to bring your student ID card and a floppy disk for your files. Lab hours are

ReplyTo: jcamel@unr.edu

Perspective: UNR Faculty/Staff

[Edit E-Mail Only]   [Submit Changes and Edit E-Mail]

4–9. An E-Mail Response May be Edited Independently

NEON Comment E-mail Response

The database record has been edited. You may:

Cancel e-mail and return to list of records!

Or continue below to send e-mail to jcamel@unr.edu regarding Comment ID 3 :

Recipients: | jcamel@unr.edu |

User
Comment:

> I am writing a research paper and would like to
> work on it in the library. Does the library have
> any computers with Microsoft Word?

Response:

> Yes, there are PCs and Macintosh computers with
> word processing software in the E. L. Cord
> Computer Lab on the first floor of Getchell
> Library. Be sure to bring your student ID card
> and a floppy disk for your files. Lab hours are
> posted at <a
> href="http://computing.unr.edu/labs/irtlab.html">h
> ttp://computing.unr.edu/labs/irtlab.html</a>. If

| Preview | Send | Clear Response |

Clicking a comment's record number displays an edit screen for that specific record. The Dean may compose his response to the comment in a text box on this screen. At the same time, he may edit out personal information that should not display to the public, and flag the comment to display in the Web archive.

After submitting the revised record and its response to the database, an e-mail editing window allows further editing before the message is actually sent. The e-mail edit window offers a preview button for a better view of the response than the edit form's text box.

The public Web display of the comment archive is a simple list in a borderless table. Options that will be added as it grows are sort preferences, a search engine, and an option to limit the display to a certain number of records per page.

Figure 4–10. Response as Written to the Database

Mark
☐ 3   Display: Yes

Word Processing in the Library?

Joe Camel

I am writing a research paper and would like to work on it in the library. Does the library have any computers with Microsoft Word?

jcamel@unr.edu   **[The response, shown below, is written to the database]**

Yes, there are PCs and Macintosh computers with word processing software in the E. L. Cord Computer Lab on the first floor of Getchell Library. Be sure to bring your student ID card and a floppy disk for your files. Lab hours are posted at http://computing.unr.edu/labs/irtlab.html. If you have questions, please call the Help Desk at 784-4320.

UNR Faculty/Staff

Figure 4–11. A Comment Displayed in the Public Archive

NEON Comment Archive

Send a comment

- **Word Processing in the Library?**
  6/19/2001 6:43:25 PM
  Comment: I am writing a research paper and would like to work on it in the library. Does the library have any computers with Microsoft Word?
  Response: Yes, there are PCs and Macintosh computers with word processing software in the E. L. Cord Computer Lab on the first floor of Getchell Library. Be sure to bring your student ID card and a floppy disk for your files. Lab hours are posted at http://computing.unr.edu/labs/irtlab.html. If you have questions, please call the Help Desk at 784-4320.

The process of capturing e-mailed comments and archiving them in a database can be visualized as a series of scripted procedures (see Figure 4-12).

As mentioned earlier, the advantage of a database for capturing questions is that it can become the basis of a Frequently Asked Questions file or Web page, and provides data for evaluating the service.

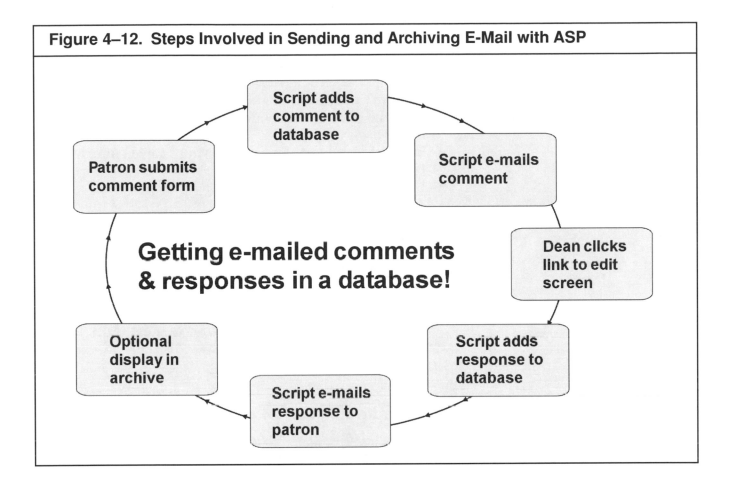

Figure 4–12. Steps Involved in Sending and Archiving E-Mail with ASP

STANDARDS AND EVALUATION OF E-MAIL REFERENCE SERVICE

A good place to find criteria for exemplary e-mail reference service is the Virtual Reference Desk's checklist for its own members: "Facets of Quality for Digital Reference Services, Version 4" (Virtual Reference Desk, 2000). The "facets" comprise 11 well-reasoned quality criteria and three levels of service for each one.

For more background information, see "Digital Reference Quality Criteria," in *Digital Reference Service in the New Millennium: Planning, Management, and Evaluation* (Bennett, Kasowitz, Lankes, 2000). The same book has a section on evaluating digital reference services, with two case studies. If your library is in a consortium, see "Quality Standards For Digital Reference Consortia," in *Reference & User Services Quarterly* (Kasowitz, Bennett, Lankes, 2000).

According to these sources, but more briefly stated, an evaluation of digital reference services should answer the questions:

- Is the service accessible to all users?
- Are the rules and procedures clear to the user?
- Is turnaround time fast enough?
- Do responses teach users how to find information in addition to answering their questions?
- Does the form elicit enough information to reduce the need for later clarification?
- Do staff members handling questions have enough experience? Expertise?
- Is referral built-in?
- Are other options available to the user? If so, are they obvious?
- Is the service promoted?

ASKA COLLABORATION

Networking questions with other libraries or AskA services could ensure that when referral is needed, patrons quickly receive more complete and accurate information. Two ambitious projects are creating innovative digital reference services on a grand scale: The Collaborative Digital Reference Service and The Virtual Reference Desk Project.

The Collaborative Digital Reference Service

The Collaborative Digital Reference Service (CDRS), sponsored by the Library of Congress, is international in scope, routing e-mail reference questions to libraries best qualified to handle them. Each participating library must submit a profile indicating its special areas of expertise and collection strengths. The CDRS Web site, at www.loc.gov/rr/digiref/, has extensive information on this expanding project. A salient feature of CDRS is the growing database archive of questions and answers.

Virtual Reference Desk Project

The VRD Network is sponsored by members of the "AskA Consortium" (www.vrd.org/network.shtml). Participants work toward creating a quality national reference service for the K–12 community. Members of the VRD network can refer difficult or out-of-scope questions to a specialist belonging to another member service. The participant list is a prestigious group, indeed:

- Ask A MAD Scientist
- AskERIC
- Ask a Space Scientist (NASA)
- Eisenhower National Clearinghouse for Mathematics and Science Education

- Environmental Protection Agency
- Internet Public Library
- American Memory (Library of Congress)
- Morris County Public Library (NJ)
- National Museum of American Art
- ScienceLine (from the UK)

COMBINING ASKA SERVICES AND VIRTUAL REFERENCE DESKS

Many frequently asked reference questions involve "ready reference" resources that are now available on the World Wide Web. A surprisingly large number of reference tools are open access, while some are subscription only. It makes perfect sense to create an organized interface for Web-based reference resources. In fact, some of the earliest efforts by libraries to expand reference service involved creating a "Virtual Reference Desk" (VRD) with sources and links.

The goal is to provide the user with high-quality reference resources equivalent to those available in the library. There are many excellent examples of VRDs on the Web. Some of the well-established sites have evolved into a combination of ready reference and e-mail reference.

The Internet Public Library (IPL) has one of the oldest and most widely known VRDs on the Web (www.ipl.org/ref/). A single Web page combines reference resource links with options to search reference resource, Ask a Question, see Frequently Asked Questions, or go to a list of Pathfinders. This combination gives users a sense of all available options in very little screen space.

EXPERT SYSTEMS

VRDs are wonderful and we should all have one, but sometimes, self-help is just not enough. A few libraries are experimenting with expert systems, which guide, cajole, and nudge the user, but do not require immediate human intervention.

Expert systems guide users by asking questions that lead them down the most likely path to the desired information. They automate decision-making, choosing the path an expert would take, if an expert were looking for the same type of information as the user. An introduction to the concept of "Expert System" is available on the Web at www.eco.utexas.edu/faculty/Norman/long.extra/Info.S98/Exp/main3.html. This site was a collaborative student project, written in an accessible style (Change, et al., 1998). Commercial technical support Web sites often channel users to the right driver or software update using a guided approach. Libraries can use a similar model to help users choose appropriate indexes or information resources.

The University of Illinois at Urbana-Champaign (UIUC) has a good example of an expert system that uses SQL to query a database of online resources and their characteristics in order to lead users through the database selection process (gateway.library.uiuc/rex/selector.htm).

Wei Ma and Timothy Cole presented information about their experimental "Article Database Advisor" service at the 2001 ACRL 10th National Conference. An informative abstract is available on the Web (Ma and Cole, 2001).

The Database Advisor invites users to choose a method for selecting resources:

- Search by keyword or phrase that describes a topic
- Browse databases by subject category
- Specify database characteristics or coverage

The developers of this project followed through with usability testing. Whatever the outcome, they have gathered invaluable data about how people look for information that will inform future efforts to improve the process of choosing the right database.

REAL-TIME REFERENCE SERVICES

Web chat software is rapidly becoming the tool of choice for delivering real-time reference service. Chat is familiar to many of our younger users, but may be alien to librarians.

Interactive chat is not a new concept at all. An early type of chat was available on VAX/VMS systems as the "phone" utility. To invite an interactive conversation, you simply typed "phone" plus a user's login name. That person could "answer phone" or ignore you. As long as you knew when a friend was going to be online, it worked very well, but limited the talkers to plain text. Unix systems also have many varieties of telnet-based chat. This arcane world of typed conversations between pairs of scholars and techies was eclipsed by Internet Relay Chat (IRC), where a *group* of users could talk to each other. Gamers embraced the bandwidth hogging virtual worlds of MUDs (Multiple User Dungeons) and MOOs (MUD, Object Oriented).

Chat went mainstream only when online services such as AOL began to offer it. Chat became extremely popular in spite of an unpleasant association with seamy and dangerous Internet activities. Commercial enterprises saw the potential of chat as a vehicle for instant technical support, shopping assistance, or a way for family or business groups to communicate. Libraries are now experimenting with chat software as a way to extend reference service.

Instant Messaging provides some of the functionality of chat, but the proprietary nature of IM software renders it unsuitable for universal access. The most popular Instant Messaging applications are ICQ (pronounced "I-Seek-You"), AOL Instant Messenger (AIM), MSN Messenger, and Yahoo! Instant Messenger (LaGesse, 2001).

Libraries are bypassing Instant Messaging for the same reason they avoid Web pages that require plug-ins: any tool that requires the user to download and register proprietary software is a barrier. Although there are libraries, such as SUNY's Morrisville College of Agriculture and Technology Library (library.morrisville.edu) that pioneered using Instant Messenger for "live" service, there are many more libraries using, or planning to use, Web-based chat services.

ADVANTAGES OF CHAT FOR YOUR USERS

Chat solves the main problem with e-mail reference: immediacy. Conducted in real-time, it can almost simulate a reference interview. Is there anything online chat can do better than telephone reference? Yes. First, remote dial-up users do not have to disconnect from their Internet connection to use the telephone. Second, if you've ever read a long URL over the phone, especially ones with tildes and underscores, you can relate to the ease of simply pasting a complicated URL into a chat window. Third, most chat systems create session transcripts, and some even e-mail them to the patron. An accurate record of exchanged information is difficult on the telephone.

Chat can be used anywhere in the library, the campus, or by students abroad. For times when chat is not staffed, a built-in e-mail component is present in most chat software, enabling visitors to send e-mail to the Reference mailbox. If you already have an e-mail reference form, no problem. Chat e-mail can go to the same destination. To identify its origin as the chat server, give it a unique subject line. This way, you can tell how many people are hitting the chat service when it is unavailable.

THE DOWNSIDE OF CHAT

The main disadvantage of chat, from the user's point of view, is the delay between transmissions. The user types a question, but it must go across the Internet, subject to existing network traffic conditions, before it appears in the chat window. There can be a delay ranging from barely perceptible to what seems like an eternity. On the operator end, the question or comment appears, and a response must be thoughtfully composed. This takes time! Even finding the right "canned" response to very common questions can take a few seconds. It helps to have some "filler" messages ready to populate "empty air time" while the user is waiting for a response. Even more confusing, the user and the operator may be typing at the same time, with messages crossing each other somewhere in cyberspace.

Since the user cannot be expected to cope with this confusion extremely well, it is up to the librarian to give visual cues that more of a message is forthcoming, or that it will take a few moments to send an answer.

Chat operators not only need to be reasonably fast typists, they must be able to multitask without meltdown, and have enough expertise to find appropriate information quickly. They need to be well acquainted with the reference interview as an art form, and accurate in their assessment of what the user is asking for. This is a tall order! The chat session is to reference as the Sumi-e painting is to art: fast, spare, confidently executed, and sometimes a thing of beauty.

Given the unfamiliar pressures of being involved in a chat session, there is legitimate concern about being able to provide consistently high-quality service. There is insufficient time to look up information in printed resources. This is becoming less of an issue because most of our reference resources have already migrated to the Web, but even with online resources, time is of the essence.

THE DARK SIDE OF CHAT

User privacy is a big issue with librarians. If patrons really thought about where their chat transcripts were, they might also be concerned. Don't assume that your library's transcripts belong to you; they may actually belong to your chat service vendor. If your chat service software runs on a host computer provided by the vendor, transcripts stored there are under the control of the host's system administrator. While your vendor may benignly guard the files, the potential for abuse exists, particularly if you cannot delete session transcripts. LSSI (Library Systems and Services, LLC), a major vendor of hosted reference chat services for the library market, has established a policy that libraries own their own Virtual Reference Desk (VRD) chat transcripts. This is a major step forward for libraries (LSSI, 2001).

Libraries that archive their own transcripts should remove personal information, such as real names and e-mail addresses, particularly if the data is reused in a publicly available Web application, such as a Knowledge Base or FAQ page.

PLANNING A REAL-TIME SERVICE

Planning for a real-time reference service is much like planning for anything else. From the idea phase to implementation can take several months to a year, depending on the way a library goes though the decision process to add a new service.

Technically, implementing chat in a single library is not difficult. The sticking points will be staffing the service and getting people to use it, issues we will discuss later in this chapter.

CHAT TECHNOLOGY AND SOFTWARE FEATURES

Chat software is not "one size fits all." Once the library has decided to plan for a chat service, a necessary step is to examine software options. For a place to start, find out what other libraries are using by visiting Gerry McKiernan's Web site for "Live Ref (sm): A Registry of Real-Time Digital Reference Services" (www.public.iastate.edu/~CYBERSTACKS/LiveRef.htm). There is other useful information at this Cyberstacks Project site, including links to surveys and comparisons, technology resources, bibliographies, and related Internet discussion groups.

Duke University Library's Digital Reference Planning Committee recently compared several real-time reference services and compiled a short, informative Web page on their features, advantages, and weaknesses. Their findings about "Live On Line Reference," are available at www.lib.duke.edu/reference/liveonlineref.htm (Blank, 2000).

Chat technology software and hosted services vary a great deal. The differences will profoundly affect the way your library does business, so it's a good idea to shop around. But, before becoming attached to a particular interface, consider the most basic options that affect everything else: How does the software handle sessions and where is it installed?

Multi-User or Private Sessions?

Some chat software creates a multi-user environment, with a chat room where people come and go and everyone can see everyone else's comments. Other programs create a single session window where a visitor talks to an "operator" but does not see other chat sessions in progress, even though the operator may be juggling several simultaneous conversations. Some high-end software, such as Virtual Reference Desk (www.virtualreference.net/virtual/), can be used for one-on-one reference chat, but are also capable of hosting interactive Web classes or meetings.

Libraries generally choose chat software that facilitates private chat sessions because confidentiality and individual service are of prime importance. However, the ability to engage in two or three simultaneous one-on-one sessions makes it possible to initiate a new chat session without waiting for one in progress to run to completion. The normal delays between comments due to typing and transmission time make it feasible for one librarian to handle two sessions at the same time. Some services allow multiple operators, but limit the number of simultaneous sessions on one account. Switching from one session window to another should take little effort. Busy services will benefit from the ability to queue chat requests and move to the next in line with one click.

Locally Installed or Hosted?

A large library with on-staff programmers may want to develop its own chat software and run it on a local server. It is definitely possible with CGI, PHP, or Active Server Pages, and should be able to provide fast response time as well as a high level of customization. Smaller institutions or those without programming staff may opt for central hosting with client software on local machines. Centrally hosted services can be up and running very quickly, and offer several advantages over homegrown solutions, especially for pilot projects or new services:

- No software development delays or costs
- No server overhead or new equipment required
- Technical support is available from the vendor
- Training manuals or on-site training may be available
- Collaboration may be possible in the future
- Commitment is generally one year or less, so it is possible to re-evaluate and switch to something better

Special Features of Chat Software and Services

After deciding on how sessions should be handled and where the software will reside, take a closer look at special features of chat software that can make the system more efficient and reliable.

Canned Responses

Brief repetitive messages should be stored and accessible from a menu in the operator's chat window, so that the appropriate one can be found and sent with one or two mouse clicks. Login greetings and end of chat messages should be standardized for a consistent, professional tone, so "canning" is an easy way to ensure consistent quality. Canned responses can be text or HTML encoded. If the chat software can handle a URL in a message, it should also work in a canned response. For example, a HumanClick operator can type "http://www.university.edu/" in the operator window and send it to the visitor's chat window, where it is clickable. This URL will also work in a canned response.

HTML Snippets

If the library has a message that needs special formatting, such as a small banner with a logo graphic that must be sent in most or all chat sessions, the chat software needs to be able to send HTML encoded messages. Otherwise, the HTML tags would appear as text in the user's chat window. That would be non-functional and ugly!

Push Pages

A "Push" option should be available in the operator window. Pushing a page is different than sending a link. "Getting pushy" means that the operator can actually cause a new browser window to open on the visitor's screen. This is very powerful and user-friendly! Choosing Push should allow the operator to type or paste a URL in a textbox and send it to the visitor's browser, which "magically" opens the Web page.

Co-Browsing

A level of functionality beyond push pages is co-browsing, which allows the chat operator to actually control a browser window on the visitor's computer. This is an advanced feature of some chat software, such as LSSI's Virtual Reference Service (www.virtualreference.net/virtual/). Co-browsing is also found in the e-commerce world. A good example is the Lands' End Web site, where you can engage the services of "My Personal Shopper" or "Shop with a friend™" (www.landsend.com/).

Repeat Visitor Identification

While anonymity is one of the attractions of chat, some chat software track visitors by IP address. Even without any personal identification, it may be useful for the chat operator to know if someone at a particular IP address has visited several times recently, perhaps working on a complex project, and what information they were given in prior sessions.

Chat Transcripts or Session logs

A nice feature in higher-end chat software is the ability to e-mail the user a transcript after the session is complete. Analyzing chat transcripts is one way to gather data on the number and types of questions being asked in chat sessions. If the same questions are asked repeatedly, canned responses, FAQ files, or user guides may help both librarians and users. Chat sessions can also help identify interface problems and areas of confusion on the library's Web page that might be corrected. Rising statistics can justify staff time and effort. Low usage may indicate that a marketing effort is needed, or that something else needs work. Users' privacy must, of course, be protected.

TRY CHAT SOFTWARE ON FOR SIZE

If a library has no prior experience with chat software, it may be instructive to try out a simple program before making a commitment to costly subscription software with a steep learning curve and options that may not be needed right away. HumanClick is a typical chat program with some nice features, offering a free version as well as two subscription options. HumanClick is available for download at www.humanclick.com/. Registration is required, but there is no time limit on use of the free version. An HTML training manual provides enough information to start experimenting with the service, and you can literally chat with yourself to evaluate the interface from both user and operator viewpoints.

The cost of chat software ranges from free to thousands of dollars, and may include:

- Setup fees
- Monthly subscription or maintenance fees
- Training costs
- Fees for multiple chat operators
- License fees based on the number of allowed simultaneous chat sessions

The more expensive services definitely have more options and capabilities. However, there is no sense in paying for more features than you can use, so decide which features are essential at the outset, and which will be nice to have later.

The logistics of running a live reference service must be dealt with concurrently or soon after deciding on software and its features.

HOURS OF SERVICE

Ultimately, 24/7 reference service may be a necessary as well as worthy goal for libraries, if we are to be the service our users think of first when they need information. Students Ask Jeeves when they could Ask a Librarian because Jeeves is available when librarians are not.

The best hours for live online reference depend on the characteristics of the user community. College students tend to get desperate between 8 p.m. and midnight. K–12 or public library patrons may get busy in the afternoon. Should a library offer real-time reference during peak times at the reference desk, in the evening after the desk is unavailable, or late at night when services have never been available? It may be reasonable to staff a pilot project when it is convenient for library staff, but a permanent service should be offered at times convenient for users. One would expect night hours to be the most popular for chat, but that may not be true for your library.

Two large university libraries, Cornell University Library's Olin/Kroch/Uris Reference Services Division (www.library.cornell.edu/okuref/) and Carnegie Mellon University Library (www.library.cmu.edu/Research/ask.html), offer reference chat service at peak times for regular reference service, Monday through Friday, 1–5 p.m. It is reasonable to expect that high-demand hours at the reference desk would also be high-demand hours for chat.

STAFFING ISSUES

Who will staff Reference Chat? If the service is offered in addition to regular reference, it is the equivalent, in staff time, of adding a new service point. Chat requires undivided attention, rarely possible at the public reference desk. Patrons are accustomed to seeing someone typing at a reference desk computer, but expect librarians to look up, drop what they're doing, and invite dialog. Chat is slow enough without that kind of interruption, which would rapidly kill the service, if not the librarians!

The considerable demands of chat for immediacy and good judgment suggest that only experienced reference staff members who are at ease with both the reference interview and technology should be chat operators. This does not mean that librarians are the only possible candidates. Experienced paraprofessional staff may welcome an opportunity to practice their skills in a new way. As the service develops, academic faculty or community experts may be excellent participants in the service, particularly as referral resources. Students, even if used as first-line information assistants in the library, are risky in the online reference environment, where too many partially answered questions without adequate referral would surely turn people away and jeopardize success.

WHERE WILL REFERENCE CHAT TAKE PLACE?

Can live-reference staff be as remote as users? Can they work from home? This is a loaded question for administrators, bringing up inevitable concerns about "credit" for working at home, especially for classified or paraprofessional staff, who may not work more than 40 hours per week. For perceived "fairness" issues on the part of non-participating staff, it probably will not be done without a great deal of thought at any library. Librarians, on the other hand, are usually exempt from a rigid 40 hour per week schedule, and have enough flexibility in their daily calendars to handle odd hours of being "on call" or occasionally taking compensatory time.

The question of whether online reference is doable outside the library is open for discussion. At the University of Nevada, Reno, it was decided that chat operators involved in the pilot project would be online from the location of their choice. Consequently, all of the initial volunteers chose to work from home. Two have dial-up connections, and one has cable Internet service. There were several complications arising from being off-campus:

- Personal home computers may not be as fast or have as much memory as library computers
- A slow dial-up connection can cause a slightly sluggish response time to become glacial if Internet traffic is high
- Authenticating with the library proxy after logging in to a remote chat server suddenly changes the operator's apparent IP address and may freeze the chat program. Authentication is a huge policy issue as well as a technical problem

Resource sharing has worked well for physical library materials and expensive electronic resources. Expertise and information in unique local collections are vastly more rare and costly than journal subscriptions. Why not share them too? Apparently, many librarians have come to the same conclusion because we're starting to work together to extend virtual reference hours and to share expertise.

COLLABORATIVE REFERENCE CHAT PROJECTS

Just as with e-mail AskA services, reference chat offers opportunities to improve service by collaborating with other libraries or experts. Three noteworthy projects are listed here.

Real-Time Reference for Undergraduates in Science, Mathematics, and Engineering

This proposed project will provide real-time reference for science students, who tend to use the Web for most of their research. The goal is to provide quality 24/7 service, so that students will have a more reliable alternative than "Ask Jeeves." Principal investigators are: University of Arizona, Carnegie Mellon University, University of Hawaii, OCLC, Oregon State University, and University of Texas. LivePerson chat software will be used. The intent is to provide a service something like CDRS, but for a more limited audience, science students. The range of time zones of the participants will help them cover the 24 hours. See the Executive Summary and Project Report for more information (www.library.cmu.edu/Libraries/24x7.pdf).

QandACafe

QandACafe is a project of San Francisco and Monterey Bay area public libraries. The QandA Web site is professional looking, user-friendly, and a model of simplicity. Visit the service at qandacafe.org/, where you will find a menu designed to put novice users at ease. Buttons prominently offer information "About Us," "What to Expect," and "Technical Problems," as well as a library directory and contact information. Librarians are available for chat Monday through Friday, 3 to 9 p.m.

Reference 24/7

Reference 24/7 (www.247ref.org/) began as a project of the greater Los Angeles Metropolitan Cooperative Library System, administered by the California State Library. In July 2001, members included 13 public libraries and eight university and college libraries. The service enables libraries to provide after-hours reference service, with the goal being round-the-clock, real-time reference. The system runs on Java applets, so it's completely Web-based, with nothing for the library to install. It is also sophisticated, offering co-browsing, session transcripts e-mailed to patrons, customization of scripted answers to frequently asked questions, referral for complex questions, and usage statistics.

Overcoming Barriers to Collaboration

Collaboration across time zones may provide part of the solution to the difficulties of staffing 24/7 services. Participating libraries could be in states or provinces on opposite coasts, or in language-compatible countries on the other side of the globe. But there is an obvious problem: how do we deal with local information in a global environment?

Transaction logs will indicate the demand for local versus general reference information. Depending on the library's clientele and collection strengths or weakness, it is prudent to consider the kinds of questions that could realistically be shared with other libraries.

The biggest obstacles to functionality for collaborative digital reference projects are licensing and copyright. If collaborating libraries share an Integrated Library System and have a way of authenticating users, the licensing issues involved in pushing pages, co-browsing, and even sending articles are less of an issue. For libraries joined only to facilitate digital reference, working around authentication problems is going to be a major challenge. We will have to band together to work this out with vendors and content producers.

HOW DO WE EXCEL AT REFERENCE CHAT?

Practice, Practice, Practice!

It is absolutely necessary to chat with other library staff in order to get the hang of chat before chatting with library visitors. Buddy up with a partner and do some role-playing. Switch from operator to user. Try opening windows, searching for information while someone is waiting, sending messages, sending URLs, and generally pushing the envelope to see what breaks. This is no time to be self-conscious. You just have to get in there and do it. If someone has a problem with the software, compare notes. If only one person is experiencing difficulty, it may be a problem with the operator's ISP or personal computer. If everyone is having the same problem, contact the service's technical support representative and be prepared to describe, in great detail, the conditions that cause it.

All chat volunteers should read the service's user manual or help files. It's fine to skim the overly technical parts of the manual, but everyone who serves as a chat operator should know what the system can do and how it works.

Training can be simple or elaborate, depending on the learning curve of the chat service software. HumanClick and LivePerson are reportedly easy to use. Other services, such as LSSI's Virtual

Reference Desk software, are more complex and may require formal training. LSSI provides training sessions as part of the setup procedure. The LSSI training manual, *Establishing a Virtual Reference Service*, is excellent for any library preparing to offer reference chat. Of course, it is a tutorial specifically for VRD software, but the additional background information, resources, and advice make it generally useful (Lipow and Coffman, 2001).

Refer and Follow Up

A good online reference service cannot leave questions unanswered or only partially answered. Referrals and follow-ups are every bit as important here as they are for the reference desk or the telephone reference service. Why would anyone ask a second question if the first one left them dangling somewhere in Web space? Most chat services do store session transcripts, which make it possible to go back after the chat session and capture the question and response, which could then be forwarded to another resource person, not necessarily a reference librarian, for follow-up.

GETTING THE SERVICE NOTICED

The response to a new reference chat service may be underwhelming. If you build it, they will NOT come unless they know about the service and have a reason to use it. Encouraging people to use the service is a bit tricky. Librarians would like regular library users, occasional library users, and non-users to be made aware of the service and to take advantage of it when they need information.

Users, or people who think of the library Web page and visit it occasionally, should be confronted with a noticeable visual cue on the home page that the service exists. Put the chat or AskA icon on as many pages as possible. There should be some discussion about whether to put direct links to the chat service or to an intermediary page throughout your Web. For new users, it may be less intimidating to read a little about the service before actually trying it. People are reluctant to be thrown into a chat session with one click if they have never used chat.

Even if the icon is obvious and ubiquitous, visitors may not realize that the service could benefit them. It may seem intimidating or formal. Today's users may not want to interact with a librarian; they have learned how to use a computer, have Internet access, and know how to get a list of results from a search engine. They know about Yahoo! or other Web directories, and can find simple reference tools, such as dictionaries and maps, without help.

Therefore, it helps to present the service throughout the Web site so that there is an underlying awareness of it. And, when people turn to it in a moment of frustration, it is very non-threatening, very friendly, and very inviting. We can expect that chat users will often be tired, frustrated, and experiencing failure. Why would you bother with reference chat if you were experiencing great success on your own? Remember the last time you had to find a video or printer driver or had a question about your software that you couldn't answer?

What about people who never visit the library Web page or even know that it exists? Obviously, promotional efforts on the library Web site will elude this potential audience, so other methods of increasing awareness of library services need to be employed. Every library environment and community is different, so the following list of suggestions is just fodder to start the process of thinking about how to approach marketing this service to your particular audience.

Some ways to promote the service are:

- Partnering—one of the reasons people know about Ask Jeeves, WebHelp, and other commercial services is that there are links to these services on lots of other "partner" Web sites. The library might be a "natural" for partnering with the local school system, government agencies, or businesses
- News Articles—write an article for the local newspaper, student newspaper, or library newsletter. Contribute a short article to the "What's New" Web page for the library
- Flyers—do many of your students commute? Put postcards, flyers, or bookmarks on cars in your parking lot. Annoying, perhaps, but the audience is targeted, and most people will look at a flyer in hand long enough for their minds to register the content. Put flyers in campus computer labs where machines have fast Internet access and students are working on projects
- Working with faculty—get instructors to mention it in their classes. Contact instructors who are teaching online or distance education courses
- Library orientations—mention it in all library orientation sessions and in orientation packets for new students
- Sidewalk chalk—it is temporary, but hard to ignore. Of course, it has to look good, so those of us who still draw stick figures will not do any better on the sidewalk
- Bookmarks—good because people will voluntarily pick them up and keep them longer than a flyer

- Signs on bulletin boards—can contribute to a general awareness of library services
- A huge "grand-opening" style banner across the front of the library—an attention-grabber, but only for those who see it
- Mouse pads with the library URL—would look great in computer labs, and so would the library Web site as the home page

EVALUATION

Focus groups can be helpful in both the planning and evaluating phases. They can be used to determine what people will expect or want from a real-time reference service, and contribute to success by indicating the best hours of service.

Surveys, questionnaires, and polls can elicit anonymous feedback. Most of us are not statisticians or social scientists. It is difficult, without training, to design a scientifically valid survey or questionnaire. However, with some thought and a little homework, it is possible to conduct a survey that will yield useful, if not scientifically valid, information. The goal is to identify user needs and preferences and to move towards meeting them by making whatever changes are indicated in the way the service is delivered.

A generic framework for evaluation of chat service might do the following:

- State objectives—What, specifically, do we want to accomplish by offering chat service?
- Measure performance of the chat software or system— Does it work? Is it fast enough? Is it reliable?
- Identify usage patterns—Who is using the service and why? Do users come back?
- Identify needed improvements—What is keeping people from using the service? Are there any trends in user feedback that point towards specific changes?

Librarians love statistics. They can tell us where we are succeeding and where we are going wrong. Using session logs or transcripts, the RefeXpress Committee of the University of Florida Library analyzed the type of questions received in the first year of service (RefeXpress, 2001). After stating hours and sample questions, the committee categorized 375 "real" reference questions. This type of analysis would be useful in deciding what FAQs or "canned responses" need to be created right away, and generally, what difficulties people have using library Web pages or Web-based resources. Creating FAQ or help pages would then serve to speed up response time during a significant number of chat sessions, since the operator could "push" to the visitor an already well-phrased and thought-out response. The RefeXpress status report is not available on the Web, but you can visit the RefeXpress itself at smathersnt11.uflib.ufl.edu/. It's available 56 hours a week, and uses e-Share Communications Net Agent software.

It's tough to accomplish real assessment! It's even tougher to determine whether the service has increased student research competence. How can you tell if students are writing better papers or finding better resources? It is easier to collect information on users' perceptions of the service, how they feel about its value, or just how they react to it generally. They may perceive themselves to be better or more confident users of information, or better prepared to find materials independently. They may have an opinion about whether or not the service saved them time. These are not objective measures of success, but they can be general indicators. For our purposes, that may be good enough.

If you believe that anything really worth doing is worth doing badly (provided you make an effort to improve), it is certain that you will get better at it, and possibly achieve excellence. In any event, digital reference and real-time services are here to stay, so we need to pay attention to how we're doing.

THE FUTURE OF DIGITAL REFERENCE

Digital reference is still in its infancy; the Web itself has only been around a few short years. Changes in technology, user expectations, and library priorities will result in more highly developed services.

MORE COLLABORATION

Libraries are closely watching the big projects, such as the Collaborative Digital Reference Service and the Virtual Reference Desk Project. More will sign on as participants. For those that do not, their development will provide a model for other, more local, projects. In the future CDRS will surely offer chat as well as e-mail reference, making it even more relevant to libraries and their communities.

MORE NON-LIBRARIAN EXPERTS WILL BE INVOLVED

The Web has also taught us that AskA experts don't have to be librarians at all. Some of the best AskA services are staffed by non-librarian subject experts. Anyone can "Ask-a-Scientist" at the MADSci Network (www.madsci.org/) or Ask Shamu at Sea World (www.seaworld.org/AskShamu/asintro.html). Unfortunately, less credible services also attract huge numbers of Web visitors. Results may be mediocre, but branding is clever and supported by aggressive marketing.

Community experts or academic faculty who are enthusiastic about sharing their knowledge could be referral sources or active partners in digital reference services. It helps if enthusiasm is paired with a knack for explaining complex topics in accessible language. In return, the subject expert would benefit from the prestige and credibility of being associated with your library.

LIBRARIES WILL GET BETTER AT MARKETING

Librarians have the advantage of a reputation for credibility and altruism, but most of us are pathetic at marketing. We need to develop efficient, reliable services together and market them like crazy. Realistically, only a few of us now have an interest in marketing, or time to do it. Some libraries are lucky enough to have a dedicated public relations officer who can coordinate such efforts. Collaborative marketing, with some professional guidance, will be driven by necessity.

REAL-TIME SERVICES WILL BE EXPECTED

The idea of chat will become less intimidating, more comfortable, and expected. Already, many young people routinely use chat to communicate with friends back home. More and more consumers are becoming familiar with online help desk services, which frequently offer e-mail and real-time technical support.

Libraries will be practiced in the art of efficiently delivering information in real-time over the Web, and real-time services will evolve and diversify, seamlessly tapping into collaborative digital reference projects as needed.

NEW PROTOCOLS WILL HANDLE INTERACTIONS

QuIP (Question Interchange Profile), which uses multiple protocols, could make Web reference services much easier and more efficient. "QuIP is a proposed metadata scheme to allow AskA services and other digital reference type services to interoperate and exchange questions and answers in a threaded manner" (Lankes, 1999). An overview of QuIP is available at the Virtual Reference Desk Web site at www.vrd.org/Tech/QuIP/.

VoIP, Voice-Over-Internet Protocol, may be the next big thing. For consumers, it will enable high-speed data and voice services. For businesses, it will facilitate Web-based communication portals, providing central access to e-mail, fax, and instant messaging, create virtual phone extensions for inexpensive remote conferencing without long-distance calls, and allow users to receive messages from any type of device, including PDAs. VoIP could play a major role in making "high-tech" "high-touch." For information on the technology behind VoIP, see Texas Instruments' press release, "*Texas Instruments' New Voice-over-Internet Protocol (VoIP) Products Enable Next-Generation Telephony*" at www.ti.com/sc/docs/news/2001/01029.htm. Some chat software, such as LiveHelper (www.livehelper.com/) and LSSI's Virtual Reference Desk (www.lssi.com/) are already capable of VoIP. Details about VoIP are available at the Protocols.com Web site (www.protocols.com/voip/index.html).

XML WILL MATURE

XML (eXtensible Markup Language) will make the delivery of organized content to the browser much easier than it is today. By completely separating content from format, developers will be able to code content once and simply change the style of presentation for as many platforms as needed, from PCs to PDAs.

XML can be also used in concert with Active Server Pages (ASP) technology to manage content. Formatting will be accomplished with XSLT (eXtensible Stylesheet Language Transformation), which transforms XML to HTML, or XSL (eXtensible Style Language) style sheets. Right now, most XML is formatted with standard CSS (Cascading Style Sheets) because XSL is not yet ready for prime time.

BROADBAND ACCESS WILL IMPROVE

Within this decade, in most places, bandwidth will cease to be a barrier to speedy access or the transmission of large files. People are impatient with slow services. It hasn't been feasible to even seriously consider Web chat as an option until recently, when the market for "always on" cable modem services and DSL services took off.

By June 1, 2001, there were 9.3 million residential broadband Internet subscribers in the United States and Canada. Of these, 6.4 million households were cable modem customers and 2.9 million were DSL subscribers (*Cable Modem Market Stats & Projections*, 2001).

According to a press release from NetValue.com, 11.1 percent of Internet households in the United States had a broadband connection in February 2001 (Jaeger, 2001). In February, 2001, a Nielsen//NetRatings press release reported that "high speed Internet access, including ISDN, LAN, cable modems and DSL connections, jumped 148 percent among home users in December 2000 as compared to the same period in 1999. Nearly 12 million home Web users accessed the Internet with a high-speed connection in December 2000, as compared to five million people a year ago."

In addition, the press release states, "More people currently connect at 56 Kbps than any other Web speed, jumping 87 percent in the past year" (Nielsen//NetRatings, 2001). Last year, most people connected to the Internet at 28.8/33.6 Kbps.

Wider broadband access might make videoconferencing a realistic option for reference services. Whether video provides any advantages for real-time reference is a question that has not been answered.

BETTER KNOWLEDGE BASES AND EXPERT SYSTEMS WILL BE DEVELOPED

It is inevitable that the mountain of data captured from libraries' digital reference experience will be the foundation of better knowledge bases. The databases themselves will become a virtual librarian comprised of the cumulated experience of a large number of information and subject specialists.

Already, there is OPAL (Online Personal Academic Librarian), a visionary project taking shape in the Open University Library, in the United Kingdom (oulib1.open.ac.uk/). OPAL's first goal is to create a system that can immediately answer routine, repeat questions asked in natural language from a user base of 200,000 distance learners. The service will be extended to other institutions, so the OU is working with project partners. The ultimate goal is to create an artificial librarian that can answer complex questions using artificial intelligence. For more information see oulib1.open.ac.uk/wh/research/opal/artificial.html.

In the United States, the Collaborative Digital Reference Service (www.loc.gov/rr/digiref/) is building a knowledge base from questions submitted to the service. On a smaller scale, individual libraries and collaborative projects will build FAQ files and databases. Some of these databases will eventually be merged, mined, and manipulated to create better self-help systems to supplement live reference services.

FROM FRAGMENTATION TO CONVERGENCE

Convergence is the opposite of fragmentation. It is desirable, for example, to offer e-mail and chat from the same interface, and to connect to these services from many different points. One database search that finds all relevant electronic journals, books, documents, and media on a topic is better than 20 searches for the same information (provided that the results are arranged in some useful hierarchy, of course). It should be possible to immediately view an article to which the library has access, no matter which index the user searches. If the library cannot provide a particular title, interlibrary loan forms should be no more than a click or two away. Referrals of complex questions to those best qualified to answer them should be easy and instantaneous.

This is where we are headed, toward integration of services that are easier to use and easier to find. Advances in technology will surely affect the way libraries interact with patrons and the way patrons expect to interact with us.

Technologies that separate content from presentation will make it possible to code once and reuse many times. Content will be interpreted for personal computers, digital phones, standards-compliant browsers, wireless devices, and things that do not yet exist. These advances will make it possible for reference librarians to quickly get information to people who need it no matter how or when they connect to the Internet.

REFERENCES

Bakken, Stig Sæther, and Egon Schmid, eds. 2000. *PHP Manual*. PHP Documentation Group [Online]. Available: www.phpbuilder.com/ [2001, July 9].

Bennett, Blythe Allison, Abby Kasowitz, and R. David Lankes. 2000. "Digital Reference Quality Criteria." In *Digital Reference Service in the New Millennium: Planning, Management, and Evaluation*, edited by R. David Lankes, John W. Collins III, and Abby S. Kasowitz. New York: Neal-Schuman.

Blank, Phil. 2000. *Live On Line Reference*. Duke University Library. Digital Reference Planning Committee [Online]. Available: www.lib.duke.edu/reference/liveonlineref.htm [2001, July 10].

Cable Modem Market Stats & Projections. 2001. Cable Datacom News. Kinetic Strategies, Inc. [Online]. Available: www.cabledatacomnews.com/cmic/cmic16.html [2001, July 13].

Change, Hsien Chun, Heidi Cheung, Anthony Chu, and Derek Lio. 1998. *Artificial Intelligence: Expert System*. University of Texas at Austin [Online]. Available: www.eco.utexas.edu/faculty/Norman/long.extra/INFO.S98/Exp/main3.html. [2001, May 5].

Gottesman, Ben Z. *Portals*. 1999. ZDNet Reviews. Originally published in PC Magazine. [Online]. Available: www.zdnet.com/products/stories/reviews/0,4161,2354132,00.html [2001, July 11].

Jaeger, Annabelle. 2001. *NetValue Worldwide: Press Release: Korea Leads World in Broadband Usage.* NetValue [Online]. Available: www.netvalue.com/corp/presse/cp0028.htm [2001, July 12].

Kasowitz, Abby, Blythe Allison Bennett, and R. D. Lankes. 2000. "Quality Standards for Digital Reference Consortia." *Reference & User Services Quarterly* 39, no.4 (Summer, 2000): 355–63.

LaGesse, David. 2001. "U.S. News.com: Instant Message Phenom is, Like, Way Beyond E-mail." *U.S. News & World Report* (March 5): 54–56.

Lankes, R David. 1999. *The Virtual Reference Desk: Question Interchange Profile, White Paper, Version 1.01d* [Online]. Available: www.vrd.org/Tech/QuIP/1.01/1.01d.htm [2001, July 13].

Lipow, Anne Grodzins, and Steve Coffman. 2001. *Establishing a Virtual Reference Service: VRD Training Manual.* Berkeley, CA: Library Solutions Press.

LSSI (Library Systems & Services, LLC). 2001. *Virtual Reference Desk: Frequently Asked Questions* [Online]. Available: www.virtualreference.net/virtual/21b.html [2001, July 10].

Ma, Wei, and Timothy Cole. 2000. *Testing & Evaluation of a Database Selection Expert System.* Presented at the ACRL 10th National Conference: Crossing the Divide, Denver, Colorado (March 15–18) [Online]. Available: dli.grainger.uiuc.edu/Publications/TWCole/ACRL_2001/abstract.htm [2001, July 10].

Nielsen//NetRatings. 2001. *Broadband Access Soars Nearly 150 Percent At Home, According To Nielsen//NetRatings* [Online]. Available: 209.249.142.22/press_releases/PDF/pr_010208.pdf [2001, July 12].

RefeXpress Committee. University of Florida Library. 2001. *RefeXpress Status Report.* March 27, 2001. Unpublished photocopy, 1 sheet.

Virtual Reference Desk. 2000. *Facets of Quality for Digital Reference Services, Version 4. Revised October 27, 2000* [Online]. Available: www.vrd.org/facets–10–00.shtml [2001, July 5].

APPENDIX: EXAMPLE OF AN E-MAIL WEB FORM WITH AN ASP FORM HANDLER

This simple Web form illustrates basic steps involved in capturing and e-mailing user input to a specified recipient. An Active Server Pages file (named mailplay.asp) displays an HTML form, transforms user input into a format suitable for e-mail, sends it to to the mail server, and displays an acknowledgment to the user. This form could be used on an "Ask A Question" page, as described earlier in this chapter.

This code displays and processes the e-mail form:

```
<%@language="VBScript"%>
<html>
<head>
<title>Simple E-mail Form</title>

<script language="JavaScript">
//This script checks for an empty e-mail address field
//A real form would include more error-checking functions
```

Figure 4–13. A Generic E-Mail Form for Asking a Question

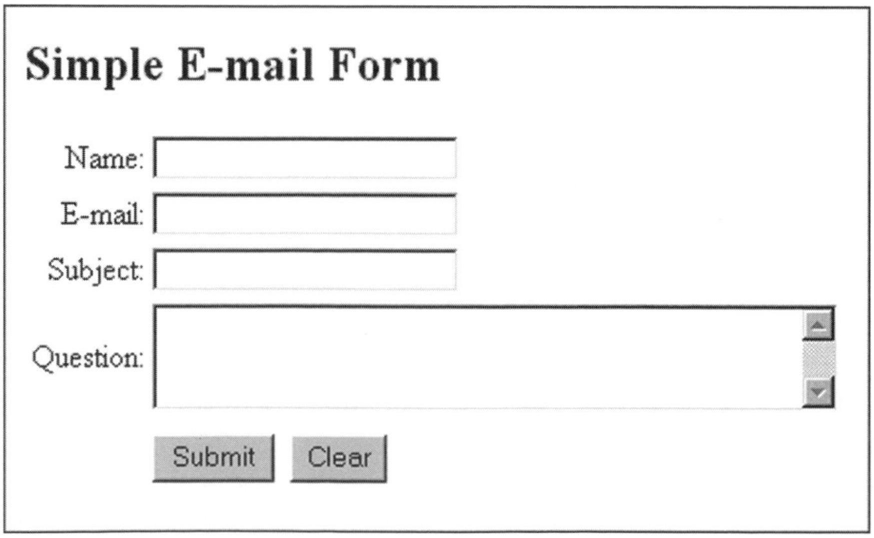

Simple E-mail Form

Name:

E-mail:

Subject:

Question:

Submit   Clear

```
function validator(theForm) {
if (theForm.user_email.value == "")
{
alert("You must enter an e-mail address!");
theForm.user_email.focus();
return (false);
}
}
</script>
</head>
<body bgcolor="#ffffff">
<h2>Simple E-mail Form</h2>

<!-- Beginning of form. Results are sent to this page, named
mailplay.asp -->

<form method="post" action="mailplay.asp" onSubmit="return
validator(this)">
<table border="0"><tr><td align="right">Name:
</td><td><input type="text" name="user_name"></td></tr>
<tr><td align="right">E-mail: </td><td><input type="text"
name="user_email"></td></tr>
<tr><td align="right">Subject: </td><td><input type="text"
name="user_subject"></td></tr>
<tr><td align="right">Question: </td><td><textarea cols="40"
wrap="virtual" rows="3" name="user_text"></textarea></td>
</tr>
<tr><td> </td><td height="40"><input type="submit"
value="Submit">  <input type="reset" value="Clear">
</td></tr>
</table>
</form>
<!-- End of Form and Beginning of ASP Form-Handler Script -->

<%
'Declare variables for the e-mail script
dim strAddr
dim replyTo
dim strSubject
dim strText
'Next, declare itsReady variable so e-mail will be sent to
'ASP script only if 'user has entered an e-mail address.
dim itsReady
itsReady = ""
'Get input from the form and assign it to script variables
 strAddr = Trim(Request.form("user_email"))
```

```
 if strAddr <> " " then
    replyTo = cstr(strAddr)
end if
strSubject = Request.form("user_subject")
strName = Request.form("user_name")
strMsg = Request.form("user_text")
strText = "E-mail from: " & strName & vbCrLf &_
"Concerning: " & strMsg

'Note: use vbCrLf (as above) to add line breaks in the e-mail
'Next, determine that we are ready to trigger e-mail function

if replyTo <> " " then itsReady = send_email()

'The send_email function creates a mail object and sends it
function send_email()
'Create an object or container for your mail
    Dim objMail
    Set objMail = Server.CreateObject("CDONTS.NewMail")
'Format the e-mail using fields from the HTML form
    objMail.To = "araby@unr.edu"
'Assign any e-mail address to From field to identify origin
objMail.From = "ref_visitor@unr.edu"
objMail.value("Reply-To") = replyTo
objMail.Subject = strSubject
objMail.Body = strText

'Send the e-mail
objMail.Send

'Release system resources after message is sent
Set objMail = Nothing

'Display an acknowledgment
Response.Write "<h3>Thank you for using e-mail!</h3>"
end function
%>
</body>
</html>
```

To avoid repeatedly validating a form on the server, JavaScript was used to check user input on the client side. In this form, we have checked only for a blank e-mail address field. If the user_email field is blank, the script displays an alert box:

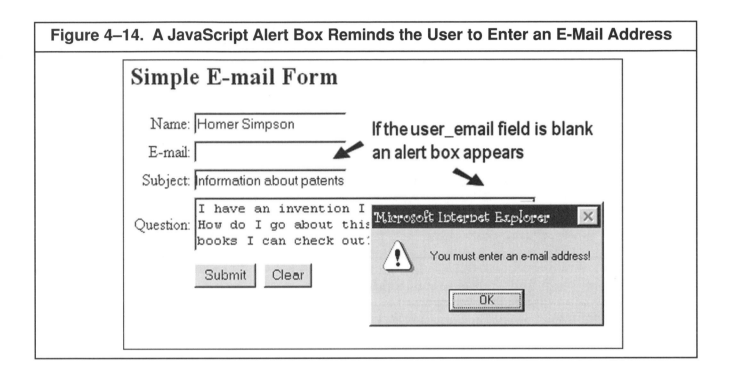

Figure 4–14. A JavaScript Alert Box Reminds the User to Enter an E-Mail Address

If this form were actually used for e-mail reference the JavaScript would contain similar functions to check other fields for missing or invalid values. Error checking can also be written into the server-side ASP script.

After successfully sending the e-mail, the user sees a confirmation:

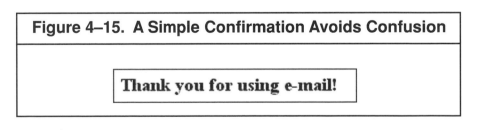

Figure 4–15. A Simple Confirmation Avoids Confusion

Since we have not specified a format for the e-mail, it will be plain text. In Pine, a popular e-mail program on campus servers, the recipient of the form-generated e-mail would see something like this:

Figure 4–16. Form-generated E-Mail Message

```
Date: Tue, 24 Jul 2001 20:46:54 -0700
From: ref_visitor@unr.edu
Reply-To: doh@springfield.com
To: araby@unr.edu
Subject: Information about patents

E-mail from: Homer Simpson
Concerning: I have an invention I want to patent.
How do I go about this?
Do you have any books I can check out?
```

This sample form will work on most Windows NT/2000 Web servers with installed ASP support and e-mail services that allow access by the default Internet user account (IUSR). This script creates a CDONTS mail object, so it will not work if your server uses a different e-Mail component, such as JMail or ASPmail. CDONTS is a free Microsoft component for Internet Information Server (IIS), so it is widely used.

5 MAXIMIZING CURRENT AWARENESS AND DOCUMENT DELIVERY SERVICES

by Margret J. Ressel and Millie L. Syring

CHAPTER OVERVIEW

- Alert Services
- Scientific Communities, Preprints, and Other Current Awareness Tools
- Document Delivery Via the Web
- Receiving and Processing Requests
- Mediated Document Delivery
- Resource Sharing—How the Library Networks Do It
- Unmediated Document Delivery Projects
- Managing Document Delivery and Current Awareness Services

Libraries of all types and sizes have the challenge of serving the needs of their primary, and often secondary, clientele. Document delivery and current awareness are an important part of that service. No library can collect every journal, book, conference proceeding, or report that its users may need. Nor can a library user browse through tables of contents for every journal that may have new information in their field of study. Contrary to many library users' impressions, not everything is available for free on the Web, either.

Current awareness tools are Web-based sites and/or services that provide tables of contents, article alerts, or new research information. They can inform library users of new research in their subject areas or in favorite publications, or by known authors, and alert them to the contents of journal issues before they are published. Current awareness tools and services available on the Web allow even the most remote users to keep current on research in their areas of interest. Students and faculty at colleges, universities, and research centers are the most prevalent and obvious users of such services, but they aren't the exclusive users. Many library clients from small businesses, large corporations, and governmental agencies, as well as side-line researchers, inventors, and teachers may also be interested in keeping up with a particular area. Current awareness tools can be useful in all types of libraries. Some examples of current awareness services are:

- general tables of contents and alert services
- publisher-based tables of contents, searching, and alert services
- preprints

Document Delivery services provide the needed materials, regardless of whether the library actually owns the publication. The virtual library, for the remote user, becomes infinitely bigger than without these services.

ALERT SERVICES

These cross-disciplinary and specialized Web-based services enable users to find out the current research being published in a certain subject area or industry, by a certain author, or within a specific journal. The Web availability of these tools and resources enables night, weekend, and holiday researchers, as well as remote clientele, to access the latest information whenever they need it most. Initiating a request for the library's intervention in the delivery of an item identified through a current awareness service is the user's logical next step. The library needs to make users aware of these tools and services, as in Figure 5–1.

GENERAL ALERT SERVICES

Commercial tables of contents (TOC) services provide users with notices of new and upcoming publications in their areas of interest. Users can set up profiles of keywords, subject categories, authors, or journals to keep current with, and they passively receive notice of new material matching their profile when it enters the database. These services provide a way to easily monitor a field of study, with many ways to go about it. Contents of current awareness databases can also be browsed, or searched by authors' names or keywords. The main difference between a TOC database and an abstracting and indexing (A&I) database is that

Figure 5–1. A Sample Web Page for Bringing Current Awareness Tools to Users

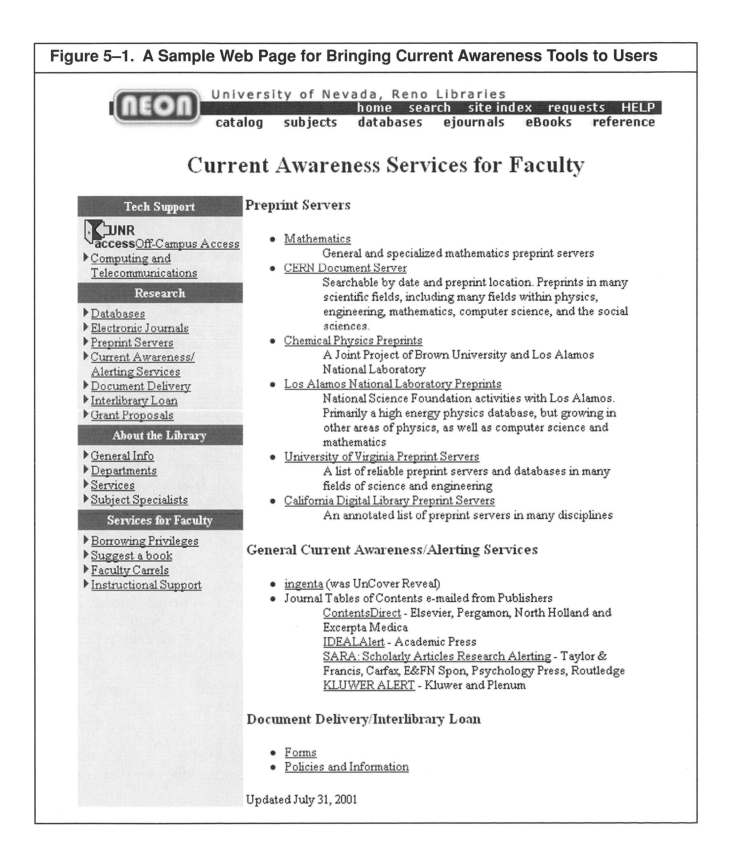

Figure 5–2. An Alert E-Mail Message from Ingenta

```
Date: Thu, 14 Jun 2001 21:26:03 +0100 (BST)
From: search.alerts@ingenta.com
To: *********
Subject: ingenta: search alert

ingenta: search alert

Dear Reveal Customer:

Please find below your Reveal Search Alerts.

Ti:[DOCUMENT DELIVERY](tka)

Record 1.
Library-Subsidized Unmediated Document Delivery
Haslam, M; Stowers, E
Library Resources and Technical Services, 2001, vol. 45, no. 2, pp. 80-89
ALA AMERICAN LIBRARY ASSOCIATION
http://www.ingenta.com/isis/searching/Expand/ingenta?unc=1013782627

Record 2.
Beyond the photocopy machine: document delivery in a hybrid library environment
Dekker, R; Waaijers, L
Interlending and Document Supply, 2001, vol. 29, no. 2, pp. 69-75
MCB UNIVERSITY PRESS
http://www.ingenta.com/isis/searching/Expand/ingenta?unc=1013598761

copyright  2001 ingenta
```

---

the former has no mediated indexing or assigned subject headings. In some TOC databases the only access point for keyword searching is the title field; in others it is possible to search for words in abstracts. Most of these services are scholarly and professional in orientation. See Figure 5–2 for an example of an e-mail alert for a profile with the phrase "document delivery" in the title of articles.

For most current awareness tools and services, providing access through subscriptions or Web links is enough. Some services may require workshops, information sheets, and orientations in order for users to get the most out of them. Many others are self-explanatory to those working in the field. Currently, the most prominent multidisciplinary services are Ingenta, Current Contents, CISTI, and Infotrieve.

Ingenta (formerly UnCover Reveal)—www.ingenta.com

Ingenta is a service covering over 25,000 journals going back to the late 1980s and even earlier for some titles. The Reveal Research Alerts service provides tables of contents by e-mail to a user for up to 50 selected journal titles. Weekly results from a pre-defined search for author or title words can also be e-mailed. The cost for the service is currently $25.00 per year for each subscriber, but many libraries are purchasing site licenses to Ingenta, lowering the price significantly. With UnCover, libraries were able to personalize the message users receive with their alerts. Many notified their local users of their own low-cost or free document delivery services, diverting users from the fee-based UnCover delivery option. At press time for this book, Ingenta customers no longer have this customization option.

Ingenta features:

- coverage of 25,000 titles, incorporating UnCover and CatchWord journal listings
- free searching—no subscription necessary
- keyword (title word) searching, author searching, and journal browsing
- MyIngenta, which allows a user to set up a profile and personalize the site
- $25.00 per year for a single user alert account (not currently available, but slated for 2002). Site licenses available for a significant discount
- article ordering (with credit card or deposit account) available
- online (for HTML or PDF files), FAX, and ARIEL delivery
- weekly updates

Current Contents (ISI)—www.isinet.com/products/cc/

Current Contents began as a print publication in 1958, and in 1988 became a computer file as well. It has been available on the Web since 1998. Current Contents' main advantages over its competitors are its inclusion of abstracts, compatibility to bibliographic management utilities (most of which are owned by ISI, supplier of Current Contents) and ability to store multiple sophisticated search profiles. Users run their profile against the Current Contents Database and retrieve results from their selected dates of coverage.

An optional product from Current Contents, Journal Tracker, enables users to have alerts e-mailed to them on a regular basis. The 8,000 journals in Current Contents are selected to be the most authoritative and reliable in each of the disciplines of coverage. The costs of Current Contents are dependent on the number of users and which sections a library wishes to subscribe to. Overall, it is the most expensive of the current awareness tools. Users cannot search the database without being part of a subscribing library or institution unless they have an individual subscription. Current Contents features:

- coverage of 8,000 scholarly journals, cover-to-cover and over 2,000 books
- discipline-specific coverage (take only what your user population needs)
- easily navigable, flexible searching, including author abstracts
- availability of print or online subscription to individuals institutional site license

CISTI Source—tucuxi.cisti.nrc.ca/

CISTI Source, from the Canada Institute for Scientific and Technical Information, is both a current awareness system and document delivery provider. It includes a journal TOCs database, and an article database of 15,000,000 articles from those journals and conference proceedings. Users can choose to receive alerts via e-mail and/or their personal Web page on the CISTI site. CISTI features:

- coverage of 17,000 journals, 2,000 with abstracts (life sciences only)
- easy access to full-text articles from subscribed e-journals
- document ordering online
- institutional site licenses
- weekly updates
- delivery of alerts via e-mail and Web page

Infotrieve—www4.infotrieve.com/

Infotrieve is primarily a commercial document delivery provider, offering full-text journals online as PDF files. Their current awareness service is free, as a means to publicize the fee-based document delivery service. Users can register and set up profiles to receive TOCs and topic alerts through their e-mail account. Libraries can set up accounts with multiple users for document delivery of articles from the database. There are several searchable databases on the Infotrieve Web site, including Medline and the proprietary e-content databases of electronic journal articles. Searching is always free.

Infotrieve features:

- coverage of over 20,000 journals
- free TOCs, alerts, and searching
- advanced searching available
- browsable and searchable e-content database (full-text online) with PDF files
- document ordering online
- alerts and contents delivered via e-mail

SPECIALIZED ALERT SERVICES

In addition to general current awareness tools, there are many specialized tools and sites, including publisher-specific services. Many publishers make it possible to set up individual accounts for current awareness alerting. Most enable their journal databases to be searchable and browsable without subscriptions to the journals. TOCs, abstracts, and selected feature articles are available for view without subscription on most of these sites. Subscriptions to the publishers' journals are necessary for full-text access. Some publishers have a separate archive subscription for online access to older issues, as well.

Elsevier ContentsDirect and Scirus

Elsevier has two services that provide current awareness of articles published in Elsevier journals.

ContentsDirect—www.elsevier.com/

Anyone interested can register for ContentsDirect and receive e-mail alerts for forthcoming books and articles in 1,085 journals from Elsevier, Pergamon, North Holland, and Excerpta Medica. Subscriptions to the journals are required for full-text access, but sample issues are available for any registrant of the ContentsDirect service. ContentsDirect also includes alerts of recent and soon-to-be published books from Elsevier imprints. Users can register for subject categories of alerts (which they can then forward to their librarian for suggested purchase).

Scirus—www.scirus.com

Scirus is an Elsevier site for searching the Web and subscription sites for scientific content. It currently covers Web sites (focusing on scientists' home pages), ScienceDirect, MEDLINE on BioMedNet, Beilstein on ChemWeb, Neuroscion, and BioMed Central. The search engine can search non-HTML formats as well as regular Web pages, giving it an advantage over other search engines. It does not cover non-scientific sites, limiting the false hits a user may get. The advanced search screen assists users in refining their searches within categories, to specific fields (author, journal title, etc.), and to specific date ranges for published material.

IDEALAlert (Academic Press)—www.idealibrary.com/

IdealAlert is a free alert service for finding journal articles and tables of contents for IDEAL Library journals. Users can select digests, search strategies (up to 20 per user), and lists of new journals issues. The database covers the 353 journal titles in Academic Press and its imprints: Churchill Livingstone, W.B. Saunders, Mosby, and Baillière Tindall. Subscription to their journals is not required for registration for the alert service.

KluwerAlert—www.wkap.nl/

KluwerAlert gives users three choices for alert services: subject categories, journal titles (tables of contents), and book series. A user can subscribe to any or all of the services, but must register individually for each one. Nearly 800 journal titles and over 1,000 book series are covered in the KluwerAlert service, from the publishing companies of Kluwer Academic Publishing and its imprints, including Plenum.

SARA:Scholarly Articles Research Alerting (Taylor and Francis Group)—www.tandf.co.uk/sara/

540 Taylor and Francis journals are covered in the SARA alert service. Users can subscribe to subject category alerts and/or journal title alerts. Both alert formats e-mail tables of contents for current issues. Users also receive occasional notices of meetings or special offers on published materials (i.e. advertising).

SCIENTIFIC COMMUNITIES, PREPRINTS, AND OTHER CURRENT AWARENESS TOOLS

Scholars, researchers, and scientists in many fields have developed virtual communities through collections of preprints, e-mail lists, and Web sites consisting of current research updates and news articles, job announcements, journal article TOCs, and many other services within a specific discipline or field. It is helpful for librarians to link to these sites for new researchers, students, and those who are interested but not active in a field of study.

PREPRINTS

Sharon Jordan, of the U.S. Department of Energy, Office of Scientific and Technical Information defines a preprint as "a document in pre-publication status, particularly an article submitted to a journal for publication" (Jordan, 1999). Preprints on the Web, or e-prints, are a way for researchers to put out their work in progress for peer consideration and comment. For the most part, these works have not gone through a peer-review process prior to publication on the Web. Because of the delays for print publication and the peer-review process, e-prints enable the researchers in an area to share ideas, results, and processes quickly. Often, the preprint process can be a catalyst for new research, or improvements on older research.

How Do You Find Them?

Preprints are available on many Web sites around the world. Collections of links to preprint servers are provided on many reliable library Web sites. A good example is the list provided by Iowa State University (www.lib.iastate.edu/services/ref/preprint.html). A search in Yahoo! or Google will generate a list of preprints in a variety of subject areas. No single location provides access to all preprints, but many authors use their personal or professional Web sites to share their work, and there are several good gateway sites for locating preprints in a particular area:

- Chemical Physics Preprints (www.chem.brown.edu/chem-ph.html)—a joint project of Brown University and Los Alamos National Laboratory, modeled after the xxx.lanl.gov site, provides easy access for submitting and retrieving preprints in TeX or LaTeX format.
- Los Alamos arXiv (arxiv.org or the mirror site at xxx.lanl.gov)—primarily a high energy physics database, but growing in other areas of physics, as well as computer science and mathematics, this is the premier preprints database. It was started in 1991 as a forum for sharing National Science Foundation funded research via the Internet. Since use of the Web has become widespread, access has gotten significantly easier. In 2001, the database moved to Cornell University.
- University of Virginia Preprint Servers (viva.lib.virginia.edu/science/guides/s-preprn.htm)—this list of reliable preprint

servers and databases covers many fields of science and engineering. The site is continually updated with links to authoritative preprints in many areas, including cognitive sciences.

- California Digital Library (www.library.ucsb.edu/cdl/preprint.html)—this annotated list of preprint servers covers many disciplines, including psychology, political science, and economics.
- Department of Energy Preprint Network (www.osti.gov/preprint/)—these preprints are of interest to the U.S. Department of Energy—mathematics, physics, chemistry, biology, environmental sciences, and nuclear medicine
- American Mathematical Society Directory of Preprint and e-print servers (www.ams.org/global-preprints/)—the AMS attempts to maintain a complete and current listing of math preprint servers, including retired servers.

Using Preprints

Most preprint servers provide databases that are searchable by author, title, and subject or keyword, as well as by date of posting. Preprints are available in many different file formats (TeX, postscript, PDF, etc.), depending on the research area. Usually, these formats are readable from a Web browser, word processor, or free software available for download. For the new preprint user, some extra information about formats and readers may be necessary. Some preprint servers have alert features that enable users to see new preprints as they are submitted to the database. Most users should have an idea of keywords and authors to search to get the best results for their field of interest. It may be appropriate to provide lists of preprints in different subject areas, depending on the clientele.

DISCIPLINE-SPECIFIC WEB-BASED COMMUNITIES OF SCIENTISTS

Some vendors (usually publishers) have developed sites with resources for scientists in a specific field. The scientists who "join" the Web-based community must register; afterwards, they use a password to access selected high quality resources such as full-text journal articles, job announcements, and oftentimes current awareness services targeted to their interests. The registration information may be used to display very targeted advertisements or to send the "members" e-mail announcements of new books or services (from the publisher) that might interest them. Some examples of these communities are:

- Chemweb (www.chemweb.com)—services for members include preprints, news articles, job ads, and structure searching
- BioMedNet (www.bmn.com)—provides registrants with TOC alerts from Elsevier journals, research news, journal articles, Web links, and more geared towards scientists in the biomedical fields
- Engineering Village 2 (www.ei.org/eicorp/eicorp)—any interested subscriber can sign up for e-mail updates on a number of subjects and save search strategies in a personalized folder on the site.
- Physicsweb/tiptop (physicsweb.org/TIPTOP)—alerts, job ads, Web search engine, research news, links to important sites, directory of members, etc.

In addition, many professional organizations have robust and informational Web sites for their members, some giving access to anyone interested. Librarians should definitely link to these sites for current awareness of new publications, news, job announcements, meetings and conferences, etc. Some examples of these sites are:

- American Anthropological Association—www.aaanet.org
- American Chemical Society—www.acs.org
- American Psychological Association—www.apa.org
- American Sociological Association—www.asanet.org
- American Management Association—www.amanet.org
- American Association for Artificial Intelligence—www.aaai.org
- Association for Childhood Education International—www.udel.edu/bateman/acei
- College and University Personnel Association—www.cupahr.org
- International Society for Political Psychology—ispp.org

OTHER CURRENT AWARENESS TOOLS

Researchers can utilize many tools to stay current with research and news in a subject area, field of study, or industry. Reading or scanning published and preprint literature is only one way, although very important, to stay on top of things. Libraries can provide links to other current awareness resources for their users, particularly remote users who cannot or do not come to the library on a regular basis. Some examples of other types of current awareness tools are:

- Listservs—e-mail forums for discussion and information dissemination. A large, but not comprehensive list is available from Topica at www.topica.com
- Personalized Web pages—through commercial Web sites, universities, and perhaps through the library, users can create Web pages that are automatically updated to give them current information of personal interest according to their profile. For an example, see my.yahoo.com. Also, refer to the section on portals in Chapter 3
- Push technology—Once thought to be a dead horse is now re-emerging in various manifestations. For a discussion of the issues, see Robin Peek's article, "A Renewed Battle for the Desktop" (Peek, 2001)
- Web site current awareness tools—Northern Light— www.northernlight.com Northern Light offers a search alerts service. This free service allows a user to set up a search profile, like in other current awareness services, to receive e-mailed Web page updates; articles are available for purchase

DOCUMENT DELIVERY VIA THE WEB

The information seekers of today expect to easily discover and download what they need from the Web. We information providers in the library world know that not everything users seek is on the Web or easily discovered there. Budget limitations, space considerations, and sheer common sense keep libraries from purchasing every virtual or physical resource that its users *might* need.

Document delivery services assist users when we do not have what is needed within our collection (physical or virtual), or when our users cannot locate what we own, or when they find it inconvenient or impossible to visit the library in person. They do not care how or where we get it. Getting needed materials to our users is the goal, and for today's users, that means offering services via the Web.

WHAT IS DOCUMENT DELIVERY?

Document delivery is the umbrella term that describes various supply lines for needed information and research materials. Mediated services include:

- interlibrary loan, which supplies materials from other libraries

- staff use of commercial document delivery suppliers for copies of articles and like materials
- in-house copying and delivery services from the resources of the home library

Many former interlibrary loan departments are now called Document Delivery Services to reflect the mediated use of commercial suppliers, expedited services for their users, and copying and delivery services.

End-user initiated reciprocal borrowing, sometimes called resource sharing, is a quasi-mediated service that allows users searching a shared online union catalog to request materials from other libraries in the catalog. The materials are pulled at the owning library and sent to the user's home library for pickup or sometimes the materials are mailed directly to the user.

Unmediated document delivery services are usually subsidized totally or partially by the user's library. Users access the document suppliers on the Web and place their own requests. Materials are usually faxed or mailed to the requestor.

Implementing, upgrading, and promoting document delivery services via the Web to your users will give you the ability to provide excellent service when they say "Get it for me."

GET IT FOR ME—USER NEEDS DRIVE THE SERVICES

Libraries strive to offer their users relevant, quality information in a timely fashion. Many libraries, especially academic ones, have been able to obtain access to greater numbers of electronic journals through consortial purchasing agreements. Statewide multi-type library consortia have licensed databases containing (mostly) full-text articles on a broad array of topics suitable for a wide range of users. So, with all the full-text information available online, interlibrary loan (ILL) and document delivery are no longer needed, right? It depends.

The proliferation of online resources provides more full text, but also provides access to more abstracting and indexing of sources that are *not* available as full text to all of our users. Depending on your clientele and your budget, you could be satisfying their information needs online and your interlibrary loan requests are decreasing, or you could be fueling their needs for information that is not available online, and your interlibrary loan requests are increasing.

Researchers often need materials that were published decades ago and up to this point have not been digitized. Mary Jackson, Senior Program Officer for Access Services, Association of Research Libraries, offered statistics showing that " . . . half of the [interlibrary loan] requests on the OCLC ILL system are for materials older than ten years" (Jackson, 2000). Not everything ever published is available online, nor are all periodicals available online. It appears that document delivery services will be around for a while.

Some library users cannot visit the library to pick up materials. They may live far from the library in rural areas or in another state if they are distance learners. They may have physical disabilities. They may not have time in their busy schedules to make it to the library during its open hours. The online journals and full-text databases that libraries provide on their Web sites allow users who cannot visit the library to access information from their homes or offices. But even when they have access to these resources, they cannot always navigate the systems that provide them. Despite our best efforts to provide user-friendly, seamless interfaces, our users routinely request articles through interlibrary loan that are available to them as articles in databases and electronic journals through the library's Web site. An in-house document delivery service could help these users by filling their requests and delivering the articles to them, whether or not they might be able to get them more directly.

Libraries have many opportunities to add value to their delivery services, whether that means augmenting existing interlibrary loan services with expedited document delivery, adding an in-house copying and delivery service, or developing unmediated document delivery projects.

RECEIVING AND PROCESSING REQUESTS

In the past, any kind of document delivery service required that the library user come to the library, fill out a paper request form, and then return to the library to pick up the materials he or she ordered. If the item requested were a book, the user would then return to the library with the item so it could be checked in. More and more, libraries are automating their document delivery services so that users do not need to appear in person to place requests.

THE ONLINE REQUEST FORM REVOLUTION

The emergence of the online request form has revolutionized document delivery. The goal should be to have request forms on the library's Web site that can be accessed from anywhere via the Internet.

For security reasons, Web forms usually require an authentication method to identify eligible users, such as a logon name and password or library card number. In most cases, users must visit the library to register for their library cards, but even library card registration can take place on the Web. Usually, cards are mailed to the users and they become activated when brought to the library. Some libraries that have instituted Web registration are:

- The Henderson (Nevada) District Public Libraries— www.hdpl.org
- The King County (Washington) Library System— www.kcls.org/libcards/card.html
- The National University—www.nu.edu/library/card.html

With the exception of those using resource sharing systems that have built-in requesting mechanisms and unmediated document delivery projects using commercial document delivery suppliers, libraries will need to devise or acquire some kind of online Web request system to automate and streamline their delivery service.

HOME-GROWN WEB REQUEST FORMS

On the simplest level, a Web form can be created using any of the methods described in Chapter 4. Mailto links and CGI script Web forms can be easily created by library systems staff or other network support staff. These simple forms result in an e-mail message that can be printed off and used as a retrieval tool. What will be lacking is a method of tracking requests and keeping statistics.

On a more complex level, libraries with programmers on their staff can devise more sophisticated forms with ways to populate the patron section from their patron database. The growing use of the OpenURL and the development of new tools such as SFX open up possibilities for populating the requested item section from bibliographic databases.

INTERLIBRARY LOAN MANAGEMENT SYSTEMS

Libraries of all types and sizes can benefit from off-the-shelf software or special modules of their integrated library system (ILS) that provide user-friendly Web request forms for interlibrary loan and document delivery. Not only will users benefit from being able to place requests remotely, but subsequent underlying processes initiated by the users' requests will be efficient and streamlined. While interlibrary loan services were the impetus for the development of interlibrary loan management systems (ILLMS), their use can go beyond the library-to-library supply line of interlibrary loan if you can adapt them for in-house document projects and the delivery of articles from commercial suppliers, too.

ILLMS evolved from the need to automate the paper-based, labor-intensive processes of interlibrary loan. It all started with in-house-created Web forms that sent their contents to the document delivery office via e-mail, moved onward to shareware programs that interfaced with bibliographic utilities (Hippenhammer and Reel, 1997), and ended with the ILLMS provided by many library vendors today. These systems streamline the communication and procurement processes, saving staff time and getting items to the requestors more rapidly.

Libraries that can utilize interlibrary loan management systems will be providing the most user-friendly and efficient document delivery services. Users gain from ease of use and the convenience of placing requests from anywhere via their computer, and the staff behind the scenes will have the tools needed to speed the request through the process.

Web request forms provided by an ILLMS create online records of the users' transactions while providing interactivity with bibliographic utilities and lending libraries for ordering materials and tracking the requests. Staff will no longer need to start from scratch when ordering materials—the information about the request is already keyed in and little extra keying is necessary to produce a request that can be sent to potential lenders. Having an ILLMS can mean the difference between having a backlog of paper request forms waiting to be ordered and being able to complete the ordering process within a day or two.

What Should You Look for in an ILLMS?

Interlibrary loan management systems available at this time are constantly evolving to incorporate new standards, such as the ISO ILL Protocol (www.nlc-bnc.ca/iso/ill/standard.htm), and added features such as delivering documents to the user. Ease of use for users and ILL staff should be at the top of the list when selecting software. Important features to consider are the ability to

- customize request forms
- authenticate users
- allow users to view and check the status of requests
- communicate with users via e-mail
- communicate with bibliographic utilities, document delivery suppliers, and lending libraries (for ordering materials)
- process and check out received materials
- generate statistics

Vendor Name	Product Name	URL
Clio Software	Clio, ClioRequest, ClioWeb	www.cliosoftware.com
Endeavor Information Systems	Voyager ILL Module	www.endinfosys.com/
epixtech, inc.	Resource Sharing System	www.epixtech.com
Ex Libris	ALEPH 500	www.exlibris-usa.com
Fretwell-Downing Informatics	Virtual Document eXchange	www.fdgroup.com
Innovative Interfaces, Inc.	Interlibrary Loan Module	www.iii.com
OCLC	OCLC ILLiad	www.illiad.oclc.org
Research Libraries Group	ILL Manager	www.rlg.org
The Library Corporation	Library.Request	www.tlcdelivers.com
WebZAP	ZAP ILL	www.webzap.org

Libraries in the market for an ILLMS should also keep in mind the lending function, which can benefit from automated catalog searching, checkout, and statistical reports. A recent summary of the features of the major ILLMS can be seen in *Library Technology Reports,* November/December 2000. This issue includes information gathered from a survey of vendors that provide these systems.

The table above includes a representative list of vendors that provide ILLMS and is not inclusive. See *Library Technology Reports* for a complete list.

Prices vary for ILLMS depending on their features and the size of library. Some vendors base their prices on the number of ILL transactions an institution produces a year. So even a smaller ILL service could probably afford to invest in one. Choosing just the right ILLMS or combination of systems can be time-consuming and the decision to purchase a particular system can be a difficult one, but worth the effort in what it will mean to provide a user-friendly online interface and efficient work flow for staff.

OCLC ILL DIRECT

For interlibrary loan, as an alternative to purchasing an ILLMS, OCLC offers a service through its FirstSearch databases that allows users to place requests at the citation level. Libraries must subscribe to the FirstSearch databases and use the OCLC ILL Subsystem for ILL requesting. One advantage to using OCLC ILL Direct is that the WorldCat database is the actual union catalog used in the staff mode for verification and producing ILL requests. OCLC provides a method of customizing lists of potential lenders so that once users place the requests in FirstSearch they can be produced automatically without staff intervention. Statistics are available on the numbers of direct produced requests. See www.oclc.org/oclc/drill/drpis.htm for more information.

MEDIATED DOCUMENT DELIVERY

Retrieving and delivering materials to library users are services that have long existed in libraries to some extent. Serving users via the Web gives libraries new opportunities to transform traditional services into ones that can be accessed over the Web and result in direct delivery to users. Library document delivery services departments retrieve materials for their users through interlibrary loan, document delivery suppliers, and increasingly, through their in-house collections. Expedited document delivery is available at most larger libraries, and especially at academic libraries.

Photocopies requested through the ILL process are now received mostly electronically and can be forwarded directly to remote users. Document delivery suppliers have become an integral part of the supply chain for library document delivery services today, especially when materials are needed quickly. Users have come to expect that we will get things to them quickly, if not immediately. Web-based ordering sites, customized user gateways, and enhanced management features have made fee-based document suppliers attractive for staff ordering or for end-user unmediated document delivery projects which will be discussed later in the chapter.

DEVELOPING AN IN-HOUSE SERVICE

In smaller academic libraries and public libraries, an in-house document delivery service can be an adjunct to the interlibrary loan service. As an example, the usual document delivery services offered at the University of Nevada, Reno have been consolidated with the in-house document delivery service. Both services use the same Web request forms that run on the Innovative Interfaces Interlibrary Loan System (see Figure 5–3).

If you are thinking of setting up a Web-based in-house document delivery service, you will need to answer the following questions:

- Will the service charge a fee?
- How will fees be collected or billed to the users?
- Who will manage the service or can it be an adjunct to ILL?
- How will the request forms be created and/or can existing forms associated with the ILLMS be used if the ILL department manages the service?
- How will the materials be delivered?

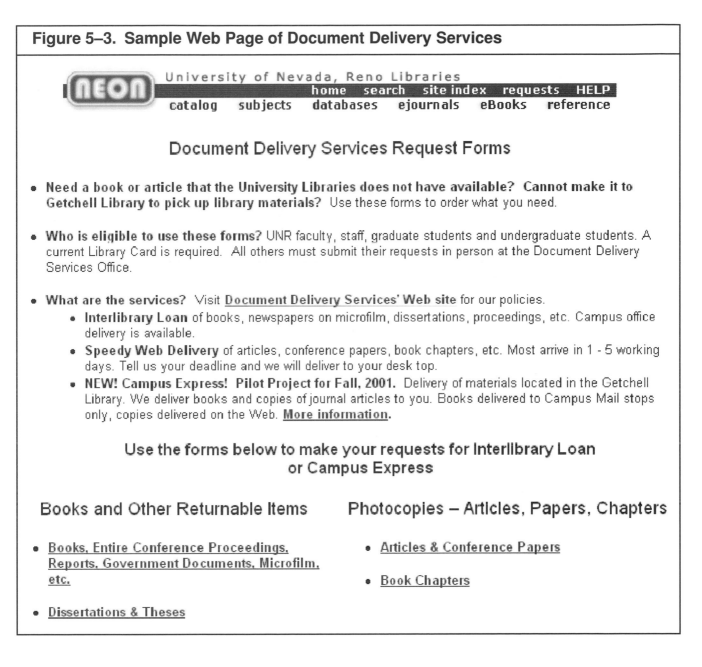

Figure 5–3. Sample Web Page of Document Delivery Services

University of Nevada, Reno Libraries
home   search   site index   requests   HELP
catalog   subjects   databases   ejournals   eBooks   reference

Document Delivery Services Request Forms

- **Need a book or article that the University Libraries does not have available? Cannot make it to Getchell Library to pick up library materials?** Use these forms to order what you need.

- **Who is eligible to use these forms?** UNR faculty, staff, graduate students and undergraduate students. A current Library Card is required. All others must submit their requests in person at the Document Delivery Services Office.

- **What are the services?** Visit <u>Document Delivery Services' Web site</u> for our policies.
  - **Interlibrary Loan** of books, newspapers on microfilm, dissertations, proceedings, etc. Campus office delivery is available.
  - **Speedy Web Delivery** of articles, conference papers, book chapters, etc. Most arrive in 1 - 5 working days. Tell us your deadline and we will deliver to your desk top.
  - **NEW! Campus Express! Pilot Project for Fall, 2001.** Delivery of materials located in the Getchell Library. We deliver books and copies of journal articles to you. Books delivered to Campus Mail stops only, copies delivered on the Web. <u>More information</u>.

Use the forms below to make your requests for Interlibrary Loan or Campus Express

Books and Other Returnable Items

- <u>Books, Entire Conference Proceedings, Reports, Government Documents, Microfilm, etc.</u>

- <u>Dissertations & Theses</u>

Photocopies – Articles, Papers, Chapters

- <u>Articles & Conference Papers</u>

- <u>Book Chapters</u>

MEDIATED DELIVERY OF BOOKS

In some cases, delivering materials from our collections directly to our users is the only way they can get them. In other cases it is a value-added service some libraries are willing and able to provide for their users' convenience. For years, libraries have been sending books directly to users, through resource sharing systems, special services for rural or homebound users, or arrangements for distance education students. These examples show a variety of approaches libraries have taken to the delivery of books to their users' homes or offices:

- Some libraries require a physician's signature before they will mail books to those who are unable to visit the library because of illness or disability (see, for example, the Ocean County (NJ) Library form at oceancounty.lib.nj.us/Services/booksbymail.htm)
- The University of Pennsylvania will mail books to faculty and graduate students who are "living away from campus" if they are at least 75 miles away (see details at www.library.upenn.edu/services/borrowing/booksbymail.html)
- The Eastern Counties Regional Library in Nova Scotia provides a Web form for a "Books by Mail" service for "persons in the more isolated areas of our region" (see ecrl.library.ns.ca/request.htm)
- Residents of Multnomah County in Oregon are encouraged to do a remote search of the library's Web-based catalog for a book or video and choose the option "Deliver by Mail." There is a $2.00 shipping charge for each item that either can be paid using an envelope that is sent with the item or "charged" to the library card (see www.multcolib.org/about/mcl-bkmail.html)

In general, academic libraries that deliver books tend to limit their service to campus offices, whether the books are in the library's collection or obtained through ILL. Home delivery is usually limited to distance learners, agricultural extension faculty, and other special circumstances. Users of special delivery services must be willing to accept the extra responsibilities associated with books and other items that need to be returned (that is, short duration of checkout for ILL books, the time it takes to receive mailed materials, and time to return them the same way).

Book Delivery Essentials

Some practical tips for sending books to users at home are to

- send items in padded envelopes or zippered bags that can be re-used for return of the items
- send items to the users via First Class Mail or other shipper that has expedited delivery
- find a way to generate an address label from the user's request
- affix a book strap to each item that gives the details users

need to know; for example, the due date, any fines that will be charged if the item is returned late, instructions on how to re-package the book for mailing, and the phone number or e-mail address where users can request a renewal
- include a return address label. Decide if users will be required to pay for shipping on the way back. Include a pre-paid shipping label to assure that books return to the correct address and specific department if the library will pay the return postage
- give users the option of bringing items back to the library if they desire

For academic libraries, delivery on campus can be made in some sort of re-usable mailing envelope or bag. Most of the tips mentioned above can apply, too. Delivering items to campus offices using the campus delivery system already in place (for example, campus mail or inter-office mail) seems a logical method. Campus mail may not be the perfect solution in all cases, however. Using such a service would depend on the level and frequency of its operation. Implementing a library-based delivery service to campus offices might be the best solution in some situations, especially at smaller institutions, but keep in mind that instituting new services requires adding or shifting staff for successful outcomes.

MEDIATED DELIVERY OF COPIES

Libraries have many options for delivering copies of articles and other research materials. Libraries retrieve photocopies from various supply lines that include:

- interlibrary loan
- document suppliers
- their in-house collections, including full-text electronic journals and licensed databases

Delivering photocopies directly to users is a service that can be easily instituted, especially because of their "disposability." Unlike books and other "returnables" that need to be returned to their home library, photocopies can be replicated if lost or merely tossed when their usefulness passes.

Some kind of photocopying service is usually available in most medium to large academic libraries. Some (mostly large) public libraries also offer fee-based information delivery (Coffman, 1999). Though not every service of this kind has an online pres-

Institution	Name of Service	URL
County of Los Angeles Public Library	F.Y.I.	www.colapublib.org
Univ. of California, Santa Cruz	Slug Express	bob.ucsc.edu/library/access/SlugExpress.html
Univ. of Wisconsin—Madison	Library Express	www.wisc.edu/wendt/libexp/about.html
Arizona State University	Library Express	www.asu.edu/lib/ill/DocDeliveryHelp.html
Hardin Library for the Health Sciences, University of Iowa	Distance Education Document Delivery Service	www.lib.uiowa.edu/hardin-www/ildeds.html
Univ. of British Columbia	UBC Library Document Delivery Service	www.library.ubc.ca/home/about/instruct/gtdocdel.html
Univ. of California, Berkeley	Baker Document Delivery Service	www.lib.berkeley.edu/ILS/baker.html

ence, many academic libraries offer Web-based request forms. Some services are free and others charge a fee. When fees are charged, they vary but seem to fall between $1.00 and $3.00 per request. Some examples of the Web presence for this kind of service are listed above. Note that some of these services also deliver books.

Desktop Delivery

Increasingly, the majority of photocopied documents received via ILL and document suppliers are in electronic format. Use of ARIEL, Research Libraries Group's software for sending and receiving scanned images over the Internet, has become widespread in all types of libraries, but especially academic and medical libraries. Documents arrive as TIFF files and they can be sent to users as e-mail attachments. Users need to have TIFF viewer software on their personal computers to open the documents. Later versions of operating systems include TIFF viewers, but for those who do not have that software, DocView, a free-ware product developed by the National Library of Medicine, comes to the rescue.

Responding to some users' dissatisfaction with the TIFF format, the National Library of Medicine developed DocMorph to help libraries convert TIFF files to PDF (portable document format), a more popular and available document format. The DocMorph Server has the ability to convert more than 40 types of files to PDF. ARIEL TIFF files can be loaded onto the DocMorph server, converted to PDF, and then the documents can

Software Name	URL
ARIEL	www.rlg.org
DocView	docmorph.nlm.nih.gov/docview/
DocMorph	docmorph.nlm.nih.gov/docmorph/default.htm
Prospero	bones.med.ohio-state.edu/prospero/

be sent as e-mail attachments. TIFF and PDF files tend to be large, often more than 1MB, so users need robust e-mail accounts to handle these files.

Once again the medical library community, that is the Prior Health Sciences Library at The Ohio State University, came up with a solution to overloaded e-mail boxes and developed Prospero (Schnell, 1999), an electronic document delivery system. Prospero interacts with ARIEL by converting TIFF files to PDF format, sending the files to a Web server where users can view and/or print out the documents, and notifying users via e-mail that their documents are ready for viewing. Taking the Prospero model a step further, ARIEL version 3.0, released in 2001, integrates the document format conversion, Web server access, and user notification into one software package. Information about the software and free-ware mentioned above can be viewed from these Web sites.

For in-house document delivery services you can utilize the same process of scanning and sending documents to your users' desktops. Paper documents from the library's collection can either be scanned and sent as TIFF or PDF e-mail attachments or, using Prospero or ARIEL, sent to a secure Web server for access as a PDF document. With requests for items that are already available to the user on the library's Web site from licensed databases and electronic journals, check the license agreements to make sure forwarding electronic files to users is allowed. Most databases have a feature that allows articles to be e-mailed by the user for output, and perhaps the library can forward articles to its eligible users the same way.

Printing out articles from online resources and then scanning them for delivery via a secure Web server as suggested above might seem silly and labor intensive, but it might be the only allowable way to solve some delivery problems. For online resources that have persistent URLs, it is simpler for everyone if you send the URL to the user via e-mail for direct access, although users will then need to go through the authentication process required for off-site access of licensed resources. Document delivery personnel may find themselves in an instructional position at times.

Management Considerations

While DocView, DocMorph, and Prospero are freely available, ARIEL has a cost. ARIEL is the standard document transmission method utilized by libraries in North America and increasingly around the world. The major document suppliers use it, too. For libraries that have not yet made the step to electronic document delivery, purchasing ARIEL or finding other methods to scan and send documents electronically to your users would be optimal for serving users via the Web. Users will need access to the software that reads PDF format, Abobe Acrobat, but PDF is such a common format on the Web that this is no longer a big obstacle for users. Nevertheless, you should feature the Adobe download Web site prominently where users will find it when they need to access a document (www.adobe.com/support/downloads/main.html).

Other Delivery Methods

Mailing and/or faxing documents to users are standard procedure for some academic libraries, many special libraries, and any library that has a fee-based service. Some users will still want to visit the library to pick up their documents, and that should be an option.

Fax quality has improved over the years but is dependent on both the sender's and the receiver's equipment. Fewer libraries use fax to transmit routine documents to other libraries now that ARIEL has become the standard. Still, fax is an option available and document suppliers and libraries make that delivery method available if requested. Many unmediated document delivery projects depend on fax for end-user delivery. Re-faxing faxed documents can literally destroy document readability. Mathematical and scientific notation become unreadable. It is best to send faxed documents to the user via U.S. Mail or campus mail.

RESOURCE SHARING—HOW THE LIBRARY NETWORKS DO IT

If your library is part of a network or consortium that shares an OPAC whose software does not offer users the ability to request books from any of the libraries included, then this part of the chapter is for you. Otherwise, skip to the next section. Library networks and/or consortia with pooled holdings in a shared catalog have the ability to use software that will allow users from any of the libraries to request materials from any network library through the online union catalog. In most cases, courier systems have been set up to pick up and deliver materials between the participating libraries. Sometimes the couriers are part of the library system's internal delivery system or commercial couriers are contracted to make the deliveries.

All types of libraries participate in these regional/statewide consortia. There are:

- multi-county networks of multi-type libraries; for example, the North Bay Cooperative Library System in northern California (www.nbcls.org), which includes public, academic, and special libraries
- state-wide networks; for example, OhioLink (www.ohiolink.edu), which includes academic libraries and the State Library of Ohio, and Pioneer (pioneer.lib.ut.us/), which includes academic and public libraries in Utah
- regional networks; for example, ORBIS (orbis.uoregon.edu), which includes academic libraries in Oregon and Washington

SOFTWARE TOOLS

Several vendors have developed software that enables end-user-initiated requesting. INN-Reach from Innovative Interfaces, Inc. is one example. Here is how INN-Reach works: a user searching the shared catalog

- finds an item not held locally
- views the locations of the libraries holding the item if needed
- requests it via a "Request Item" icon
- receives the item via his or her home library

The process involves placing a hold on the desired item at the owning library.

Requests for journal articles and other photocopying requests cannot be processed through this online-catalog-based system. However, epixtech, Inc.'s Universal Resource Sharing Application (URSA) offers the ability for users to request books and journal articles with the ability for requests to be routed to staff for processing if desired. Photocopies of journal articles or items not located in the union catalog can be requested via URSA and are forwarded to the ILL department for fulfillment. See the issue of *Library Technology Reports* mentioned above for more information on these and other vendors of resource-sharing software.

An example of an integrated resource sharing and document delivery requesting service developed by a public entity is one that has been created by the University of California for the California Digital Library (www.cdlib.org/guides/request/). The "Request" feature from within the Melvyl Catalog and some online bibliographic databases allows users to request materials from their campus library if that campus has an in-house document delivery service or request materials from other libraries in the system.

UNMEDIATED DOCUMENT DELIVERY PROJECTS

Libraries began to experiment with subsidized unmediated document delivery projects in the mid-nineteen-nineties. These projects were inspired by the development of online requesting mechanisms available through bibliographic databases, such as CARL's UnCover database and OCLC's FirstSearch. Academic, medical, and special libraries have tried unmediated document delivery projects as an adjunct to mediated interlibrary loan. The reasons for initiating unmediated projects are varied and include reducing the workload of interlibrary loan departments while providing streamlined service (Sellers & Beam, 1995), reducing staffing costs for ILL (Crowley, 1999), and compensating for serials cancellations (Haslam & Stowers, 2001). All of these reasons for initiating subsidized unmediated document delivery projects are still valid today as libraries often struggle with providing what their users need while trying to live within shrinking budgets for ongoing subscriptions and staffing.

DOCUMENT SUPPLIERS

Document suppliers on the Web are a ready source for finding articles that can be purchased by anyone with a credit card or deposit account. Libraries sometimes refer unaffiliated people who need articles quickly to one of these commercial services. Direct access to document suppliers through licensed bibliographic databases has recently re-emerged as a way to give users the opportunity to obtain items that are not available as full text in the database. An example of this feature is the ability for libraries to select this option to appear in the EBSCOhost databases with the user being directed to Infotrieve for articles in journals not held by the library. Depending on the library's willingness and ability to subsidize the service with a deposit account, users might request and receive the articles freely, or they might have to use their own credit cards to obtain the articles.

Unmediated document delivery (UDD) projects usually allow a selected user group direct access to document suppliers for ordering needed articles. Most current awareness vendors (see the earlier part of the chapter for specific vendors) offer online articles and/or delivery of copies of articles on a pay-per-view basis as an integral part of their services. A few suppliers cover broad subject areas and have access to large research library collections:

- The British Library's Document Supply Centre— www.bl.uk—click on "Document Delivery"
- CISTI (Canada Institute for Scientific and Technical Information)—www.nrc.ca/cisti/docdel
- Infotrieve—www4.infotrieve.com
- Ingenta—www.ingenta.com

Document suppliers come in several varieties. Some suppliers are library-based that rely on their in-house collections, for example, CISTI and the British Library's Document Supply Center. Some commercial suppliers use research library collections for document retrieval, for example, Infotrieve and Ingenta. Infotrieve and Ingenta also have publishers' content available in their online databases that is delivered as PDF files. CISTI specializes in the subjects of science, technology, and medicine, but has a "Global Supply" service that can search for documents beyond its holdings and its partner libraries. Infotrieve is the most "full-service" of the suppliers mentioned. In addition to its database and the resources of the research libraries to which it has access for document supply, Infotrieve uses other document suppliers and publishers to track down needed documents.

Services vary, but some vendors have built-in account management tools that facilitate your ability to customize the service. In some cases a "gateway" can be set up for a fee to help administer users' accounts. Some suppliers give you the ability to enter eligible users' delivery information, set limits on the numbers or costs of articles that can be ordered, and produce status reports and statistics. Some suppliers can load the library's serial holdings to keep participants from ordering titles owned by the library, thus reducing the cost. Per-article prices vary, from $10 and up, and copyright fees are added according to the copyright holder's set fee. Rush delivery usually adds another $10 or more to the cost. Delivery of offline articles is usually via the user's fax machine, though courier and U.S. Mail are other options. ARIEL delivery is usually available and could be implemented if your unmediated project had a central delivery site, for example, to a specific academic department's office.

PLANNING AND MANAGEMENT

Budgeting for unmediated projects is the first step. Sometimes grant monies can support a pilot project. Public libraries could initiate a project directed at user groups with special information needs and apply for grants from local foundations or the Library Services and Technology Act program in their states. For the most part, funding can come logically from the library's materials budget. Libraries use materials funds for buying access to online full-text databases and electronic journals. In the unmediated document delivery model, users select the resources they need, thus buying information "by the drink" instead of committing the library to long-term subscriptions that may not get the expected use. Use of the materials fund leads to the same outcome—users get what they need. Questions to consider when setting up a UDD project include:

- How will the project be funded?
- What suppliers will be used?
- Who will manage the project and train users?
- What user group(s) will participate?
- What statistics will be collected?
- How will suppliers be evaluated during the project?
- How will you get feedback from users during and after the project?

Initiating an unmediated document delivery project involves setting goals and solid planning for positive outcomes. Regular communication with users is necessary to make sure they know how to search the document suppliers' databases and submit requests. Getting the users' feedback about the quality of the services they are receiving from the document suppliers is essential. Plan to contact users for input on a regular basis. At the end of pilot projects provide an evaluation tool so participants can evaluate all aspects of the project. With good information and statistics at hand, pilot projects can become regular services. Do not be afraid to experiment.

MANAGING DOCUMENT DELIVERY AND CURRENT AWARENESS SERVICES

Implementing new current awareness and document delivery services generates new management tasks and the need for oversight. Some tools require only verification of URLs, some services are staff intensive, taking staff away from other services they will still need to support, others take little time or effort, but require equipment and technology. While some tools and services are free, others are very costly, and funding must be determined and developed before implementation. Libraries should make sure to get the most bang for the buck by promoting and publicizing their services effectively.

STAFFING ISSUES

When a library takes on new initiatives, staff is affected. Rarely are any new staff positions allocated to implement them. Fortunately, most current awareness tools and services do not require much staff intervention. A librarian already making links and conducting training workshops can take on the additional duties of finding and linking to preprint servers, alert services, and other relevant sites. Existing training workshops can incorporate tips for getting the most out of Ingenta or Infotrieve profiles.

Implementing new document delivery services, on the other hand, can be much more staff-intensive. Clerical, technical, student staff, and volunteers will most likely be taking on the bulk of additional work of in-house delivery of materials, programming of Web forms, and processing the likely increased volume of requests. Libraries starting up new projects should analyze closely potential effects and plan accordingly. Things to consider from the staffing perspective when starting up a new service include:

- who will train the staff to use and manage the service
- who will train the users, if necessary
- what low-priority tasks can be disposed of in favor of the new service
- when the new services will be implemented (slow times are often good for test phases, so staff can get used to a new project before a deluge of requests come in)
- how the services can be integrated with existing processes

BUDGET ISSUES

With the exception of services such as Current Contents and Ingenta, most current awareness tools and services have no or low implementation costs. Most document delivery services have initial as well as ongoing costs in staff, supplies, software, and equipment. These costs are necessary for a successful service and must be anticipated and budgeted before implementation. Unmediated document delivery can have a high cost for the documents themselves, implementation and user training, but may save staff time in the long term. Some costs involved in providing new current awareness and document delivery services include:

- subscriptions or site licenses for current awareness services
- deposit accounts with document suppliers for mediated and unmediated delivery
- additional student or clerical staff to implement in-house delivery services
- additional equipment, hardware, and software
- postage, which can be significant for mailing materials directly to users

Where do you get the money? Many libraries are writing grant proposals to institutional, state, local, and private entities in order to implement new services. Some are reallocating existing funds from materials, equipment, and staff budgets to enhance or initiate new services and subscriptions. These services are very arguably part of the collection, and should be budgeted along with any other materials. It is clear that by offering these services, users have access to more information. Be creative and seek money wherever it is, through

- federal funding agencies
- state funding, including LSTA grants
- institutional funding, such as campus instructional enhancements grants
- private donors and foundations

PUBLICITY AND PROMOTION

Using the Library Web site to publicize and promote current awareness and document delivery services is essential. Some ways to promote new or enhanced services on the Web are to

- create Web page(s) for document delivery and current awareness services available to users. Link to the page(s) from multiple locations

- list the services (Ingenta, Current Contents, or preprints databases, for example) on existing pages of bibliographic databases, services, and research information
- incorporate the services into subject-specific Web pages for classes or constituencies
- advertise new Web pages and services with a temporary (or permanent) link from the library or institutional home page.

Other ways to publicize new, enhanced, or underutilized services are to

- use existing lists of e-mail addresses for remote (and/or on-site) users and send announcements of services, training sessions, and Web pages
- take advantage of existing methods of reaching users, such as registration materials, printed notices such as hold-pickup and renewal notices
- use signs, bookmarks (some vendors will provide printed materials), and fliers for your on-site users
- provide orientation sessions for complicated services, such as unmediated document delivery and personalized current awareness services
- attend departmental meetings of faculty or researchers

If users do not know services are available, they will not use them. Students and non-professional researchers may not even know these services and tools exist until the library notifies them. Put these services in front of your users where they are likely to go anyway.

EVALUATION

Any new service must be evaluated for success or failure in order to be justified. For projects requiring funding or ongoing staffing, in particular, assessment must be made that it is worthwhile. For unmeasurable services and enhancements, like many current awareness tools and specialized Web pages, feedback can be found in focus groups and surveys of users. Satisfaction is the bottom line and can garner overwhelming support for a new service. Statistics gathering is essential to prove to administration and external funding sources the value and use of new services.

Implementing and enhancing existing services in document delivery and current awareness via the Web is important to keep libraries relevant to remote users. Libraries need to know what is possible and constantly strive for the best service utilizing the technology and tools available.

REFERENCES

Coffman, Steve. 1999. "Special Considerations for Fee-Based Services in Public Libraries." *Journal of Interlibrary Loan, Document Delivery & Information Supply* 10, no.1: 13–28.

Crowley, Gwyneth H. 1999. "Unmediated Document Delivery: A Project Using FirstSearch and EBSCOdoc." *Interlending & Document Supply* 27, no. 3: 122–127.

Haslam, Michaelyn, and Eva Stowers. 2001. "Library-Subsidized Unmediated Document Delivery." *Library Resources & Technical Services* 45, no. 2: 80–89.

Hippenhammer, Craighton, and Keith Reel. 1997. "Interlibrary Loan Web Forms and IPT." *Journal of Interlibrary Loan, Document Delivery & Information Supply* 7, no. 3: 35–44.

Jackson, Mary E. 2000. "Research Collections and Digital Information: Will There be a Role for Interlibrary Loan and Document Delivery Services?" *Journal of Library Administration* 31, no.2: 15–25.

Jordan, Sharon M. 1999. "Preprint Servers: Status, Challenges, and Opportunities of the New Digital Publishing Paradigm," *InForum '99* [Online]. Available: www.osti.gov/inforum99/proceed.html [2001, July 31].

Library Technology Reports 36, no. 6 (November/December, 2000).

Notess, Greg R. 1999. "Internet Current Awareness," *Online* 23, no.2 (March/April): 75–78.

Peek, Robin P. 2001. "A Renewed Battle for the Desktop," *Information Today* 18, no.2 (February): 30–31.

Rowley, Jennifer, 1998. "The Changing Face of Current Awareness Services," *Journal of Librarianship and Information Science* 30, no.2 (September): 177–183.

Schnell, Eric H. 1999. "Freeing Ariel: The Prospero Electronic Document Delivery Project." *Journal of Interlibrary Loan, Document Delivery & Information Supply* 10, no.2: 89–100.

Sellers, Minna, and Joan Beam. 1995. "Subsidizing Unmediated Document Delivery: Current Models and a Case Study." *Journal of Academic Librarianship* 21, no.6 (November): 459–466.

Tomaiuolo, Nicholas G., and Joan Garrett Packer. 2000. "Preprint Servers: Pushing the Envelope of Electronic Scholarly Publishing," *Searcher* 8, no.9 (October): 53–61.

6 PROVIDING LIBRARY INSTRUCTION TO REMOTE USERS

by Amy W. Shannon and Terry A. Henner

CHAPTER OVERVIEW

- Special Challenges for the Remote User
- Instruction of Remote Users—On Their Turf
- Remote Instruction of Users
- Special Technologies for User-Centered Instruction
- Many Opportunities

An early episode of *Star Trek* has Captain Kirk roaming a deserted starship in search of the crew. The crewmembers, we eventually learn, are still present on the ship, but are trapped in a dimensional rift, rendering them invisible. An invisible population similarly surrounds librarians working in an increasingly digital environment. The proliferation of networked resources has created a largely unseen, but very active contingent of remote library patrons. As the proportion of remote library use increases, so too does the challenge of providing bibliographic instruction. While there is clearly a surge in access to digital information resources, we don't generally know who the users are, where they are, or what problems they face in using electronic resources. Fortunately, some of the same technological developments that tend to isolate patrons from library staff can also be employed to overcome the difficulties inherent in supporting remote library users.

SPECIAL CHALLENGES FOR THE REMOTE USER

Scholarly information resources have never been easy to use, which is why instruction has been a key service component of the mission of most academic libraries. In recent years, with the glut of available online information, libraries have also assumed the responsibility for educating students in information literacy. The fact that many of our users now do not come to the library does not free us from those responsibilities. In fact, remote users have other obstacles of their own that we need to help them overcome.

Often, the first hurdle for remote patrons is not which database to use, but how to log onto the library network, or how to authenticate their access to the system. So the instructional needs of remote users goes beyond choosing information resources, negotiating search interfaces, and navigating Web sites; it also includes the problems imposed by the networked environment itself. These students need to master various aspects of the operating system, Web browser, supplemental "plug-in" programs, dial-up connection settings, and other issues inherent in a networked environment. The teaching of computer literacy and telecommunications essentials has for many libraries become a fundamental component of library instruction for remote users.

The fact that remote users are geographically dispersed from the physical library and library staff creates a basic dilemma:

- Who do they ask for help?
- How do they know what help is available?
- Do they even realize they could benefit from some help?

The classification of remote user should not be reserved only for those who are miles away. Given the presence of inexpensive and ubiquitous network access, even users in close physical proximity to a library, or within the library itself can be classified functionally as remote users. The library Web site can provide an excellent opportunity to make the connection with users who have instructional needs. It offers a unique advantage over traditional methods of classroom instruction in that librarians, through a variety of methods, can offer instruction that is tailored to the individual and takes into account their particular environment and learning styles and is available to them at their convenience, at their own pace.

INSTRUCTION OF REMOTE USERS— ON THEIR TURF

In this new era of information delivery, library users are coming to expect information to travel to them. Along with this new era of delivery comes an even greater need for instruction and help in accessing and using information resources. Library users often have to navigate a morass of technical details just to get online and access the library's licensed products. Once online, students are faced with more competition for their attention than ever before. They need to learn to become careful information consumers, making choices between information coming from the entirety of the Internet. To reach these new remote users, library instructors must find a way to take the instruction to where their students are.

Students, wherever they are located, and whether they are using the physical or the virtual library, can benefit from traditional library instruction. Regardless of the setting, library instruction teaches patrons how to identify, evaluate, select, and use information resources, despite their format and location.

There were good reasons for library instruction to be held in the library in the past. Not only were the necessary resources housed in the building, but it was good to orient the students to the location of materials and services in the building. This is no longer true. A walk through the reference department is no longer a necessary or even desired part of library instruction, and librarians are starting to be sited far from their native habitat.

In some cases it still makes sense for on-campus students who will be using library resources and services to come to the library as a class for an instruction session, particularly if the library has the most wired facilities on campus. But sometimes students are not able to come to the library for formal instruction, and sometimes even if they could, it makes more sense to teach on their turf. Increasingly, students are not coming to the library to do their research, and even when they do come, they may not stray far from the computer nearest to the entrance. Sometimes the class is too large to fit into a library classroom. The advent of distributed access to information resources has freed library instructors from the confines of the library buildings.

TAKING TO THE ROAD: INSTRUCTION IN THE WIRED CLASSROOM

Most institutions are putting in a raft of "wired" classrooms.

These classrooms can have anything from an Internet connection to all the latest bells and whistles. With the minimum of an Internet connection and decent projection system, these rooms are more effective for today's library instruction than any walking tour of the library could be. When librarians travel to classrooms to provide an orientation to information resources, they are able to meet with larger groups than the library can accommodate, and they are proving by their demonstrations that library resources are accessible from outside the library.

Content of the Internet-Era Class Instruction Session

First and foremost, in this new era of remote use, students are rarely interested in hearing about what the library has in paper or microform, no matter how central it may be to their research. It helps to avoid thinking of what you are doing as an overview of library resources. Instead it is an overview of accessible information resources. The distinction is in the word "accessible." Paper resources are no longer considered very accessible.

The most common question on the minds of students is usually "how can I get access?" and unless you handle this question up front you will have a hard time getting their full attention no matter how eloquently you cover the important aspects of research strategy or critical thinking skills. A simple promise that you will handle or refer these questions at the end may be enough to bring their attention back. Discussing access at the beginning of the session has the added benefit of informing some students that remote access is possible for them. Plus, explaining that some resources are licensed drives home the idea that not all information is free—a handy concept for when you get around to discussing evaluation of information sources.

Because Web use is so ingrained in the habits of remote library users, they are particularly susceptible to the mindset that open-access Web sites alone will suffice for all information needs. Remote users often have heightened expectations of the Web (and a lack of critical judgment) and are less likely to explore bibliographic databases and full-text collections. Not only should a library instruction program targeting remote users draw attention to the full array of resources available electronically, it should help students learn to evaluate the quality of information retrieved. There are numerous Web sites available to help students to learn evaluation skills. For access to a number of these sites, check out "Evaluation of information sources" at www.vuw.ac.nz/~agsmith/ evaln/evaln.htm. But let's be realistic. Few students will be self-motivated enough to spend much time there, unless it is part of a graded assignment. So, it will be up to you, their library instructor, to impart what you can of the basic concepts for evaluating Web-based information.

As with traditional library instruction, you will want to point students in the direction of the best licensed databases and full-text resources for their particular needs. But you can customize library Web pages for a particular course and/or develop tutorials to help students effectively use the recommended resources. We all know that if you try to teach too much in a session, none of it will stick. Some library instructors believe that we should try to teach no more than three basic concepts during a formal session. Naturally, we adjust the complexity of the instruction to the level of the course and the average attention span, experience, and capabilities of each group. For inexperienced students who will be remote users of information resources, the important three concepts might be that

- the library has a mission to provide resources that will support student learning and research and has acquired certain online information resources that will be especially useful to them in this particular course, and these resources can be found on the Web at . . .
- they can make use of these special resources in the library or outside the library, but outside the library they will need to go through a certain authentication process, which is . . . and if they need help accessing or using these resources, they should . . .
- there are other useful resources on the Web besides what the library provides. But not all Web pages are equally valuable or credible. Some tips for evaluating the quality of Web sites are . . .

After spending the appropriate amount of time that is needed to thoroughly impart these concepts, you can move on to other topics for those who can manage more information, or if you are in a hands-on lab you might want to let the students explore the library resources as you remain available for one-on-one assistance.

Web Pages vs. Handouts

The era of the handout is over. What we once tried to accomplish with reams of soon-to-be-lost-or-tossed pages can now be more effectively accomplished through customized Web pages. These Web "handouts" cannot be lost and are always available at hand when needed. Like traditional paper handouts, customized Web pages can be as specific or general as needed. Also like

Figure 6–1. Web-based Course "Handout"

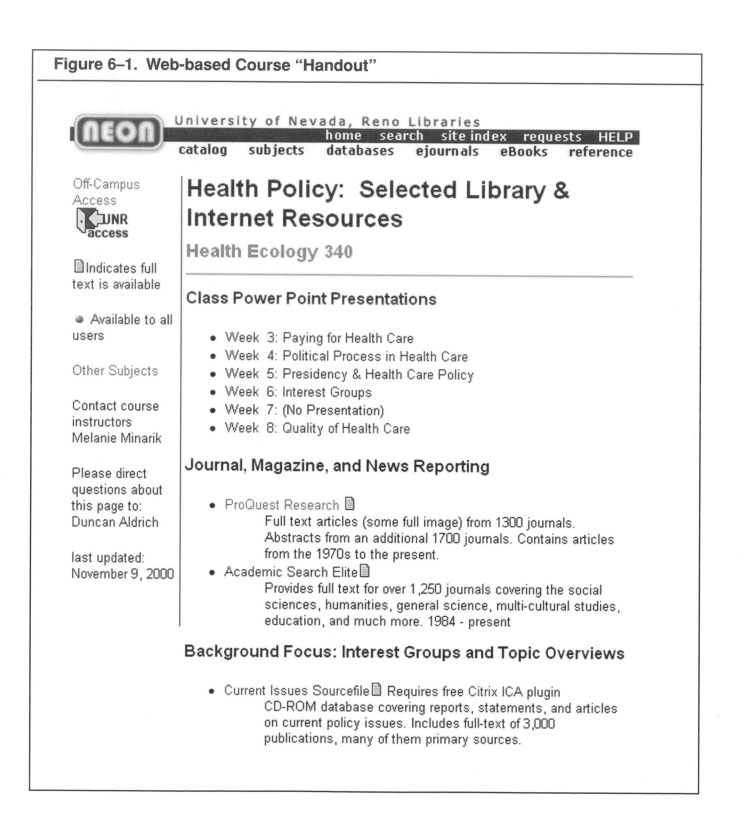

Figure 6–2. Another Web-based Course "Handout"

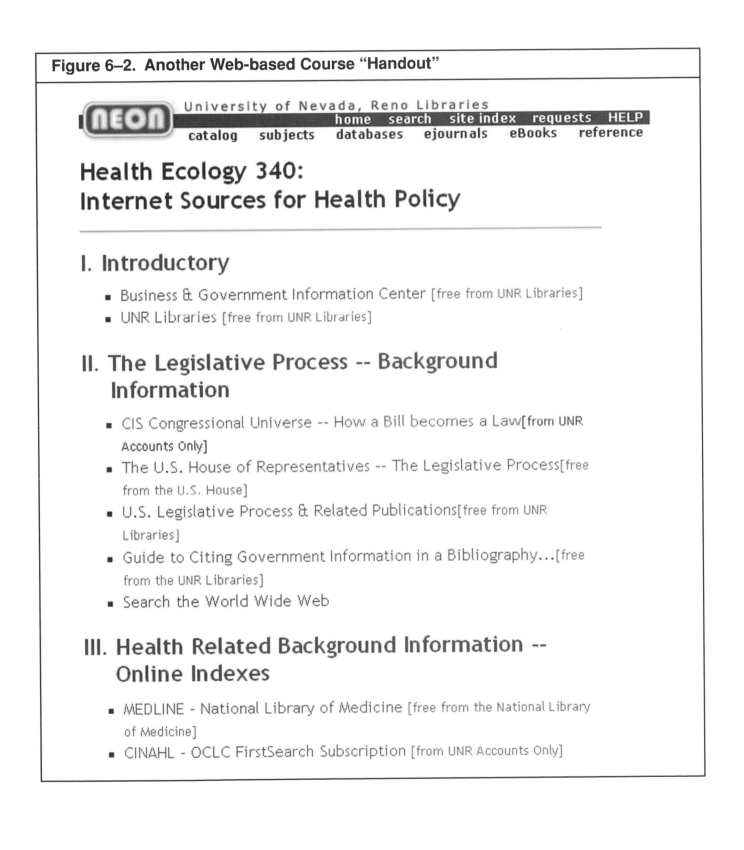

University of Nevada, Reno Libraries

home   search   site index   requests   HELP

catalog   subjects   databases   ejournals   eBooks   reference

Health Ecology 340:
Internet Sources for Health Policy

I. Introductory

- Business & Government Information Center [free from UNR Libraries]
- UNR Libraries [free from UNR Libraries]

II. The Legislative Process -- Background Information

- CIS Congressional Universe -- How a Bill becomes a Law[from UNR Accounts Only]
- The U.S. House of Representatives -- The Legislative Process[free from the U.S. House]
- U.S. Legislative Process & Related Publications[free from UNR Libraries]
- Guide to Citing Government Information in a Bibliography...[free from the UNR Libraries]
- Search the World Wide Web

III. Health Related Background Information -- Online Indexes

- MEDLINE - National Library of Medicine [free from the National Library of Medicine]
- CINAHL - OCLC FirstSearch Subscription [from UNR Accounts Only]

traditional handouts, some libraries maintain a collection of standard pages for use in a variety of teaching situations. Better than paper handouts, Web "handouts" can link the user directly into online resources, without their having to write down call numbers or URLs. Also, these pages can be updated and added to as often as needed throughout the semester.

Although Web "handouts" can take almost any format, the most common forms are the laundry list and the annotated laundry list. Some examples are given in Figures 6–1 and 6–2.

For greatest impact, course-specific Web pages need to be easy to find by their target audience. Links to these pages should be added to courses' online syllabi, to the library's appropriate subject pages, and to courses' electronic reserve readings. Where appropriate these pages can be designed to act as a customized gateway between a course's Web site and the library's Web.

When Things Go Wrong

No discussion of our new online world can be complete without acknowledging that things do not always go as planned. You would be hard put to find an instructor who has not had to tap dance in the face of suddenly slow or nonexistent Web connectivity. A situation as simple as a lack of an extension cord can be a calamity when you are facing 30 or more bored, but expectant students. Unfortunately, the more our message is about online research, the fewer alternatives we have to fill in awkward gaps.

In addition to the obvious suggestion of checking all equipment and connections ahead of time, there are some things you can do to help lessen the impacts of uncertain technology:

- memorize or keep with you the phone numbers of all available technology support personnel
- choose databases and Web pages to demonstrate that are usually quick to load
- prepare backup examples in case your primary example sites are down or slow to load
- use disappearing Web sites as a lesson in the transient nature of much of today's Web
- ditto for sites that have suddenly reorganized, leaving you stumbling about
- limit the number of examples you plan to demonstrate from a single Web site
- "can" a few examples by downloading them to your hard drive ahead of time
- open an additional browser session so that you can show other things while a slow database loads

- prepare a discussion of Web page evaluation that can be fitted into slow load times
- maintain a sense of humor and, if all else fails, be prepared to reschedule

A LAPTOP AND A SMILE: TAKING INSTRUCTION TO THE UNWIRED ENVIRONMENT

Despite the seemingly ubiquitous nature of online access, many venues for instruction are not yet wired. The denizens of these environments are still remote library users, logging in from home, work, or computer lab, and are as in need of instruction as any other remote library patrons. But is it effective to try to take instruction in the use of online resources to an unwired classroom? Although not ideal, if can be effective.

A common strategy is to prepare a "canned" presentation that can be taken to the classroom on a laptop and presented using a digital projection system. Some libraries maintain portable equipment for just this purpose. Although a canned example is never quite as exciting as a live demonstration, it can mimic what the students will see when they log on from home.

Another approach is to combine a brief class appearance with online instructional materials that the students access outside of class, such as a tutorial or online assignment. This strategy allows for the personal connection developed through face-to-face contact with the librarian, while acknowledging the limitations of teaching online resources without Internet access.

Future improvements in the speed and quality of wireless modems may make the unwired classroom a thing of the past. Librarians will be equipped to carry the network to the students.

INSTRUCTION IN THE HANDS-ON COMPUTER LABORATORY

When teaching labs with a room full of computers were first unveiled, they were heralded as the beginning of a new era of hands-on learning. It soon became apparent to anyone who tried teaching in these labs that a new teaching style was required. When faced with an instructor 20 feet away and a glowing computer monitor 15 inches away, students nearly always focus on the computer. Therefore, you will need to do less talking and more directing. Many a library instructor has given an eloquent overview of computerized research tools only to find that many of the students were busy surfing the Web or reading their e-mail. Even when all students are paying attention, invariably some will get lost and spend the entire session trying to make it to the right screen.

Technology is available to give the instructor control of all the computers in the room. This eliminates the problem of students getting lost or not keeping up, but still is not optimal. It can be hard to maintain an intellectual connection with students whose attention is sucked into the glowing video screen. Computers that are locked into the instructor's control can fail to maximize the hands-on learning experience. It can be a bit like riding the kiddy cars at an amusement park: as long as the car is locked onto tracks, you won't get a true driving experience.

A particularly good setup includes combining both a traditional overview with hands-on training. In this scenario, for the first half of the session the students focus on a screen at the front of the room, then try out these skills on the computer in front of them during the second half of the session. To keep them focused on the lesson, turn off their monitors before they enter the room, and have them leave them off until needed. During the second (hands-on) half do not try to regain the class's attention. Instead, work one-on-one with the students as they try out the various resources using their own topics. This scenario has proven to work particularly well in sessions longer than the traditional 50 minutes. It can also be split into two sessions.

If you are faced with teaching in a hands-on lab with no projection screen and no software to control student computers, consider team teaching. One instructor can lead the session while the other moves about, helping lost students to regain the appropriate screen.

One more note about teaching in hands-on labs. Students often learn as much or more from each other as they do from the instructor. Pairing the students, two to a computer can be extremely effective. Students working together will often answer each other's questions and work out problems together before you have a chance to get around the room to them.

If your library is designing or updating a hands-on computer classroom or if you have a choice of these rooms to teach in, consider the following:

- computers should be positioned so that the students are seated facing the front; it is nearly impossible to teach effectively to students' backs
- computers should be spaced so that a pair of students can work at each, with adequate seating and elbowroom available
- the spacing between rows should be adequate for the instructor to easily move between rows to help students at any station

- the overhead projection unit should provide an image that is easily read from any station in the room. The best bet is projection onto a screen, rather than a large monitor
- the instructor's station should be at the front of the room and should not require excessive pacing about between keyboard and pointer distance to the screen
- pay attention to acoustics and ventilation. Twenty or more computers can make more noise and generate more heat than a walled-off area can comfortably handle

REMOTE INSTRUCTION OF USERS

Taking instruction to the class works when the class is accessible. There are many cases where taking part in a class session is either not practical or not possible. Many institutions have turned to creating computerized help for remote library users. This help ranges from context-sensitive help in the form of research tips that pop up as the user reaches a critical point in the library's Web site, to full-blown interactive tutorials with live searching demonstrations and grading systems.

WEB-BASED TUTORIALS

Tutorials can be used to fulfill a myriad of objectives. They can be aimed at pretty much any audience and can be used to cover large or small topics.

Consider Your Objectives

Before launching into building a tutorial, consider carefully what you are trying to achieve. Is there an instruction gap to be filled and is a tutorial the best way to do it? Tutorials work best when they are used to teach the student a series of steps. If your need is to illustrate a number of unrelated facts or instructions, then your users may be better served with context-sensitive help screens, or even an FAQ.

Consider Your Intended Audience

Build it and they will not necessarily come. Consider carefully the audience you are trying to reach and how they will encounter the tutorial. How will it be linked into the library's existing Web structure? Placing a link on the library's main Web page that says "Tutorial" is bound to result in disappointing use statistics. Typically library users will only go through a lengthy tutorial if they perceive an overwhelming reason to do so. In the case of the general research tutorial built for use through freshman English classes, that reason may be course requirements. In the case of tutorials designed for use by the general public, you will need to focus on answering specific problems and advertising the benefits of the tutorial.

Consider Your Resources

Good tutorials can take massive amounts of staff energy and time to create and maintain. This is especially true if you are including screen shots from online databases. These databases change their look and feel on a regular basis, making it virtually impossible to keep the tutorial up to date. As the library adds new resources, it will take time to integrate information about them into an existing tutorial. This is not to say that a tutorial won't be right for your library. Each library will need to weigh the cost against the expected benefits. Brief tutorials covering fairly stable topics or tutorial projects that replace large amounts of in-class staff time may reap the greatest benefit for the library.

Tutorial Design Concepts

It is tempting to try to create a tutorial that is all things to all library users. And it is certainly reasonable to want to make your efforts as universally useful as possible. One way to maximize the flexibility of a tutorial project is to build it in modules. Examples of modules you might find in a tutorial designed to teach general research skills would be

- narrowing your research topic
- using the library catalog
- choosing a subject index
- searching for full-text availability
- requesting an interlibrary loan
- citing your references

The flexibility of the module design allows instructors to add or subtract modules as needed and to direct library users to just the parts of the tutorial they need.

Just as in the classroom, online teaching is most effective when a variety of techniques are used to reach students with a variety of learning styles. If possible and appropriate to the subject, consider adding video or audio elements to the tutorial. An example might be a streaming video tour of the library. Breaking up the tutorial with a mix of media will considerably enliven the activity. At the least, be sure to add a lot of pertinent images to illustrate points and break up the text. When using screen shots, be sure to include the browser frame. This helps students to mentally link the example with what they encounter on the library Web.

The great advantage of an online tutorial over a classroom presentation is the ease with which you can intersperse interactivity. Regardless of how many canned examples you may provide, linking into a live search of the database in question is always optimal. Tutorial designers often struggle with how to link out to a database for an example, and still retrieve the student to finish the tutorial. One way to do this is to open the live example in a Web frame or a new window. Another approach is to set the live searching examples apart at the end of each module, along with information on how to return.

When a tutorial is a required course assignment, you may be called upon to create a system of grading, or at least of registering that each student has completed the assignment. The needs and desires of the course instructor will affect the best way to accomplish this. Pretty much anything you devise will not be proof against the ingenious student who wishes to cheat, but at least you can require some effort to do so. The simplest solution is to have the system create a "certificate of completion" as the last screen in the tutorial. This can be printed out or e-mailed to the instructor. Slightly better is to have the system query the student for name and password or number at the start, so that the resulting certificate or e-mail message is customized. Some systems have been designed to ask for class number or instructor's e-mail address as well as the student's personal information, and will automatically forward the student's score. A drawback to such systems is that students must complete the tutorial in one sitting. Additionally, experience has shown that many students are hard put to know their course number or even their instructor's name. If there are sufficiently small numbers of classes involved, a drop box with options may solve this problem.

Example of a Successful Tutorial

The University of Arizona Library has an award-winning tutorial named RIO or Research Instruction Online (www.library.arizona.edu/rio/). It is designed as a general overview and, in addition to information about the library's branches and services, includes information on research, paper writing, critical thinking and even campus computing resources (Figure 6–3). The tutorial is divided into modules that can be accomplished in any order. Each module has an associated self-quiz. There is information given on how to use the tutorial. English Composition

Figure 6–3. Tutorial Divided into Easy-to-Learn Modules

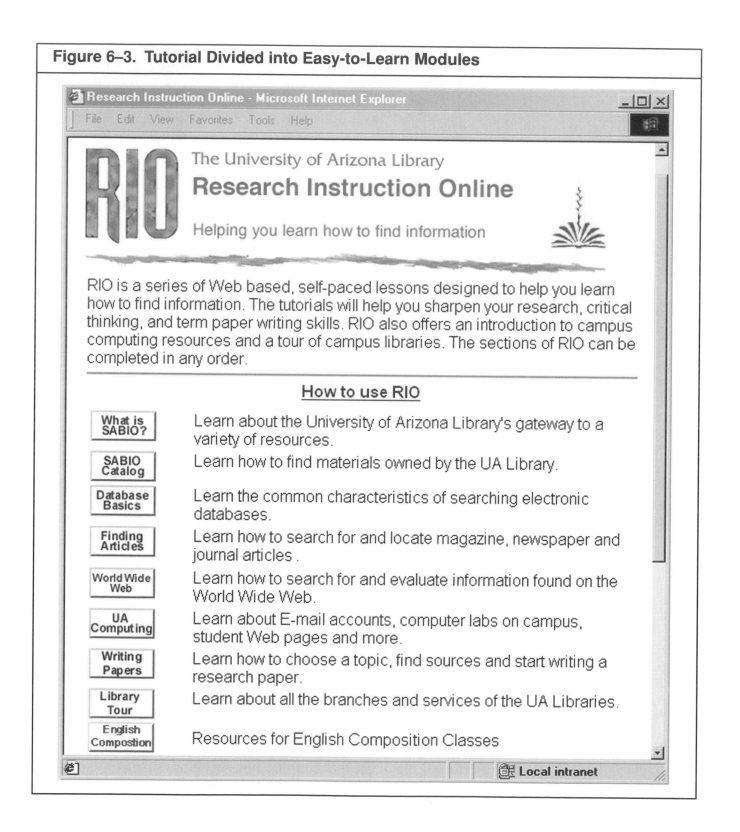

Figure 6–4. Tutorial Module with Clear, Simple Text, Interspersed with Examples

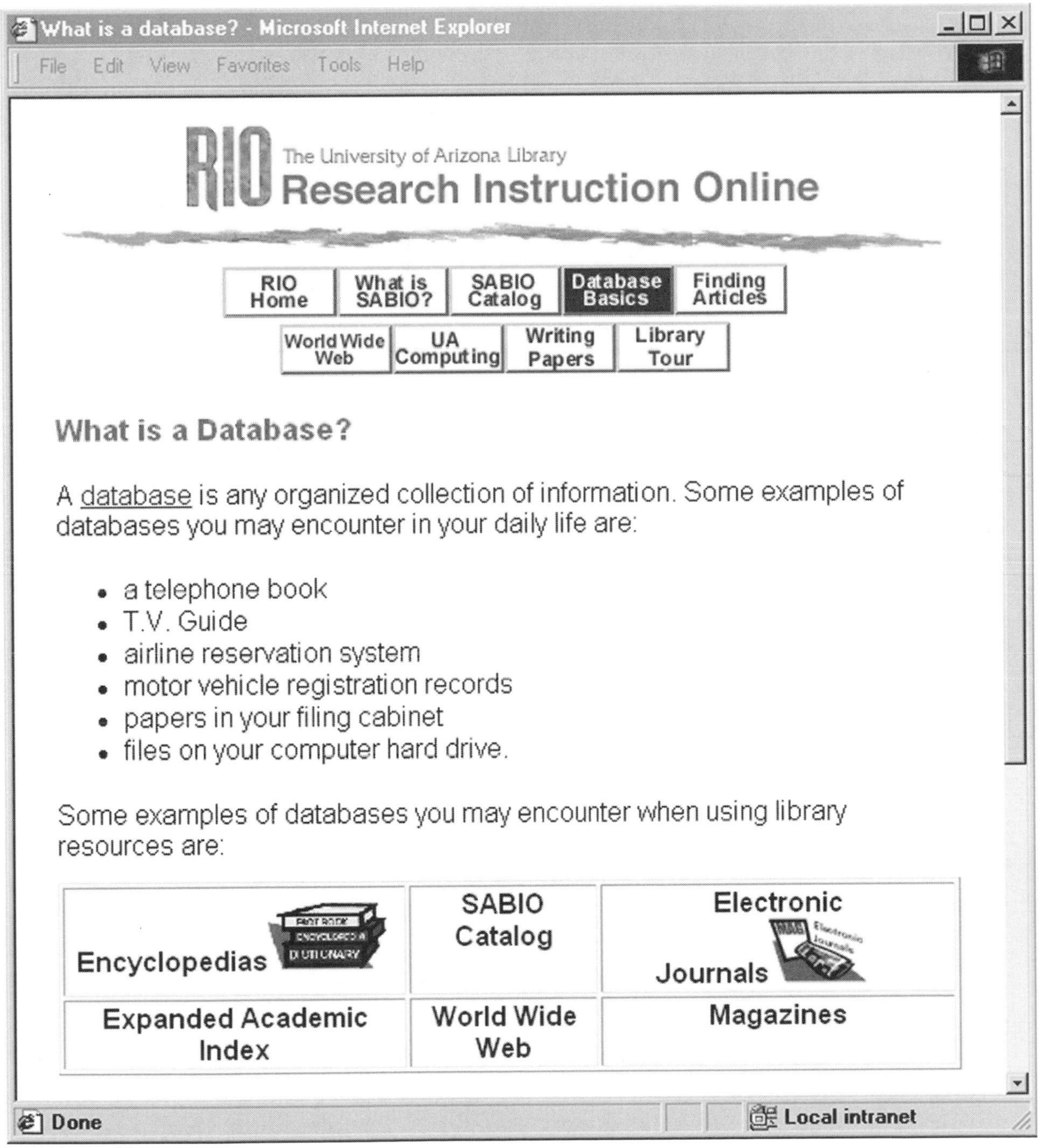

What is a database? - Microsoft Internet Explorer

File   Edit   View   Favorites   Tools   Help

RIO The University of Arizona Library
Research Instruction Online

| RIO Home | What is SABIO? | SABIO Catalog | Database Basics | Finding Articles |

| World Wide Web | UA Computing | Writing Papers | Library Tour |

What is a Database?

A <u>database</u> is any organized collection of information. Some examples of databases you may encounter in your daily life are:

- a telephone book
- T.V. Guide
- airline reservation system
- motor vehicle registration records
- papers in your filing cabinet
- files on your computer hard drive.

Some examples of databases you may encounter when using library resources are:

| Encyclopedias | SABIO Catalog | Electronic Journals |
| Expanded Academic Index | World Wide Web | Magazines |

Done   Local intranet

Figure 6–5. Page from a Special Subject Tutorial Graphically Illustrating How to Set Up Proxy Access

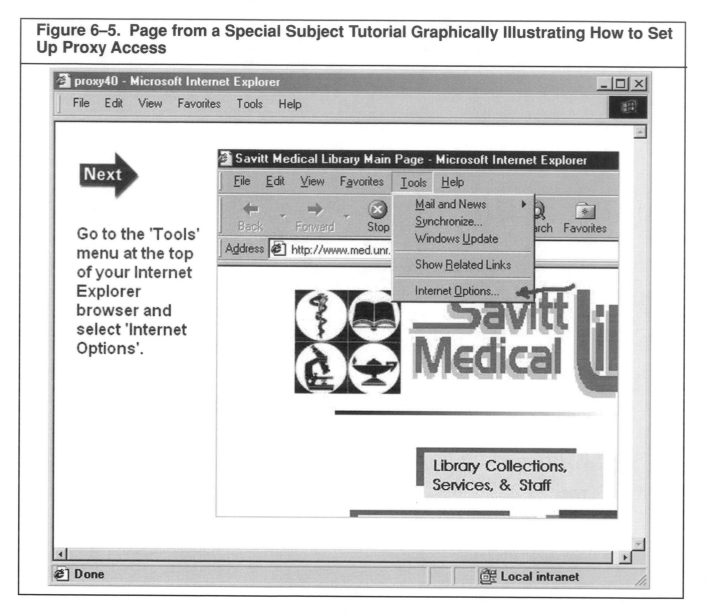

students can link from the main page to a customized assignment. All information is given in short, digestible chunks and the text is interspersed with many examples (Figure 6–4).

Special Subject Tutorials

There are plenty of other uses for tutorials than to teach freshmen to do research. Brief tutorials can be created to fill specialized instructional needs, such as how to request an interlibrary loan, how to download helper applications, or how to set the proxy in Internet browser software (Figure 6–5). These types of tutorials are designed to go a step or two beyond context-specific help screens, yet may be offered in a similar way. They can be offered at the point of need by linking them into the appropriate parts of the library's Web.

Building In Feedback

Since tutorials can be large, resource-intensive projects, you will probably want to collect information on who is using it, how it is used, and how it can be improved. Whoever is responsible for your library's Web site is probably already monitoring use of the site. If not, there are a number of software choices available that will create reports listing time of use, pages visited, site users' domain names, and other interesting statistics. That takes care of whom and how often, but it doesn't give feedback about how the site can be improved. Only the users can tell you this. You may want to consider adding a place for comments into the end of the tutorial. A less obvious, but more labor intensive idea is to add a point in various tutorial modules where you ask the student to formulate questions that a librarian will answer via personal e-mail. Not only does this plan provide the opportunity to answer some of the students' questions, and to let you know what is absent or unclear in the lesson, but it has the added advantage of providing a one-on-one personal connection between student and librarian. Regardless of how you gather feedback, it is always a good idea to place a statement in a prominent position in the tutorial, requesting comments and offering contact information for those with further questions.

INSTRUCTION FOR SPECIALTY GROUPS OF USERS

As libraries become more accessible to the remote patron, the variety of our users is growing. Increasingly, libraries are developing programs to help specialty community groups make the most of Internet resources. Some examples of these groups include:

- local social organizations
- groups of medical professionals
- local small businesses
- environmental and political groups
- Master Gardener Programs
- Elderhostel classes

Although licensing restrictions usually limit remote access to many of our resources for these patrons, there are lots of additional Web-based tools that are freely available. A good starting point for libraries wishing to develop this clientele is to label free resources on their Web. Some libraries create Web pages specifically for community groups.

If serving community groups is part of your library's mission, then consider taking instruction to places where these groups gather, such as community centers, nursing homes, schools, or even meeting rooms in shopping malls. If your library has a publicity or public relations officer, consider asking them to assist with publicity.

SPECIAL TECHNOLOGIES FOR USER-CENTERED INSTRUCTION

Expanded computer capabilities now make it possible to extend options for instruction beyond the straightforward handout or tutorial. Instructional aspects of computer use are often comprised of many closely linked steps that do not lend themselves to the static presentation of a frame-by-frame tutorial.

VIDEO CAPTURE PROGRAMS

An effective alternative is to use a video capture program such as Lotus ScreenCam, which in effect makes a full-motion video of all events taking place on a computer desktop. The programs are capable of capturing audio as well, so it is possible to include voice-over narration to augment the screen activities. The "movie" can then be presented to users by linking from a Web page. Programs of this type generally require that a free client program be installed on the user's workstation in order to view the video. This ability to animate a "teachable moment" gives instructors a powerful simulation tool to illustrate complex, multi-step activities.

VIDEOCONFERENCING SYSTEMS

The basis of most bibliographic instruction is the presentation of computer images in order to demonstrate the operation of various catalogs, databases, and Web resources. Videoconferencing systems are quite capable of transmitting acceptable screen images from a computer, though additional hardware, specifically a scan converter, must first be installed. Those considering a videoconferencing implementation should be aware that scan converter technology has improved dramatically in recent years, and an older model may likely yield unacceptable transmission quality.

Other considerations in presenting videoconference sessions are the availability of support staff, conferencing equipment, and bandwidth on the conference network. A broadcast definitely benefits from the aid of an assistant trained in operating and managing cameras and sound, and switching between broadcast sources at the correct times during a presentation. Users on the remote end must also be familiar with operation of the equipment, or much time can be spent just getting things to run properly. Perhaps the greatest deterrent to use is the competition for scheduling. Classrooms from which broadcasts can emanate are often few in number and always in demand. Coordinating the availability of a classroom with the availability of a remote facility adds a level of complexity to the instructional process.

DESKTOP VIDEO SYSTEMS

An alternative to dedicated videoconferencing systems is a desktop conferencing system. These transmit communications over the Internet, but employ ordinary computers rather than dedicated compression hardware and video monitors. Some of these include:

- NetMeeting—www.microsoft.com/windows/netmeeting/default.asp
- VideoLink Pro—www.smithmicro.com/videolinkpro/
- CUseeMe—www.cuseeme.com/products/cuseeme5.htm

Microsoft NetMeeting is gaining attention because, in addition to possessing an impressive array of capabilities, it has the added advantage of being included in Windows 98-Second Edition, Windows 2000, Windows ME and Internet Explorer 5.1 and above. The current release, NetMeeting 3.01, is also easily downloadable from the Microsoft site as a 2MB compressed file. Hardware requirements are minimal: a 133 MHz Pentium processor and 32 MB of RAM. To use audio features with any of these products, it's necessary to have a sound card, speakers (or headphones), and a microphone. Video requires a video camera that can connect through your computer's parallel or USB port. And with all these products, expect poor quality video relative to dedicated conferencing systems such as PicTel. Expect frame rates of around 8 frames per second. Even with DSL, cable, or high-speed local area network (LAN) connection, the video will not be smooth because it cannot send the approximately 30 fps required for broadcast-quality video.

Features of Desktop Videoconferencing Systems

Desktop conferencing software allows for real-time interactive communication and the capability to maintain face-to-face relationships with remote library users. The array of options for hosting virtual meetings or providing instruction include:

- text chat
- shared whiteboard
- sharing of an application or desktop
- file transmission
- interactive video and audio transmission

NetMeeting, for example, allows text, whiteboard, application sharing, and file transmission work with up to eight simultaneous users. In application sharing you can bring up a word processing document on one computer and it can be viewed simultaneously by the other participants in the conference. Text messaging will appear instantaneously on all participant desktops. Diagrams drawn on the desktop whiteboard will similarly be shared among all participants.

Sharing an application is an especially powerful teaching tool, as it lets you deliver a mirror image of your desktop and display it in real time on a remote user's PC. By providing an "over the shoulder" view of your use of a particular database, you can conduct a virtual instruction session to anyone running NetMeeting.

Limitations of Desktop Conferencing Software

In addition to shaky video quality, there can be other drawbacks to watch out for in conferencing software packages. NetMeeting will not run on a Macintosh. Smith Micro's VideoLink Pro works only on Macintosh computers, and requires broadband connection for video. First Virtual Communication's CUseeMe Conference Server is designed to work across platforms, but the cost for server and end-user software packages can be limiting.

Security factors are another concern. Those operating behind firewalls or through proxy servers can experience incompatibility problems.

Most restrictive, perhaps, are limits on simultaneous users. A true conference situation should allow a flexible number of participants. NetMeeting, by itself, only supports audio and/or camera-generated video between two persons. CUseeMe has plug-ins available to extend its number of users.

Multipoint Control Units

It is possible to exceed the NetMeeting's two-person limitation by using third-party products called conferencing servers, or Multipoint Control Units (MCUs). These software/hardware devices bridge three or more clients to allow participation in real-time conferencing, employing both audio and video. This does, however, introduce an additional level of expense, complexity, and necessity for technical support. MCUs are available from a variety of vendors, and will be an add-on to Microsoft's Exchange 2000 product line. A new product, CUseeMe's Video-ware, dispenses with the need for additional hardware, and may prove to be worth its hefty price tag.

MANY OPPORTUNITIES

Technology is clearly driving significant changes that affect the way users gain access to library resources, and correspondingly, how librarians are addressing the instructional needs of the growing class of remote users. Library instruction programs will be most effective if they are taken to the user, and take into account the variability of individual learning styles. Network technology, by offering many modes of synchronous and asynchronous instruction, has the potential to create positive teaching opportunities and advance the level of support for library users.

As collections move towards electronic format, and patrons stay away from the library in droves, the need for instructional programs delivered via networks becomes more critical for the success of library users. Partnerships with computing support departments can help libraries meet users' increasing need for computer literacy skills. A mixed program of in-person sessions, online tutorials, videoconferencing, Web "handouts," and context-specific help pages can reach the widest of remote audiences.

REFERENCES

Anderson, Judy, and Lynne DeMont. 2001. "Treading Carefully Through the Murky Legalities of Electronic Reserves." *Computers in Libraries* 21, no.6 (June): 40–45.

Brandt, D. Scott. 1997. "The Multiple Personalities of Delivering Training via the Web." *Computers in Libraries* 17, no.8 (September): 51–53.

Cottrell, Janet R. 2001. "Teaching Students to Evaluate Web Resources More Critically: Implications from a Faculty Workshop." *College and Research Libraries News* 62, no.2 (February): 141–143 [Online]. Available: www.ala.org/acrl/cottrell.html [2001, November 13].

Grimes, Deborah J., and Carl H. Boening. 2001. "Worries with the Web: A Look at Student Use of Web Resources." *College & Research Libraries* 62, no.1(January): 11–23.

Hinchliffe, Lisa Janicke. 1998. "Resources for Designing Library Electronic Classrooms." *MC Journal: The Journal of Academic Media Librarianship* 6, no. 1 (Spring) [Online]. Available: wings.buffalo.edu/publications/mcjrnl/v6n1/class.html [2001, October 8].

Johnson, Anna Marie, and Phil Sager. 1998. "Too Many Students, Too Little Time: Creating and Implementing a Self-Paced, Interactive Computer Tutorial for the Libraries' Online Catalog." *Research Strategies* 16, no.4: 271–284.

Mosley, Pixey Anne. 1998. "Making Library Instructional Handouts Accessible through the World Wide Web." *Research Strategies* 16, no.2: 153–161.

Pival, Paul R., and Johanna Tunon. 1998. "Netmeeting: A New and Inexpensive Alternative for Delivering Library Instruction to Distance Students at Nova Southeastern University." *College & Research Libraries News* 59, no.10 (November): 758–760.

Scigliano, John A., and Jacques Levin. 2000. "One-Stop Shopping in an Online Educational Mall: A Multimedia Web-Based Teaching/Learning Environment." *T.H.E. Journal* 27, no. 11 (June): 72–80 [Online]. Available: www.thejournal.com/magazine/vault/A2881.cfm [2001, November 13].

Swaine, Cynthia Wright. 2001. "Developing, Marketing, and Evaluating Web-Based Library and Information Skills Tutorials." *Virginia Libraries* 47, no.3 (Fall) [Online]. Available: scholar.lib.vt.edu/ejournals/VALib/v47_n3/swaine.html [2001, November 13].

Unruh, Don L. 2000. "Desktop Videoconferencing: The Promise and Problems of Delivery of Web-Based Training." *Internet and Higher Education* 3, no. 3: 183–199.

Young, Rosemary M., and Stephena Harmony. 1999. *Working with Faculty to Design Undergraduate Information Literacy Programs: A How-To-Do-It Manual for Librarians.* New York: Neal-Schuman Publishers.

7 INTEGRATING LIBRARY RESOURCES INTO ONLINE INSTRUCTION

by Amy W. Shannon

CHAPTER OVERVIEW

- Connecting With Instructors and Students
- Courseware 101 for Librarians
- Library Involvement
- The Online Library Instruction Session (or Not)
- Document Delivery, Electronic Reserves, and Copyright
- Final Thoughts
- Appendix: Levels of Involvement in Online Courses

Increasingly, colleges and universities across the United States are adding online courses to their catalogs. These courses may be taught either partly or exclusively through the Internet. In many cases the student may never come to campus, may never meet the instructor face to face, and may even be taking the class from a radically different time zone. What can libraries do to meet and exceed the information needs of these students? How can librarians work with instructors of online courses to integrate information-gathering skills and appropriate resources into the curriculum?

CONNECTING WITH INSTRUCTORS AND STUDENTS

The first step in convincing an instructor that you should take an active role in an online class is to evaluate what you can bring to the equation. Many instructors new to online teaching may consider the library even less relevant to an online class than to a traditional class due to increased geographic restrictions. It will be your job to sell your services. You will need to let them know exactly what you can do for their class.

A great starting point is the wealth of technical expertise that librarians have available. Many new online teachers are starting with less computer expertise or confidence than you would expect. They may have minimal or no Web authoring experience. Even template-based courseware requires some level of technical know-how to develop an interesting, varied course environment. Offering to help find missing files, fix broken Web links, add a few images, or help with the odd HTML tagging problem can be a godsend to the instructor with limited expertise or limited troubleshooting time. Even if your institution is able to provide instructional design assistance, another computer-support shoulder to lean on is usually more than appreciated and it can get you in the door to offer other services.

The availability of relevant full-text materials is sometimes more of a secret than we would like. Just as libraries need to advertise online resources and services to students, you will need to inform instructors about the wealth of full-text resources, finding tools and services available to their students. The instructor is the main link to the university for remote students in online courses. Sometimes the quickest way to an instructor's heart is to inform them of online resources that support their research rather than their teaching. Once you have their attention, you can then present the pedagogical advantages of a variety of library online resources and services as they relate to student needs in online courses.

Overall, the most valuable resource the library has to offer an instructor is time. Given sufficient time the instructor could search out the best information resources, surf the Web for new sites of relevance, and learn to troubleshoot even the trickiest courseware. But, like everyone, instructors have limited time. Librarians can help with all of these time-consuming tasks.

Making the first connection with the instructor can be as simple as letting them know you're interested and would like to devote some time to their class. If they are skeptical, don't be afraid to offer unsolicited examples of resource lists, assignments, or even interesting Web sites. Maggie Ressel, at the University of Nevada, Reno, has developed a workshop and a Web page, informing instructors of the library services available to online classes (Figure 7–1). Understand the instructor's/course goals and address them. Some libraries collect copies of all course syllabi, online and otherwise, in order to facilitate in providing targeted services and resources.

Figure 7–1. Web Site to Inform Instructors of Library Resources for Online Classes

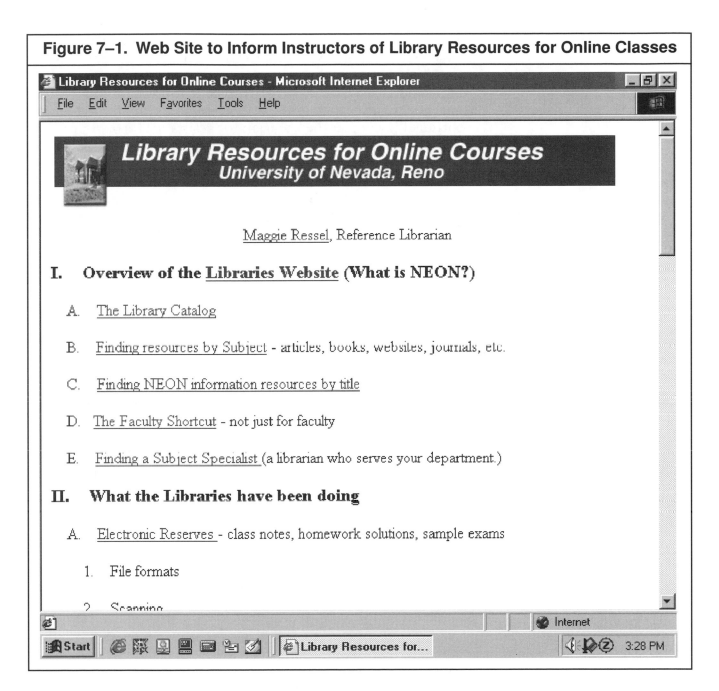

BECOME A TEACHING PARTNER

In the best of all worlds the librarian has the opportunity to become a teaching partner, collaborating on assignments, course readings, and class discussion. Only the instructor's receptiveness and the librarian's time budget limit the level of involvement possible. Success with one instructor invariably leads to a raft of requests for the librarian to be involved with other classes. You can use examples of your work with the first class as a selling point in your negotiations with other instructors. At the University of Nevada, Reno technical assistance with a department's earliest online course led to extensive involvement in the building of the department's online program, and students from that first course continued to contact the librarian for assistance throughout their later classes.

REMOTE INSTRUCTORS

Along with the increasing numbers of remote students, we are starting to see increasing numbers of remote instructors. An online class can be run from anywhere there is a reliable Internet connection, so instructors are traveling far and wide. One University of Nevada, Reno professor answers e-mail from his students while chasing rhinos in Africa. Another UNR professor moved her home permanently to another state, committing to teaching all her future courses online.

Although it takes a bit of initiative, you can still be involved in these classes. Check the course schedule for upcoming online classes and make an effort to contact the instructors as early as possible. Your first contact with the instructor can be by e-mail or (perhaps better) by phone. Rather than just asking what assistance you can give, be sure to offer specific services. Remote instructors are even less likely to be aware of existing library services than on-campus instructors. Instructors who are not able to come to the library may be thrilled with an offer to hunt down supporting material for their class. An additional service you can provide these instructors is to be available as a face-to-face contact for students who come to campus.

STUDENT DEMOGRAPHICS

You need to consider many factors when designing services and assignments targeted at online courses, not the least of which is the demographics of online students. As with traditional classes, the average level of research expertise will vary with discipline, previous course experience, and course level. Online courses are available for all levels of students from high school through postgraduate and professional.

Online courses are particularly attractive to nontraditional students. These students may have work or family constraints that make flexible scheduling a necessity. Not only is their time in short supply, but it may be limited to odd hours of the night. They may never see the instructor face-to-face, or even correspond with them in a synchronous (real-time) manner.

Another frequent user of online courses is the rural or geographically distant student. Online specialty courses are making it possible for students to receive instruction on subjects that are not taught locally. Some courses may have participants from all around the globe.

For both types of students, variations in their available equipment and connectivity can be challenging. Although most courses require a minimum level of computer equipment and expertise, students may try to fudge, or just plain do not understand their deficiencies. Some students rely on using a computer at their place of employment, not realizing that they will need to change proxy settings or navigate through a firewall. Rural students may have difficulties with intermittent Internet connections.

COURSEWARE 101 FOR LIBRARIANS

The online course comes in a variety of forms and can be either fully online or just "web-assisted." Online content can range from just the syllabus to a fully integrated learning environment that includes:

- the syllabus
- communication tools
- links to specially created source material
- links to outside resources

Although it is still common for instructors to build online courses from scratch, the overwhelming trend is to use licensed courseware products. Many courseware packages are now available, and a single campus may use several. The Centre for Curriculum Transfer Technology's Web site provides reviews and comparisons of 55 different products (www.ctt.bc.ca/landonline). Librarians can reap great public relations benefits by familiarizing themselves with the inner workings of the packages most used on their campuses. Both of the top-selling courseware options, WebCT and Blackboard, allow instructors to download and build a course for free, so you may wish to familiarize yourself with the software by building your own "dummy" course.

COURSEWARE BASICS

Courseware is turnkey software that allows the instructor to build an online course within a single integrated environment. Within a single Internet interface, students taking courseware-driven classes can

Figure 7–2. Course Menu Page Built in WebCT Courseware

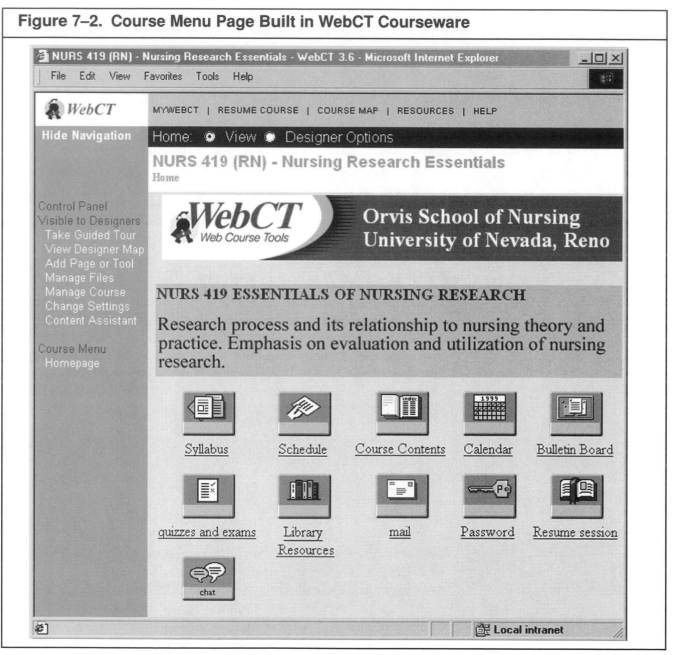

- read lectures
- correspond with the instructor and other students
- access outside readings
- take tests
- check in during office hours

These products include a menu-driven structure of templates ready for content to be inserted by the instructor.

Figure 7–3. Course Menu Page Built in Blackboard Courseware

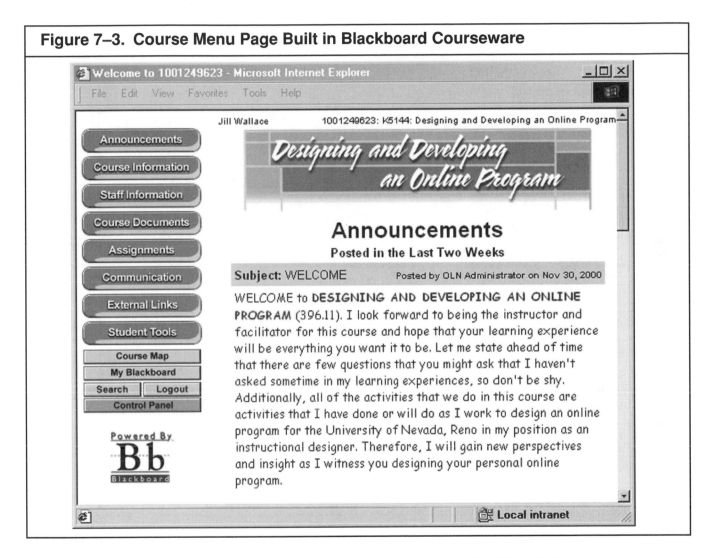

COMPONENTS OF A COURSEWARE CLASS

Although there is a wide variety of courseware products on the market, most of them have some features in common. Almost all courses will have a single entry or introductory screen. This organizes the course contents and gives access to the variety of actions available. These pages may include any links the instructor wishes, but typically include links to

- the syllabus
- readings
- assignments
- communications
- testing
- helper applications, such as glossary or calendar

Figure 7–4. Links to Outside Resources from within Lesson Text

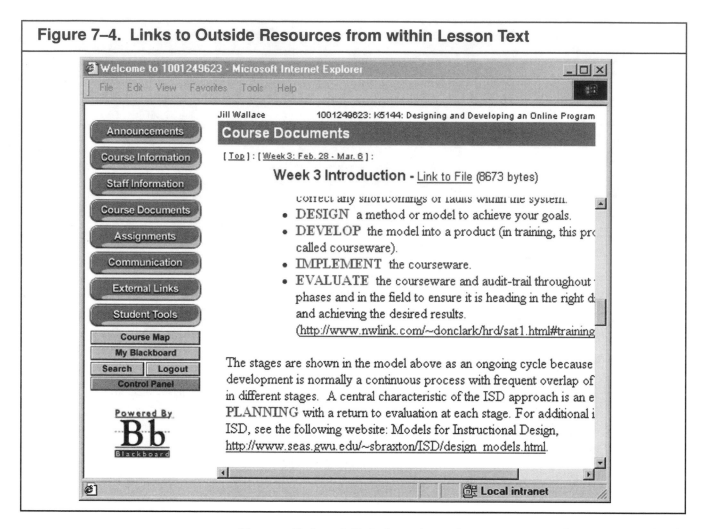

Figures 7–2 and 7–3 show introductory screens from courses built using WebCT and Blackboard.

Communications options are arguably the top selling point of individual courseware products. Most will allow the student to communicate with the instructor and other class participants through

- e-mail
- discussion lists
- a bulletin board
- real-time chat
- an online whiteboard

These options are usually laid out for the student in a single section of the interface, along with an address list. Active online classes will often have the bulk of their activity centered on the course bulletin board.

Although most courseware-driven courses are confined behind passworded student accounts, they can all link to outside Internet resources. Instructors may choose to embed links into almost any part of the class, from the introductory screen to individual bulletin board messages (Figure 7–4). Outside links are commonly used to provide students with optional additional readings.

In addition to providing testing and other assessment options, the more sophisticated courseware allows instructors to track students' use of each of the course's components. Finally instructors have a way of knowing if anyone reads their handouts!

LIBRARY INVOLVEMENT

The library can establish a presence in these classes in many ways. The simplest is to encourage instructors to place a link to the library's Web site on the course's introductory page. The University of Nevada, Reno has put a linked icon on the initial menu screen of the template given out to all instructors developing online classes (Figure 7–5). Although the instructor could remove the icon, most instructors are happy to have it as a basic feature. Links to the library's Web do not have to be limited to initial menus. Other good places to suggest links are in the text of assignments or on the list of additional readings.

Much as we want the link between the course and the supporting information resources to be transparent, linking directly to library resources can involve sticky issues of authentication (see Chapter 8). Students who use a password to gain access to their course usually do not expect additional hurdles to get to information from within the class. Efforts will need to be made to educate the students on how to gain access. You may wish to encourage the instructor to give an early assignment that requires the student to negotiate authentication procedures. This should help to prepare them to deal with the hurdle throughout the term.

The library may be able to provide links to appropriate online research tools, as well. The list of helper applications could include a link to an online encyclopedia, statistical database, or other reference source. Within assignments, a link to an appropriate abstracting database could help the students get started on their research.

Librarians have traditionally developed handouts listing appropriate library resources. Customized Web-based lists of available online resources can be created and linked directly into the class

Figure 7–5. Courseware Template Given to All Instructors with Preset Library Link

(Figure 7–6). These are possibly more useful than the handout ever was, since they can't be lost and they help to identify which of the myriad of related information resources are available online.

Another very effective approach is to work with the instructor to identify resources that can be linked throughout the text of lessons. These can be presented as further readings, or even as footnotes. This works particularly well with content Web sites.

Figure 7–6. Customized Web-Based Course "Handout"

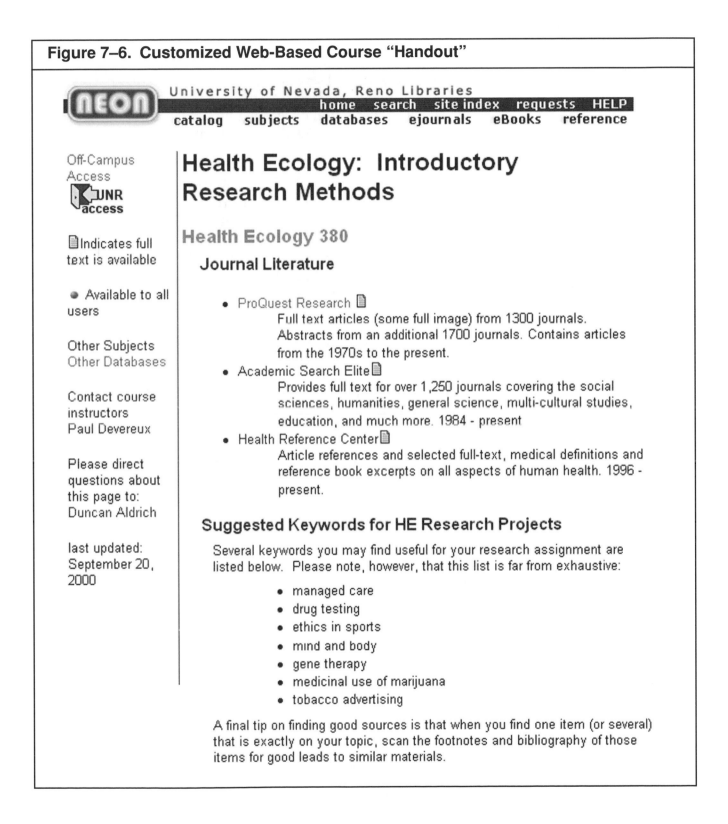

University of Nevada, Reno Libraries

home   search   site index   requests   HELP
catalog   subjects   databases   ejournals   eBooks   reference

Off-Campus
Access
UNR
access

Indicates full
text is available

• Available to all
users

Other Subjects
Other Databases

Contact course
instructors
Paul Devereux

Please direct
questions about
this page to:
Duncan Aldrich

last updated:
September 20,
2000

Health Ecology: Introductory Research Methods

Health Ecology 380

Journal Literature

- ProQuest Research
  Full text articles (some full image) from 1300 journals.
  Abstracts from an additional 1700 journals. Contains articles
  from the 1970s to the present.
- Academic Search Elite
  Provides full text for over 1,250 journals covering the social
  sciences, humanities, general science, multi-cultural studies,
  education, and much more. 1984 - present
- Health Reference Center
  Article references and selected full-text, medical definitions and
  reference book excerpts on all aspects of human health. 1996 -
  present.

Suggested Keywords for HE Research Projects

Several keywords you may find useful for your research assignment are
listed below. Please note, however, that this list is far from exhaustive:

- managed care
- drug testing
- ethics in sports
- mind and body
- gene therapy
- medicinal use of marijuana
- tobacco advertising

A final tip on finding good sources is that when you find one item (or several)
that is exactly on your topic, scan the footnotes and bibliography of those
items for good leads to similar materials.

Two examples:

- following a discussion of heart disease may be a link to the American Heart Association
- site a discussion of recent advances in cloning may have a footnote that links directly to the full text of an article on the subject

Many instructors can and are adding these links themselves, but it is a time-consuming business. Searching out resources is a service that librarians excel in providing.

Just as with traditionally taught classes, some instructors will not prepare their classes until the last minute. This will limit the type and level of your participation. You can still work with these classes using content clues gleaned from the syllabus along with discussions with the instructor. Being careful to avoid the epithet of "pushy librarian," you can offer to create a Web list of additional resources or address the course after the research assignment has been determined.

ESTABLISHING A ONE-ON-ONE CONNECTION WITH STUDENTS

Possibly the most crucial aspect of providing support for an online course is developing communication with the students. An effective online class is a community, with established modes of communication, and to fully reach this community you need to become a citizen, or, at least, a recognized visitor.

An extreme measure of service would be to take part in all aspects of course communication, from chat to e-mail, bulletin board and white board. That scenario is probably excessive, unless you are truly co-teaching the course. A more moderate approach is to choose specific points at which to become an active participant in the course. Start with participation in the course orientation, whether onsite or virtual. Students in online courses sometimes feel isolated, and need assistance in visualizing the other course participants.

Introduce Yourself

Provide an introduction to yourself, not just to the library. Remember that while the library is a large, anonymous concept, the librarian can be viewed as a research lifeline. Many online instructors will post a picture of themselves so that the students can feel more connected. Consider posting your own picture or a link to one on the library page, if available. If you are involved in a number of classes you can create a Web page for multiple uses, but be aware that a canned introduction can never replace the level of connection you will achieve with an individual introduction. During a successful introduction, students should feel that you are speaking directly to them. Another good point at which to become active in course communication is as students are beginning a research project with which you can be of help. Attention to the course syllabus can allow you to step in at just the right moment to remind the class of your availability.

Make Yourself Available to Students

Most courseware products include an address book feature that lists contact information, or at least e-mail, for all course participants. Ask to be on the list. Provide students with alternative contact information as well, such as phone number, fax number, and address. If students are on campus, let them know where to find your office, and when you are most likely to be found there. Answer all questions or requests promptly, since the online expectations of timeliness are short, and a pause is like a black hole.

Synchronous vs. Asynchronous Communication

Use the community already developed by the instructor to determine the best way to communicate with the class. Some courses excel in the use of synchronous communication, such as chat sessions or white board, where students and instructor are able to log in at the same time. For these courses you could schedule virtual office hours, using chat software, provide scheduled time for reference services, or, depending on your typing skills, give a virtual mini-lecture, with immediate response to questions. Other courses are limited to asynchronous communication, including e-mail, a bulletin board, and Web pages. In these courses, the bulletin board is usually the center of course-wide discussion. Consider hosting specific discussion threads on research strategies, or best resources.

A Little Etiquette is a Good Thing

Like all communities, an online course has its own set of rules. To maximize your effectiveness, try to follow the unspoken etiquette of the class. Do not try to contribute until you have been properly introduced, otherwise the students will wonder why you are there, rather than attend to your words. Try for an introduction as early in the semester as possible. If an appropriate response is going to take a while, at least send an acknowledgement of the question. Do not jump into the middle of a conversation, unless invited. And be sure to announce your presence if you are monitoring the discussion.

With some course subjects, such as medicine, psychology, or social work, the need for a policy of confidentiality is obvious. Often, but not always, the instructor will have set down confidentiality guidelines at the beginning of the course. It is a good rule to assume that all class discussions are to be kept within the confines of the course, and it is a good idea to state up front your willingness to do so. Most librarians are used to observing patron confidentiality, but students are not always aware of this.

TECHNICAL BELLS AND WHISTLES

Just a few words about streaming audio and video: although I believe these will soon become standard features of online learning, currently their use is problematic for students who often experience slow downloads. The librarian should check with the instructor to see if the course's minimum equipment requirements are sufficient for satisfactory use of these technologies. The instructor may have already surveyed the class about their available technology and computer expertise. If this is not the case, you may wish to do so early in the course term. This will allow you to plan what bells and whistles you can throw in without causing undue frustration on the part of the students. As you make these plans it is important to remember that extra fancy touches are only effective if they add to course content or ease of understanding the material. For example, an ornithology class may benefit from streaming audio of bird songs, but a cartoon robin hopping about and singing popular music would likely be a waste of bandwidth.

THE ONLINE LIBRARY INSTRUCTION SESSION (OR NOT)

Since many instructors' first online courses are a near direct translation of traditional courses, it is tempting to try to translate the traditional library instruction session. Resist the temptation. The one-shot BI session evolved because of the limitations of the classroom teaching model. Librarians were limited in time they could spend in the classroom and instructors were reluctant to give up precious class time. Librarians have long suspected that the overall effectiveness of such one-shot sessions is low. Wouldn't it be better to spread the information throughout the semester, providing instruction right when it is needed? And wouldn't it be nice to finally make a handout that no one loses and is always at the student's hand when needed?

The online world provides just this opportunity. It is just as easy to divide up the information into separate modules as it is to teach it all at once. Online course material provides the magic of having your examples just one click away. All teaching is hands-on and you have access to the students on their own schedule. By far the most valuable improvement is the ability to make your instruction available right where and when it is needed. Here is an example: The online chemistry student with an assignment to look up the molecular weight of a substance could have a link to the full-text version of the CRC Handbook of Chemistry and Physics right there on the assignment. The immediate success would be remembered in a positive light, creating less frustration than the traditional arrangement of trying to remember what was in a BI session, or trying to find an elusive handout.

Working with the instructor can maximize the positive aspects of distributing research instruction throughout the course. The instructional objectives can be matched to the existing assignments, and relevant outside resources linked to give the students a rich, yet pain-free learning environment.

MAXIMIZE YOUR EFFORTS WITH MULTI-USE COMPONENTS

Another advantage of the online teaching environment is the ability to share a module of research instruction between two or more classes with similar needs. Good candidates for this might be instruction on using a particular complex subject resource, instruction on creating a reference list, or information about alternative library services (Figure 7–7). Where customization is appropriate, the same module can easily be adjusted with subject-specific examples. A "library" of such modules can be collected, adapted and shared by a group of librarians, saving in overall development time.

THE PERFECT RESOURCES: EMPHASIZING FULL TEXT

The advent of plentiful full text has made online scholarship far easier and more effective. Since students of online courses seldom have a library visit in their plans, and are often learning on a tighter-than-most time budget, timely delivery of full text is just what they require. These resources can be arranged as an electronic reserve reading list or as links embedded throughout the course lectures and assignments. Since not everything is available full text the librarian may need to offer alternative readings to the instructor.

Figure 7–7. Instruction Module to be Shared between Two or More Classes

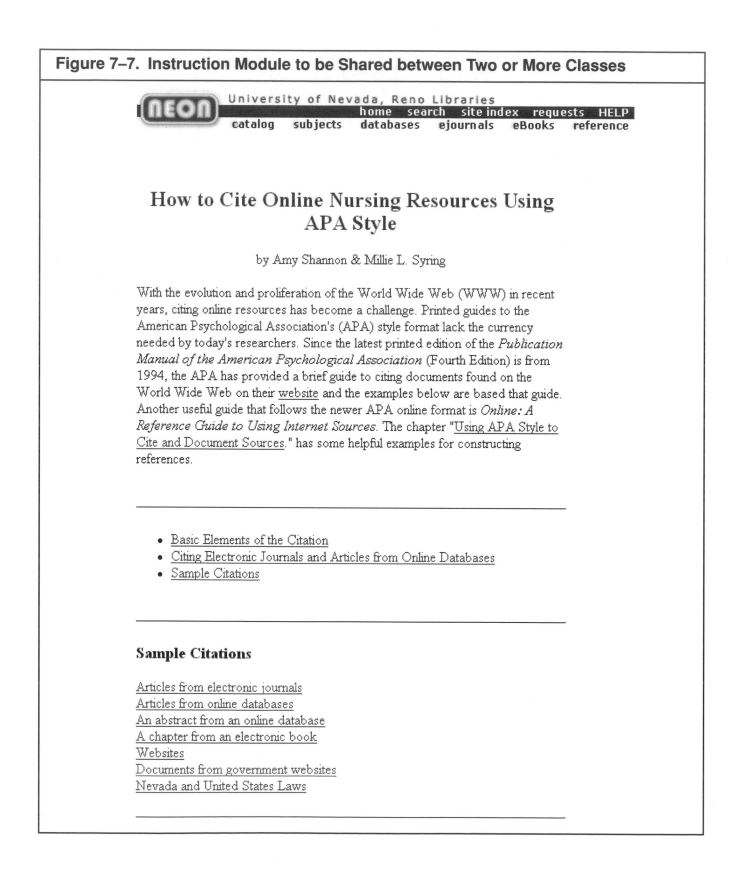

University of Nevada, Reno Libraries

home   search   site index   requests   HELP
catalog   subjects   databases   ejournals   eBooks   reference

How to Cite Online Nursing Resources Using APA Style

by Amy Shannon & Millie L. Syring

With the evolution and proliferation of the World Wide Web (WWW) in recent years, citing online resources has become a challenge. Printed guides to the American Psychological Association's (APA) style format lack the currency needed by today's researchers. Since the latest printed edition of the *Publication Manual of the American Psychological Association* (Fourth Edition) is from 1994, the APA has provided a brief guide to citing documents found on the World Wide Web on their website and the examples below are based that guide. Another useful guide that follows the newer APA online format is *Online: A Reference Guide to Using Internet Sources*. The chapter "Using APA Style to Cite and Document Sources." has some helpful examples for constructing references.

- Basic Elements of the Citation
- Citing Electronic Journals and Articles from Online Databases
- Sample Citations

Sample Citations

Articles from electronic journals
Articles from online databases
An abstract from an online database
A chapter from an electronic book
Websites
Documents from government websites
Nevada and United States Laws

Figure 7–7. *Continued*

Articles from Electronic Journals

<u>Article</u> -- This takes you to the actual article

Example:

Watson, R., & Thompson, D.R. (2000). Recent developments in UK nurse
education: Horses for courses or courses for horses? *Journal of
Advanced Nursing*, 32, 1041-1042. Retrieved January 29, 2001, from
the World Wide Web: http://www.blackwell-synergy.com

****

<u>Article</u> -- This takes you to the table of contents for the issue

Example:

Miller, S. (1997). Midwives' and physicians' experiences in collaborative practice:
A qualitative study. *Women's health issues*, 7, 301-308. Retrieved
January 23, 2001, from the World Wide Web: http://sciserver.lanl.gov

Articles from Online Databases

<u>Article</u> -- This takes you to the database to search for the article

Example:

Schwarz, J.K. (03/31/1998). Nursing care at the end of life: The link between
science and humanity; A nurse's narrative of her mother's dying.
Alternative Health Practitioner, 4, 35-39. Retrieved January 6, 2001,
from Alt-Health Watch database on the World Wide Web:
http://www.libraries.unr.edu/subjects/databases.html

****

<u>Article</u> -- This takes you to the database to search for the article

—   -

Figure 7–8. SFX Menu Linking between a Record in an Aggregator Database and Other Library Services

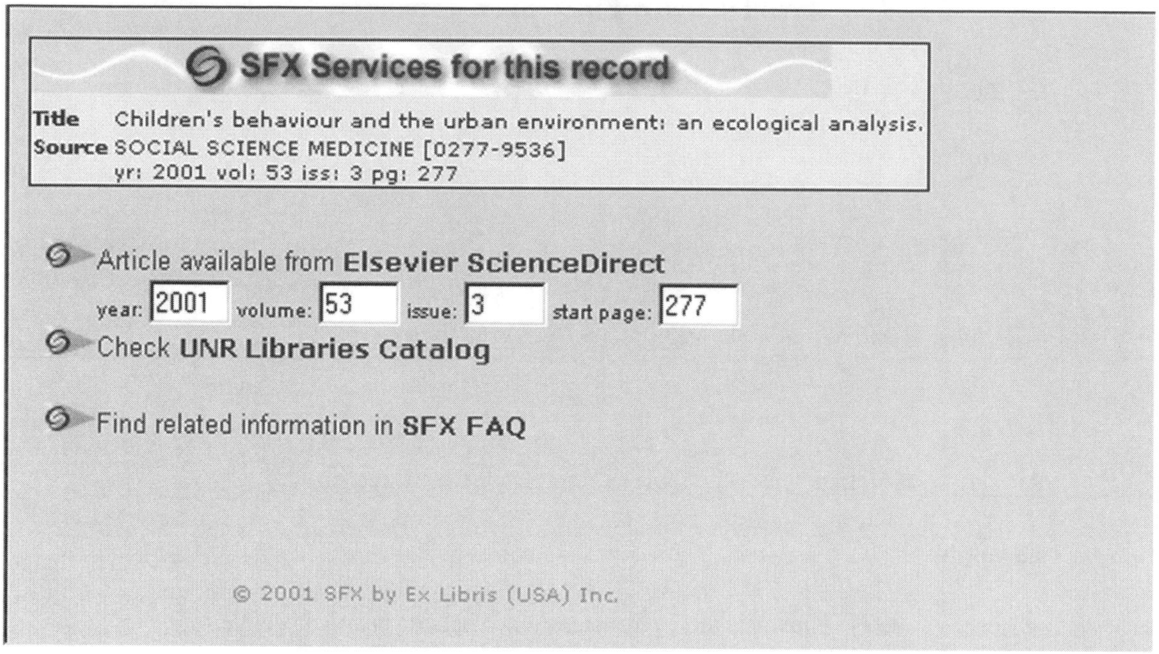

Useful full text does not need to be limited to items identified by the instructor. The librarian may put together a list of added resources, or even post a continually updated list of resources submitted by students as they find them useful.

To complete their research, students will need to have access to many more online resources than those specifically identified as additional readings. If your library does not already do so, it may wish to prominently label resources that contain full text. An additional step is to create a separate page or portal that outlines resources and services especially useful to students in online courses.

For some disciplines, and particularly upper-level courses, generalist full-text aggregator databases do not provide sufficient coverage. Students will need to be introduced to the two-step process of using an abstracting source, then checking for text availability. As the technology to link between resources evolves, this process should become easier and more transparent. Some databases, i.e. the Web of Science and Cambridge Scientific Abstracts, are offering links directly from their abstracts to full text at publisher and aggregator sites. New products and projects such as SFX and CrossRef will allow students to link directly from abstracting resources to full-text journals or books (Figure 7–8).

DOCUMENT DELIVERY, ELECTRONIC RESERVES, AND COPYRIGHT

Perhaps someday we will reach a future where all students' research needs are fulfilled by available full text at the click of a mouse. Meanwhile, students still need access to materials that are not yet digital. As institutions add online courses to their catalogs, their libraries will need to provide for all of the research needs of this new class of students. Students in online courses are the ultimate in remote users—most will never see the campus or the library building. To be accessible, all materials, including those not yet available online, must travel to the student.

DOCUMENT DELIVERY

To adequately serve these students the library needs to provide and promote a package of delivery services. If an article is not available electronically, then the library should be able to photocopy and deliver the text by fax or scanned image over the Internet. Most libraries only provide home delivery of books or other print materials as a rare exception, if at all. As long as students in online courses still need access to printed monographs, there will be a need for expanding this type of service. Be creative. If sending materials to students' homes is not practical for your institution, you may be able to set up delivery to another library in the student's geographic area. If the information needs to be borrowed from another institution through interlibrary loan, consider having it sent directly to the student. For more information on document delivery options see Chapter 5.

ELECTRONIC RESERVES AND COPYRIGHT

Just as with any other kind of class, students in online classes often need access to a wide variety of supporting materials designated by their instructor. These materials can include:

- articles
- book chapters
- documents
- sample exams
- homework problem sets and answer keys
- multimedia materials
- images

Unlike students taking traditional on-campus classes, students in online classes can not be expected to come to the library to check out reserve materials. Instead, they should be able to access everything they need from wherever they log in. Libraries have been responding to these needs by developing electronic reserve collections.

Electronic reserves are the perfect mate for online courses. The passwording function of courseware limits use of materials to course participants. The students are already dealing with the technological issues of downloading large files. Links to helper applications such as a PDF viewer can be embedded right in the course materials. The courseware allows you to provide a link directly to the appropriate reserve site so students will not have to wade through menus, or even remember to go to the library's Web site.

File Formats

Electronic reserves can consist of any type of file that can be delivered over the Internet. The most common type of file used is a Portable Document Format (PDF). PDFs are images of scanned documents and are relatively easy for libraries to create, store, and deliver. Anyone using these will need to have a helper application, such as Adobe Acrobat, to read the file. Since PDFs are scanned images, they have a couple of drawbacks. First, they can be relatively large files, slow to download, especially if the student has a low-speed modem connection. Second, they are unreadable by the read-aloud software used by visually disabled students. To offset this problem, the North Carolina State University Library offers a service where, upon request, given 2–4 days notice, they will create an HTML version compatible with screen readers from a PDF reserve document (see www.lib.ncsu.edu/rbr/disabilities_user.html).

Some other types of files delivered through electronic reserves can include:

- links to freely available Web sites
- links to articles in licensed full-text collections and databases
- TIFF, JPEG, or GIF images
- data files for use in spreadsheet or database software
- streaming audio or video files
- GIS data

These reserve files can be placed almost anywhere students can access them. They can be arranged as Web pages on the library server, as bibliographic records in the library's OPAC, or as links in a courseware package.

Increasingly, electronic textbooks are becoming available. "E-textbooks" have both advantages and disadvantages as candidates for electronic reserve. The obvious advantage is its availability over the Internet. The most common disadvantage is the one-person-at-a-time licensing restrictions imposed by some e-book vendors. Just as in dealing with a physical item on reserve, the book may be checked out at time of need.

The Big Question: Copyright and Online Classes

With the increase in online delivery of information, copyright issues are of greater concern than ever. Complicating the picture are the many myths circulating about what is covered by "fair use." It is not our intention to provide a manual on copyright compliance, other than to outline some basic concepts. The central concern of educational institutions is the law's provision for "fair use" of copyrighted material. Section 107 of the Copyright Act of 1976 provides a four-part test for determining fair use:

> In determining whether the use made of a work in any particular case is a fair use the factors to be considered shall include
>
> 1. the purpose and character of the use, including whether such use is of a commercial nature or is for nonprofit educational purposes;
> 2. the nature of the copyrighted work;
> 3. the amount and substantiality of the portion used in relation to the copyrighted work as a whole; and
> 4. the effect of the use upon the potential market for or value of the copyrighted work.

Discussion of each of these factors is available in many places on the Web, but a good place to start is Circular 21 of the United States Copyright Office, "Reproduction of Copyrighted Works by Educators and Librarians" (available on the Web at www.loc.gov/copyright/circs/circ21.pdf). It is important to note that in the fair use test, meeting the standard for all four factors is not always necessary for fair use.

Restricting access is the key to online delivery of copyrighted materials. Your library will need to find a way to ensure that only the students enrolled in the class will have access to materials you have scanned and put on the Internet. This can be done either by placing these materials behind the authentication barrier already used for access to licensed databases, or by limiting access to within passworded courseware. See Chapter 8 for authentication options.

A Few More Words about Electronic Reserves

Since sometimes the instructor is just as geographically remote as the students, consider electronically accepting requests for placing materials on reserve. You can do this formally or informally by e-mail, or you can create a Web form that prompts the instructor for pertinent information and delivers the request into a carefully planned filing system. For an example of a course reserves request form see www.library.unr.edu/comments/reserves.html.

Many online instructors are choosing to provide access to scanned articles directly through their courseware rather than using the library's reserve system. In these cases instructors are often not aware of the range of services you could provide for their classes. Be sure to contact them to promote ILL and other services. For more information about electronic reserves visit the Electronic Reserves Clearinghouse at www.mville.edu/Administration/staff/Jeff_Rosedale/.

FINAL THOUGHTS

Online classes present quite a challenge to the traditional library model. The need to serve remote students is pushing library services to evolve, making the most of the increasing availability of online information. With whole degree programs now available over the Internet, we can no longer treat remote students as an exception to the norm. What was once special service to the homebound or distance education student, may soon become our core service priority. Unless we devote resources to the development of the library's connection to online students, it may well become the librarians who are considered "remote," rather than the students.

REFERENCES

Alden, Jay. 1998. *A Trainer's Guide to Web-Based Instruction: Getting Started on Intranet-and Internet-Based Training*. Alexandria, Va.: American Society for Training & Development.

Centre for Curriculum Transfer Technology. 2001. "Online Educational Delivery Applications: A Web Tool for Comparative Analysis" [Online]. Available: www.ctt.bc.ca/landonline/ [2001, October 8].

Cervone, Frank, and Doris Brown. 2001. "Transforming Library Services to Support Distance Learning: Strategies Used by the DePaul University Libraries." *College and Research Libraries News* 62, no. 2 (February): 147–149.

CNET News.com Staff. 1997. "Online Students Fare Better" *CNET News.com* (January 17) [Online]. Available: news.cnet.com/news/0–1005–200–315893.html [2001, October 9].

French, Deanie, Charles Hale, Charles Johnson, and Gerald Farr, eds. 1999. *Internet Based Learning: An Introduction and Framework for Higher Education and Business.* Sterling, Va.: Stylus Publishing.

Getty, Nancy, Barbara Burd, Sarah Burns, and Linda Piele. 2000. "Using Courseware to Deliver Instruction via the Web: Four Examples." *Reference Services Review* 28, no.4: 349–359.

McCollum, Kelly. 1997. "A New Industry Sprouts Up to Help Professors Put Courses On Line." *The Chronicle of Higher Education* 44, no.10 (October 31): A33–A34.

Meyen, Edward L., Cindy H.T. Lian, and Paul Tangen. 1998. "Issues Associated with the Design and Delivery of On-Line Instruction." *Focus on Autism and Other Developmental Disabilities* 13, no.1 (Spring): 53–60.

Raspa, Dick, and Dane Ward, eds. 2000. *The Collaborative Imperative: Librarians and Faculty Working Together in the Information Universe.* Chicago: Association of College and Research Libraries.

White, Cheryl. 2000. "Students and Faculty Respond to Online Distance Courses at Grant MacEwan Community College." *T.H.E. Journal* 27, no. 9 (April): 66–70 [Online]. Available: www.thejournal.com/magazine/vault/A2814.cfm [2001, November 13].

White, Ken W., and Bob H. Weight. 2000. *The Online Teaching Guide: A Handbook of Attitudes, Strategies, and Techniques for the Virtual Classroom.* Boston: Allyn and Bacon.

APPENDIX: LEVELS OF INVOLVEMENT IN ONLINE COURSES

Here are some examples of how the library can be involved in online courses:

Full Service Model

- The librarian works with the department to develop a suite of activities for a program of classes
- The librarian assists the instructor with technical aspects of courseware
- The librarian participates in onsite or virtual orientation
- The course's main menu page has link to the library's subject entry page
- The librarian is on the course e-mail list, along with listing other contact information such as phone and fax
- The librarian holds office hours through chat
- The librarian monitors and contributes to the course bulletin board
- Assignments include links directly to online readings/electronic reserves
- Assignments include required research activities
- The librarian suggests Web links to be added to lectures for additional reading
- The library provides document delivery via fax or image delivery, as well as sending books as necessary
- Library services are a feature on the course evaluation

Light Service Model

- The librarian creates a course-specific page of resources
- The librarian is a "guest speaker" in a scheduled chat session or two
- A link to the library's Web portal is on the course menu page
- Library services are introduced during the course orientation
- The library makes available readings through electronic course reserves
- Contact information for the pertinent subject librarian is on the library introduction page

Self-Service Model

- The library develops modules that can be linked to several courses
- The library portal is a link on the main course menu
- Full-text resources are openly labeled on the library Web
- Canned introductory information is provided for use in course orientations
- Library contact and services to remote students information is available through a library Web page

8 SUPPORTING THE REMOTE USER OF LICENSED RESOURCES

by Carol A. Parkhurst

CHAPTER OVERVIEW

- Ownership, Users, and Technology
- Authenticating Users
- Authorizing Resource Use
- Access Management
- Methods of Controlling Access
- Content Delivery Issues
- Strategies for User Support

OWNERSHIP, USERS, AND TECHNOLOGY

As access to licensed electronic resources has become more important to library users, the challenge of gracefully linking remote users to the resources they want has become increasingly complex. And the adventure has just begun. Rapid evolution in the technical environment, emerging standards, complex policy and legal issues, and a broad range of user sophistication combine to make supporting remote users a daunting prospect for even the most sophisticated libraries.

OWNERSHIP

The concept of ownership is fundamental to a discussion of licensed resources. Libraries, as brokers for their users, enter into contractual agreements with resource providers to gain online access to proprietary materials. The terms of these agreements invariably require that the institution restrict access to those who are members of the institution's defined user base. Strategies for conclusively identifying those who are entitled to use the materials, for assuring that online access is available just to those individuals, and for protecting the rights both of the user and the owner are discussed below.

TECHNOLOGY AND USERS

Bringing licensed resources within reach of all users requires that we make every effort to reduce barriers to access. Our goals are to make online access immediate, seamless, and intuitive. The current state of the technology infrastructure in most libraries, combined with a lack of skills and a certain degree of trepidation on the part of many staff and users, makes this difficult. Think of it from the perspective of a typical remote user, who must establish an online connection, assert identity, obtain permission to use the resources, find the materials needed, and then retrieve the materials, often contending with poorly designed interfaces, slow response time, arcane technical requirements, and inadequate documentation. It's not a pretty sight!

There is hope. Most libraries have acquired at least limited experience with offering remote online access to their users, usually starting with a local online catalog. Many libraries are offering a wide array of electronic products, forging ahead to serve users the best they can within existing constraints. A few are leading the way by experimenting with less well-understood technologies, by exploring emerging standards, and by grappling with the inter-institutional relationships that must be established to succeed in this environment.

In this chapter we will examine some of the methods currently used to support remote access and discuss promising technologies that are in the early stages of adoption. This is not meant to be a highly technical discussion. The state of available technology is always changing; it is hoped that this chapter will illustrate various approaches for supporting remote users and point out issues to be considered.

AUTHENTICATING USERS

Who has the right to gain access to the resources to which your library has subscribed? The answer is unambiguous—only those who are members of the user group(s) as defined in your licensing agreement have that right. It is the library's responsibility to limit access to members of the defined group.

Meeting this obligation requires that any person attempting to gain access to a licensed resource be *authenticated*. Authentication is simply the act of verifying the identity of a person. Authentication carries with it no inherent *authorization*. It is critical to keep these two issues separate (authentication refers also to ensuring that content is what it purports to be, but that is not the topic of this chapter).

ON-SITE ACCESS

A license agreement may allow use of a licensed resource by people who are physically present onsite (such as in the library or on campus), even if they are not members of the defined user group. If your library does not intend to restrict access to anyone initiating a session from a local computer, you should ensure that license agreements allow for onsite unrestricted use. Public libraries rarely require onsite users to identify themselves, but the practice is more common in academic and corporate libraries. Local practices should reflect the nature and mission of the institution.

ESTABLISHING IDENTITY

"Who are you?" Anyone attempting to connect to a proprietary resource from outside the physical boundaries established for open access must be queried to establish identity. It can then be determined whether or not the person is entitled to use the resource as a member of the defined user group.

Elements for establishing identity can be grouped into three categories (Lynch, 1998):

- Something You Know—identity can be verified by the user's possession of a "secret" such as a password, a login ID, a student identification number, mother's maiden name, or a combination of elements
- Something You Possess—such objects might include a library card with a barcode, a smart card, or a digital certificate (located on a disk or computer)
- Something You Are—positive photo identification and biometrics (fingerprints, retinal scans, voice patterns) can be used in situations requiring high levels of security. Biometric devices are unlikely to be used in libraries during the foreseeable future

Procedures for authentication and registration may present an unexpected barrier to users. Bishop (1998) describes work associated with the Digital Libraries Initiative project at the University of Illinois. Of 1,540 user attempts to access the project during the first two weeks, 83 percent were abandoned at the initial request for a network login. The authors reach a conclusion that "seemingly 'trivial' barriers—like basic awareness and authentication and registration requirements—may prevent a substantial portion of the target audience from ever using the digital libraries designed for them."

Degrees of Assurance

"Are you who you say you are?" The degree to which we must ensure that the user is indeed who he claims to be is relative to the sensitivity of the application. For access to licensed electronic resources, a reasonable degree of assurance will suffice. For access to personal data or medical information, a much higher level of assurance is needed.

The use of retinal scans and the like offers a high degree of assurance in verifying user identity, but the technologies required to support this are unlikely to be practical for libraries any time in the foreseeable future. Smart cards and digital certificates are in use in a few libraries, and are under consideration in others. The most commonly used elements for identification are things people know such as logins and passwords.

METHODS OF AUTHENTICATION

The ideal method of authentication is easy to administer, unobtrusive to users, and secure against tampering or compromise. Users are best served by a consistent method of authenticating that can be used for all proprietary resources.

User Identifiers and Passwords

User identifiers (user IDs or logins) and passwords are still in common use for authentication. A user ID identifies the individual who is trying to access a restricted resource, and the password is the "secret something" that only the individual knows. Reliance on passwords is a legacy from the early days of computing. Before the Internet enabled desktop computers to gain access to thousands of computers worldwide, passwords provided strong protection. There was little risk that they would be intercepted in transit from the user's computer to the host, and few people had access to computers powerful enough to guess another's password. Not so today.

Employing user IDs and passwords for authentication has some advantages:

- no special software is required for the client
- users understand the concept of password

However, reliance on logins and passwords can have serious disadvantages:

- passwords are easily compromised. Passwords sent as clear text are vulnerable to packet sniffing software, which is easily obtained and can be used to capture passwords by anyone with the time and patience who has the necessary physical access. Servers can be breached and password files stolen.
- even with SSL (Secure Socket Layer) encryption, each Webserver that passes a request must handle the login and password. Information can easily be captured at these junctures.
- despite institutional policies to the contrary, users share passwords, write them down, and use the same passwords on multiple machines.
- Web applications can trick a gullible user into providing password information.
- most of us have to remember multiple passwords; the frustration of keeping track of these can further reduce any incentive to keep them safe.
- assigning logins and passwords can be unwieldy. The process doesn't scale well, especially if the library has to assign logins and passwords to a large population.

Barcodes

Barcodes can function much the same as a user ID and password scheme. An individual might be required to authenticate by typing a barcode number and name, where the barcode number is, in effect, a password.

Smart Cards

Smart cards require specialized hardware, so it is unlikely that smart card technology will be useful in a strategy to serve remote patrons. Smart cards may eventually be used as part of a digital certificate implementation (see below), making certificates more portable.

Kerberos

Kerberos can be thought of as a sophisticated user ID/password scheme. Kerberos is a network authentication protocol that is designed to provide strong authentication for client/server applications by using secret-key cryptography (also known as symmetric key cryptography) to enable a client to prove its identity to a server (and vice versa) across an insecure network connection. A free implementation of the protocol is available from the Massachusetts Institute of Technology, the developer of Kerberos (web.mit.edu/Kerberos/www/). Kerberos is also available in commercial implementations.

Kerberos has been widely implemented in academic and financial institutions. With Kerberos' inclusion in Microsoft's Windows 2000 operating system, the protocol now has the potential to reach a wider audience. Of course, Microsoft has added proprietary functions, creating the potential for interoperability problems in environments that run both Unix and Microsoft Kerberos.

The advantages of Kerberos are that

- users are authenticated against a central database; therefore, they may use a single user ID and password for resource authentication
- the system is highly secure
- Kerberos works well in a closed environment such as a university campus

Disadvantages:

- implementation requires that Kerberos support software be installed on every user's workstation
- Kerberos has been slow to be accepted in third party software, such as browsers and database management tools
- Kerberos does not scale well for large populations or for remote applications

For additional information see Tung (1999).

Digital Certificates

A digital certificate is a small computer file containing identifying information about an individual or institution. Associated with the certificate is a pair of encryption keys called *public* and *private keys*. The contents of a digital certificate are prescribed by the X.509 standard developed by the International Organization for Standardization (ISO) and adopted by the American National Standards Institute (ANSI) and the Internet Engineering Task Force (IETF). A certificate usually contains the user's name or identifier, public key, expiration date of the public key, name of the Certificate Authority (CA), serial number of the certificate, and the digital signature of the CA. The data format is compatible with Web-based security protocols.

Digital certificates are used to certify the identity of an individual or an institution seeking access to computer-based information. A digital certificate is issued using a process similar to those by which passports or student ID cards are issued; an individual must prove his identity to the issuing authority's satisfaction in order to receive a certificate. Instead of having to remember many different passwords to use online resources, individuals will use a digital certificate and a private key that are stored on the user's computer and accessible only to a person who has physical access to the computer and knows the password. Certificates and keys may also be stored on a floppy disk or on a smart card. Recognizing that individuals may be members of various user communities (e.g., banks, associations, corporate institutions), we can look forward to being holders of multiple digital certificates.

Certificate Authorities (CA) issue digital certificates. In essence, a Certificate Authority attests that the owner of the certificate is who they say they are. There are commercial Certificate Authorities such as VeriSign, Inc. (www.verisign.com/products/onsite/index.html) and Identrus (www.identrus.com). Institutions may establish their own Certificate Authorities, acting as their own CA for internal use, or acting as a CA for internal and external certificate recipients.

Certificates are usually valid for one or two years. It is difficult to expire certificates prior to their expiration date (this is the function of certificate revocation lists).

These issues pertinent to deployment of digital certificates should be considered:

- how certificates are requested, approved, delivered, and installed in a wide range of browsers
- how certificates are revoked, expired, and renewed

The U.S. government is actively encouraging the use of digital certificates. The Federal PKI Steering Committee has been charged with overseeing efforts to build a virtual "bridge" that federal agencies can use when evaluating one another's digital certificates. The bridge, to be maintained by a Federal Bridge Certification Authority, will cross-certify agencies' certificates, so that one agency can determine if a digital certificate coming from another agency has the level of assurance the agency seeks (Tillett and Yasin, 2000).

AUTHENTICATION DATABASES

Once a user has submitted a login and password or other identifying information, the elements submitted are evaluated against records in an authentication database. Comparing the elements submitted with the records in the database is the process of "authentication." If the elements match, then the user's identity is assumed to be known. However, this does not mean the user is immediately allowed to access the resource he requested; it simply means we know (or think we know) who the user is.

The database used for authentication may be a library patron database, a campus database (faculty, staff, students, alumni), a human resources database, or any other database that contains appropriate records. Determining the database to use and establishing processes for the creation and maintenance of the database requires careful consideration.

Database Characteristics

- What is the scope of the database? Will it contain records just for those who have registered with the library, or records for all eligible users? Many academic institutions have created centrally maintained databases for the purpose of authenticating users for a variety of campus services such as Webregistration, access to buildings, and charging for purchases and services. Can the same database be used for authenticating library users?
- What fields will be used? Will the information collected be minimal, to be used exclusively for authentication, or will the database also contain attributes to be used for other purposes?

Database Management

- Who will create new records? Will library staff key in individual records? Can records be loaded in batches from a central database? Can this entire function be delegated to a central authority?
- Who will maintain the records? We know that user populations can be highly volatile. Students will graduate or change status; people move around; employees come and go. It is the library's legal responsibility (by contract with the resource provider) to make diligent efforts to ensure that the authentication database is accurate and up-to-date for determining eligible users.
- Who will maintain the database application and the server? Is the database part of the library's integrated online system? Is it a responsibility of a central information systems (IS) support organization?
- Is the database secure? Will access be limited to those with appropriate credentials? Will database queries be encrypted?

As a key element in the support of remote library users, the authentication database must be highly reliable. Consideration should be given to mirroring and other methods of providing redundancy that ensure 99.999 percent availability.

AUTHORIZING RESOURCE USE

Once a user's identity has been verified through the authentication process, it does not necessarily follow that the user will be allowed to use the requested resource. Users are entitled to use resources not on the basis of *who* they are, but on the basis of their *attributes,* such as membership in a qualified group (e.g., affiliated student, member of a corporate staff, resident of a municipality, member of an association). Verification of identity is the first step as the basis for authorization; the second step is determining user attributes. It is the matrix of user attributes and the requirements for eligibility to use a particular resource that determines whether a user is *authorized* (allowed) to use the resource.

Authentication and authorization are, conceptually, two separate operations. Several working groups have recommended that the two operations not only be *conceived* as separate, but actually *be* separate.

Current implementations often appear to couple authentication and authorization. For example, an integrated library system (ILS) may be used to authenticate the user, as well as to authorize use of resources based on information in the patron record. In its most basic implementation, authorization may be granted on the basis that the user *exists* in the database, with no further examination of patron characteristics.

DEFINING USER ATTRIBUTES

An attribute is a property or characteristic associated with an individual. User attributes are used to determine eligibility to access various institutional or commercial resources. Examples:

- Nature of affiliation—in an academic institution this could be an undergraduate student, graduate student, faculty member, staff member, adjunct faculty, medical resident, alumni, donor, or member of the community. In a public library, there may be fewer, but no less important distinctions in privileges for residents of a municipality, library staff, and non-residents

- Currency of affiliation—it is essential to maintain a status attribute for current affiliation. For instance, a student who has graduated may still be in the database, but it should be noted that the student has left the institution
- Enrollment in a program or course—access to some resources may be limited to those enrolled in a certain degree program or class

Much of the discussion in the literature has focused on the granularity of distinctions that are required to determine user eligibility. Some argue that granularity should be no finer than membership in a user group as defined by the licensing institution. Others prefer to make finer distinctions, such as recording affiliation with a college or department within a university. Finer granularity is required to distinguish affiliates such as alumni and the general public, since these groups are not usually included in those eligible to use licensed resources in academic libraries. However, with fine granularity a system may unintentionally gather too much information about users and use patterns, potentially compromising user privacy.

ILS VENDOR SOLUTIONS

Some integrated library systems (ILS) offer the capability of authorizing users for access to resources based on attributes in the library patron database. For example, in the Innovative Interfaces' system, the Web Access Management (WAM) module manages rights for up to 200 resources. Rights to each resource can be assigned according to patron type (defined by the library) and location identifier. Rights can be blocked, at the library's discretion, for reasons such as excess library fines or expired borrowing privileges. The WAM module is an integrated access management solution, incorporating authentication, authorization, and session management. WAM users authenticate against the patron database by keying a barcode number, a name and, optionally, a PIN. Other ILS vendors offer similar tools.

DIGITAL CERTIFICATES

The traditional use of certificates is for authentication, not authorization. However, there are several ways in which certificates can be used as part of an authorization infrastructure.

Attributes Held Within Digital Certificate

A digital certificate can contain information about its owner, such as a user's network identifier. The certificate can be parsed by an application and the network ID extracted; the identifier can subsequently be used for querying an attributes database.

Participants in a workshop sponsored by the Digital Library Federation reached the conclusion that user attributes other than a network identifier should not be included in a certificate payload (www.ucop.edu/irc/cdl/tasw/Authentication/Architecture-3_W95.pdf). It is preferable for the institution to have a directory or attributes server that can determine eligibility for services.

Certificates and Directory Services

A directory is a database of names/identifiers and attributes of individuals, servers, and other resources that may be accessed over the network. It is likely that directories will store most of what we need to know about credential holders. LDAP (Lightweight Directory Applications Protocol) is proving to be an effective repository for user attributes, including the user's public key. Other components of certificate technology (Web servers, browsers, certificate servers) are integrating LDAP as the first choice of repository for certificates and for certificate revocation lists (Cearley and Winsor, 1997). LDAP is attractive because it:

- provides APIs (Application Programming Interfaces) for accessing directory information across a network using Java, C, C++, and Perl scripts, so that almost any application can connect to the server
- allows authentication to the directory itself using the public key
- enables authorization to very granular levels

Digital certificates can be used to initiate the authorization process. The combining of certificates and LDAP treats authorization as a network service, making it available to all applications and resource servers. The architecture for this approach requires

- X.509 certificates defined by the issuing institution
- an extension field in the certificate that serves as a pointer to a given authorization infrastructure (i.e., a directory or database)
- directory attributes that determine access rights for a user

For additional information, see *A Recipe for Configuring and Operating LDAP Directories* by Michael R. Gettes (www.georgetown.edu/giia/internet2/ldap-recipe). The document is "intended to be a discussion point toward the development of common directory deployments within the Higher Education community."

ACCESS MANAGEMENT

A strategy for access management involves three operations: authentication, authorization, and access control. Authentication and authorization have been discussed above. The final operation, actually enabling a user to connect with a restricted resource may, in some respects, be the most difficult to do well. The three operations should appear seamless to the user, but may be accomplished with different technologies and at different levels of an organization. For example, authentication might be handled at the institution level (perhaps by a Kerberos implementation), authorization handled within the library (in the ILS database), and access control managed by a proxy server (either in the library or in an information systems department).

Designing an access management system requires consideration of both technical and policy issues. In determining the best overall strategy for your library, the following should be considered.

SCALABILITY

The system must be capable of growing to serve all potential users and resources.

SECURITY

Ideally, data stored on a server must be invulnerable to compromise. Information transmitted between a client and a server on the network should be encrypted to protect user privacy. Authentication dialogs that involve transmission of confidential user identification and passwords must always be encrypted.

EASE OF DEPLOYMENT

Simplicity is a virtue. The less complex the system, the more readily it can be adopted technologically and organizationally, and the more acceptable it will be to users.

Consider the extent of technical support available to the library. Will support come solely from library staff? Is it possible to obtain support from another agency such as an information systems department? Your choice of strategy for access management hinges on the degree of technical support you can expect.

FLEXIBILITY

Change in technology is rapid and inevitable so don't box yourself in. Take nothing for granted; even circumstances that appear to be predictable may prove otherwise. Imagine that your library decides to join a consortium for resource sharing and you want to take advantage of the consortium's authentication and proxy services. Would you be able to adapt your access management scheme?

PRIVACY AND ACCOUNTABILITY

A balance must be maintained between user privacy and institutional accountability. The nature of this balance for your institution will depend on the institution's mission and values.

User privacy is a key concern, both for legal reasons (e.g., student and patient record confidentiality laws) and philosophical ones (a perceived right to privacy held by most people). Choices made in implementing technical systems can minimize the extent to which personal information and personal behavior (use of resources) are monitored and captured. Participants in the Digital Library Federation's (DLF) 1998 *Workshop on Access Management* recommend that campus-based authentication services or proxies should not relay actual identities to resource providers (Arms, 1999).

We can reassure users that their privacy is our concern by letting them know what data is being collected, what is done with that data, and what rights they have. TRUSTe, an independent, non-profit organization whose mission is to build users' trust and confidence in the Internet by promoting the use of fair information practices, offers a Model Privacy Statement at www.truste.org/bus/pub_sample.html. It is suggested that you place prominent links to your institution's privacy policy throughout your Web site.

Balancing the desire for privacy is the need for user accountability, which leads ultimately to institutional accountability. An essential part of many license agreements is a commitment by the institution to make a reasonable effort to identify and investigate sources of anomalous and possibly inappropriate use, in order to prevent abuse. Establishing *pseudonymous identifiers* (Lynch, 1998) for presentation to resource providers protects user privacy while allowing a mechanism for tracking abusers. Treating a user as an *anonymous* member of a group identity offers good privacy, but foregoes the possibility of tracking abuses.

COMMUNITY ACCEPTANCE

An access management system must be acceptable to your users. They want it to be easy; they want it to be predictable, comprehensible, and convenient. Complexity should be hidden as much as possible. It helps users if new services appear to be add-ons to existing services, so they are familiar with at least some of the procedures.

Be cautious with access methods that assume high bandwidth network connections. At home, many users still rely on low-end computers and slow modems.

AFFORDABILITY

If you can't afford to do it, you'll have to choose another solution. Strategies that leverage your existing technology base are often more cost-effective. If you have an integrated library system or a Kerberos implementation on campus, consider using those in your scheme.

METHODS OF CONTROLLING ACCESS

The server hosting a proprietary resource must be able to determine that the requesting user is a member of the defined user community. Until that determination is made, access is not allowed. Methods of access control can be considered as one of three general types: IP (Internet Protocol) source filtering, proxy server, and credential based (Lynch, 1998). The most commonly used methods of access control, and those methods being actively considered by libraries, are discussed here.

IP SOURCE FILTERING

Most resource providers support IP source filtering. It is currently the most commonly used method of controlling access. IP source filtering takes advantage of an existing network protocol. When a user initiates a session with a resource host, the host server examines the IP address of the client device that is embedded in each packet of information sent to the host. The IP address uniquely identifies the network location of the client device. The host server compares the IP address with the range(s) of addresses that cover the library's network presence.

To initiate IP source filtering, the library supplies the resource provider with a list of all IP addresses, or more commonly, ranges of IP addresses, for devices on the library or campus network.

The resource provider creates an access control list against which all requests for access are matched. If the incoming client IP address matches an address or fits within a range of addresses on the list, then access is allowed. Otherwise, the request for access is denied.

IP source filtering works only within defined institutional IP ranges. IP source filtering is not an alternative for controlling access in all circumstances. For most remote access, simple IP source filtering is not an option.

Dial-in Services

IP source filtering can be used only if (a) access to the dial-in service is limited to authorized affiliates and (b) the dial-in service uses IP addresses that are exclusive to the institution. If the dial-in service is outsourced to a commercial ISP (Internet Service Provider), IP filtering usually cannot be used.

Commercial Internet Service Providers

There is a growing trend for users to subscribe to commercial network services rather than use the institution as an ISP. Newer technologies such as DSL (Digital Subscriber Lines), ISDN (Integrated Services Digital Network), and cable-TV Internet access are superior to modem dial-in. When remote users subscribe to commercial services for network access, they have IP addresses assigned by the ISP; remote resource providers cannot use these addresses to distinguish eligible users.

Advantages and Disadvantages of IP Source Filtering

There are advantages to IP source filtering. It is easy and seamless for the user sitting at a computer in a library, a computer lab, or other on-campus location. It scales well, is simple to deploy, and requires no supporting infrastructure. There is strong privacy for users. However, the disadvantages may outweigh the advantages:

- User accountability is limited. An IP address identifies a machine on the network, not a person. While it may be possible to match an IP address to a particular residence hall room or office location, there is no way to identify the user at a public workstation or in a computing lab.
- Configuration of IP ranges for a large institution can be quite complex.
- IP source filtering does not offer fine granularity for authorization. Anyone who can physically sit down at a connected workstation can use the resources.

- The move from older class-based network addresses to Classless Inter-Domain Routing (CIDR) introduces new problems. For a definition of CIDR see webopedia.internet.com.

By most accounts, IP source filtering by itself is not viewed as a workable solution for the long term.

PROXY SERVERS

Proxy servers act as "brokers" between Web browsers and resource providers. In a proxy scheme, requests for access to an online resource are diverted to a proxy server, which in turn redirects the request to the resource provider. The proxy server also handles the response from the resource provider, returning it to the originating Web browser.

Proxy servers are widely used to support access to restricted resources, often in combination with IP source filtering for in-house user access. Note that proxy servers provide a mechanism for access control, but the institution will still have to deploy some method of authentication and authorization to control access to the proxy servers.

In a survey conducted in December 2000 by the Secure Systems and Services Interest Group (a unit of the Library and Information Technology Association), it was discovered that among responding libraries, 60 of the academic libraries and eight public libraries were employing proxy servers. The most widely used software package was EZproxy (26 libraries), followed by Innovative's Web Access Management (12 libraries), then Squid (seven libraries) and Apache (six libraries). See www.pandc.org/proxy/survey/report.html.

Advantages and Disadvantages of Proxy Servers

Advantages of proxy servers include their

- potential for packaging a request to protect user privacy
- potential for excellent usage statistics
- ease of deployment (for vendor-supplied solutions)

There are also disadvantages:

- proxy servers may not scale. Packaging and repackaging user requests takes considerable system resources. As the number of users grows, the size of the server needs to grow, as well. Some overhead may be mitigated by the use of caching, although this introduces additional complexity for server management

- proxy servers are potentially a single point of failure and a single point of security compromise
- proxy servers can be bottlenecks, causing unacceptably slow response time
- Resource providers may explicitly forbid proxy connections, or may require that each sanctioned proxy server be registered. Vendors are understandably cautious about proxies, because it is not difficult to set up a rogue proxy server that mimics a legitimate server

Mechanical Proxies

A mechanical proxy makes use of protocols built into HTTP. Mechanical proxies require a Web browser that supports automatic proxy configuration (as do most widely used browsers). Once the browser is configured, all HTTP requests are passed to the designated proxy server. The proxy server intercepts the requests and retransmits them to the destination host. Since the proxy server transmits its own IP address to the resource host, the session appears to originate from an IP source address within the authorized institution ranges. Using a mechanical proxy is essentially a method of enabling IP source filtering for off-site users. The interaction with the proxy server is transparent to the user.

Innovative's Web Access Management (WAM) system is an example of a mechanical proxy implementation. To reduce system overhead, WAM acts as a proxy only for those remote servers that appear in the "forward table." All other Web requests are handled directly by the client's browser.

Users frequently have difficulty configuring automatic proxies. We have found related user support to be highly staff intensive, although improved online instructions have helped our users to become more self-sufficient.

As of this writing, neither the America Online (AOL) browser nor Netscape 6.x supports automatic proxy configuration. Also, browsers do not support multiple automatic proxies. Services such as DSL (Digital Subscriber Lines), ISDN, cable-TV Internet, and commercial ISPs often require their own proxies. Even if it is possible to bypass or disable the service provider proxy to install an automatic proxy for remote access, the provider's proxy is usually reinstalled when a browser is restarted. The user is forced to reinstall the library proxy for every session.

A computer that is behind a corporate firewall will not be able to use an automatic proxy. Personal firewalls on home computers do not seem to interfere.

Application-Level Proxies

An application-level proxy forwards requests to a resource server without relying on protocol mechanisms within HTTP. There are several types of application proxies. Relay proxies, rewriting proxies, pass-through proxies, reverse proxies, and some gateways are application-level proxies.

This type of proxy is easier for users since browser configuration is not required, but there are disadvantages to application-level proxies:

- application-level proxies are usually not scalable for larger environments
- programming can be quite complex (Lynch, 1998)
- application-level proxies generally will not handle Web pages that contain Java-based programs or JavaScript code
- depending on the implementation, cookies may not be handled correctly
- each resource needs to be configured separately in the proxy. Some application-level proxies require that every unique URL for a vendor product be configured. For electronic journals that have unique URLs for each article, this will not be possible

An inexpensive product called EZproxy has been used successfully in a number of libraries (www.usefulutilities.com/ezproxy/). EZproxy is a rewriting proxy server and therefore requires no browser configuration. The latest version allows EZproxy services to be used through corporate firewalls. In July 2001, the University of Nebraska at Omaha library introduced an EZproxy-based system called Leo. The Nebraska system authenticates against the library's ILS database using Innovative's Patron API (Applications Programmer Interface) software. Technical staff in the library handled the scripting for the authentication module. EZproxy doesn't solve all browser-related problems. EZproxy requires that the client's browser accept cookies, and some browsers and users refuse cookies. There are still problems with the AOL browser. Leo's online instructions refer to AOL's browser as a "crippled browser," with a recommendation that the user install a "fully functional browser" (library.unomaha.edu/information/library_user/01f/leo.htm).

A thorough discussion of a pass-through proxy server implementation at Brown University is available at www.brown.edu/Facilities/CIS/Network_Services/libproxy/. Pass-through proxies require a separate proxy server for every remote resource. Fortunately, most Web servers allow port-based virtual hosting, so that many proxy servers can actually be set up on the same physical machine.

The University of Calgary has developed a relay server for remote information services. The program is written in C and the source code is freely available. The library has obtained permission from each resource provider to use relay access. The server has proved to be seamless for the vendors and for most users. It is reliable and scalable (handling 2,100 electronic products). See www.ucalgary.ca/~zhangc/webrelay.html.

A technique called "referer URL" takes advantage of the fact that any request for Web services carries the URL of the referer page (that is, the page from which the link to the server was made). The Albertsons Library at Boise State University has developed a system for enabling remote access that uses a referer URL. Choosing a resource from the library's Web site takes the user to an appropriate page for that resource. At that point the user is authenticated using a Web form with Perl scripts that queries the library's ILS database. If authentication succeeds, the user is redirected from the authentication page (using the HTTP environment variable HTTP_REFERER) to the resource provider's site. The referer URL can include a vendor-provided login and password (www.riverofdata.com/tools/authentication.htm).

Referer URL access is relatively simple to implement, but it has some disadvantages:

- not all resource providers support referer URLs
- the process may not scale well
- URLs cannot be bookmarked
- referred URLs can be easily spoofed and cannot be considered to be secure

COOKIES

Remembering multiple logins and passwords is confusing and annoying for users. For those who use a single machine, and for resources that don't require high security, it's possible to store logins and passwords as cookies on the user's computer.

Harvard's Library Digital Initiative uses cookies to store authentication and profile information on a user's browser, so that the user doesn't need to provide repeated authentication information when navigating through various resources. These cookies expire after a limited time (Flecker, 2000).

VENDOR SOLUTIONS

A number of integrated library systems vendors offer proprietary solutions for managing access control to remote resources.

The solution offered by your ILS vendor (or a vendor under consideration) should be explored in depth. Be aware that not all ILS remote access solutions support proxy services. If a resource provider supports IP source filtering as the sole access method, the library will have to employ a proxy server in addition to the ILS access management scheme.

WebExpress from OCLC is a product that supports Z39.50 compliant information resources through a locally customized gateway. Users are authenticated against a local file within WebExpress. WebExpress may be of interest to small and medium-sized libraries with limited resources for technical support (www.oclc.org/Webexpress/)

CREDENTIAL-BASED ACCESS

In this approach, the user presents some form of credential directly to the resource provider. The credential is usually a login/user ID and password or a certificate.

Logins and Passwords

There are two types of login and password implementation that can be considered to be methods of credential-based access. In the first method, a resource provider gives the library a single login and password to be used for access to the resource. Libraries have handled this method in various ways, including printing bookmarks with the logins and passwords and handing them out to eligible users. Other libraries have posted logins and passwords on a secure Web page. The password for the secure Web page is distributed to eligible users. This general method is of limited usefulness, in that it does not scale well and the potential for unauthorized resource access is high.

In the second approach, a user offers his individual user ID and password to the resource provider in order to gain access to the restricted service. The resource provider verifies that the user ID and password are valid, either by submitting a query to an authentication server at the user's institution or by comparing to an access list kept at the vendor site. This method doesn't scale well, either. Imagine the logistics of issuing individual logins and passwords to each of the library's users, potentially multiplied by the number of remote resource providers. This is practical only for resources for which access is highly restricted and available to a small number of users.

Digital Certificates and Public Key Infrastructure

Public Key is a technique that was designed to securely exchange information between strangers. Here is a basic description of how it works (Cearley and Winsor, 1997):

- a user acquires a key pair, one public key and one private key. The keys are related mathematically, so that anything encrypted by one key can only be decrypted by the other
- the public key is published. It can be listed in a directory, posted to a Web page, or sent via e-mail. The private key remains encrypted in a secure password protected file
- when someone wants to send a secret message, she finds the user's public key and encrypts a message with a public key algorithm
- the encrypted message is sent via e-mail, transmitted across a network, or posted in a public place
- the intended recipient retrieves the message and decrypts it with his private key, after unlocking the key with his local password

The public key in this example lends its name to "Public Key Infrastructure" (PKI), which refers to the software, policies, and practices for managing digital certificates. A certificate is a repository for a public key that has been digitally signed by a recognized Certificate Authority. Components of the Public Key Infrastructure are:

- a Certificate Authority that provides the services required to issue, store, manage and revoke digital certificates
- an authentication database or directory that stores information about certificate holders. Typically, the database contains a unique identifier for the user, associated demographic information, and the user's public key. LDAP is the emerging protocol of choice for authentication databases in academic institutions
- an attributes server that may be used to store information that is not contained in a certificate but may be needed for authorization. As an alternative, attributes may be stored in the authentication database

A typical digital certificate transaction between a user and a resource provider might proceed like this:

1. The user requests service from a resource provider
2. The resource provider validates the authenticity of the user's issuing certificate authority (CA), retrieves the location of the user's local directory/attribute service from within the

digital certificate, and contacts that directory service to request authorizing information

3. The directory service validates the authenticity of the resource provider's issuing authority, and then responds with appropriate classes of service permissible for the user. The directory service may also manage the Certificate Revocation lists, necessary for a fully functioning PKI

4. The resource provider delivers service to the user

A significant impediment to using digital certificates as a method of direct access control is that it requires the cooperation of resource providers in accepting certificates. To date, few providers have made a commitment to digital certificates as an access control method.

Under the auspices of the Digital Library Federation, the California Digital Library, Columbia University, JSTOR, and OCLC have developed a protocol that enables a resource provider to verify that a user bearing a digital certificate has authority from a home institution to use a requested resource. The prototype method combines the use of X.509 digital certificates for authentication with a directory service for authorization based on user attributes. See www.diglib.org/architectures/digcertpv.htm for more information.

The University of California (UC) statewide system is implementing a PKI as part of its Common Authentication Project. *Why UC Must Invest in a Public Key Infrastructure (PKI): The Case for Digital Certificates*, published by the UC Office of the President, states that "a consensus has emerged among technical experts and information managers in government and industry that a technology called Public Key Infrastructure (PKI) offers the best feasible solution to these issues" (University of California . . . , 2000) (www.ucop.edu/irc/auth/). The UC, Irvine campus is proposing a strategy that combines the use of on-campus Kerberos authentication with a Campus Certificate Authority (CCA) and an LDAP network directory. The CCA grants a certificate after Kerberos authentication is performed. An LDAP network directory will store the user's ID, attributes information for campus affiliates, the certificate, and the public key for each campus affiliate. A campus attributes server, which may or may not be the LDAP server, will contain authorization information (i.e., attributes) for applications such as library remote resources, personal benefits information, and many other campus services.

CREN (Corporation for Research and Educational Networking) is establishing itself as a higher education "bridge authority" to verify the individual certificate authorities at CREN's member institutions (www.cren.net).

Deploying a PKI has many advantages:

- X.509 is a well-defined protocol
- certificate technology is standard in the latest browsers
- certificates need not be reconfigured for every service provider. They can accommodate multiple affiliations and access rights
- PKI offers strong security and interoperability across institutions. The e-commerce community and the federal government are positioning themselves to support certificate technology
- PKI has uses besides access control. PKI provides a means of enabling "signatures" on digital documents. These can be archived, with the digital certificate providing evidence that the documents have not been altered after they were "signed." Several states have enacted legislation to permit legally binding contracts to be signed using PKI technology. PKI also provides strong encryption for information in transit over networks. Financial transactions and e-mail messages may be encrypted using PKI

PKI is not the solution for everyone. Even with its advantages, adoption of PKI and digital certificates will likely be limited for some time to come because

- deployment is expensive and complex
- digital certificates and private keys are stored on floppy disks, smart cards, and personal computers. Individuals who use multiple machines will have to install the certificate and private key on each computer
- installing a certificate into a browser is not a trivial procedure
- use of PKI on public computers serves only to identify the machine, not the individual user, the same as IP source filtering
- use of a personal digital certificate and private key on a public workstation is a potential security risk. The certificate and key must be removed after use
- individual implementations of PKI will not interoperate if not specifically intended to do so. Planning is imperative
- there is a concern that institutions could be liable for unauthorized use of digital certificates

- there are restrictions on use of high-level cryptography outside of the United States
- there are serious privacy concerns. A subclass of certificates called *anonymous certificates* offers a means of ensuring greater privacy for users (Lynch, 1998)
- institutions should consider contractual constraints that require a resource provider to respect some level of user privacy and anonymity
- use of digital certificates and PKI can be problematic for low bandwidth users. At very low network speeds, the technology is not feasible
- a PKI may be overkill. Since what we are essentially looking for is a way to determine whether somebody belongs to our designated user group and thus should be allowed to access restricted information resources, it may make sense to choose a method that is simpler and easier to support than PKI

For additional information on digital certificates, LDAP, and PKI see:

- *Digital Certificate Infrastructure: Frequently Asked Questions*, published by the Digital Library Federation and the Corporation for Research and Educational Networking (CREN)—www.cren.net/ca/faqs.html
- *A Digital Library Authentication and Authorization Architecture*, March 22, 2000. Describes a model developed by participants at a Digital Library Federation-sponsored meeting held in January 1999 (www.ucop.edu/irc/cdl/tasw/ Authentication/Architecture-3_W95.pdf)
- VeriSign's *Introduction to Public Key Cryptography* (www.verisign.com/repository/crptintr.html)
- *Guidelines for Constructing Policies Governing the Use of Identity-Based Public Key Certificates*, published by the Certification Authority Rating and Trust (CARAT) Task Force, The Internet Council, National Automated Clearing House Association (NACHA)—internetcouncil.nacha.org/ Projects/CARAT_Final_011400.doc

Hybrid Systems

Access management solutions that blend a variety of currently available technologies will be the best for most institutions. These "hybrid" systems may take various forms. Perhaps an institution will continue to support a proxy-based approach, in order to manage access to a wide range of disparate services. The institution may select a credential-based solution for authenticating users to the proxy, to gain experience in deploying such a system.

Internet2 has brought together a group of leading campus information technology architects to provide direction for creating a national interoperable middleware infrastructure for research and education. This group, called MACE (Middleware Architecture Committee for Education), aims to foster interoperability in areas such as security and directories (middleware.internet2.edu/MACE/).

Shibboleth, a project of MACE, is investigating technologies to support inter-institutional authentication and authorization for access to proprietary Web resources. The intent of Shibboleth is to support the heterogeneous security systems in use on campuses today, rather than to mandate use of any particular scheme.

CONTENT DELIVERY ISSUES

Once a remote user has connected to an online resource, there can be complications in viewing, printing, and capturing the content. Resource providers are delivering content using a variety of electronic file formats, ranging from simple ASCII text to full-motion video and VRML (Virtual Reality Modeling Language). Standard Web browsers will interpret and display many of the formats, but certainly not all. For example, Adobe Portable Document Format (PDF) is used by many resource providers for electronic document distribution. Anyone who makes use of full-text information resources must download the Adobe Acrobat Reader (www.adobe.com).

The International Coalition of Library Consortia (ICOLC) 1999 *Guidelines for Technical Issues in Request for Proposal (RFP) Requirements and Contract Negotiations* recommend that a number of content format issues be discussed with a resource provider during the purchasing process (www.library.yale.edu/consortia/techreq.html). After thoroughly exploring the product so that you understand any special requirements for content presentation, you will be better able to support users of the product. These are examples of content delivery issues that should be addressed with vendors:

- use of embedded applications such as Java and JavaScript that can limit accessibility of the vendor site to particular browsers

- maintaining compatibility with standard browsers
- consistent use of standard HTML
- ADA accessibility—services should be developed in accordance with ADA (Americans With Disabilities Act) standards (www.usdoj.gov/crt/ada/adahom1.htm)
- capturing content—users should be able to capture content by printing, e-mailing, and downloading. Preferably, content should be printable without the use of special software
- use of embedded multimedia—unless these are integral to the product, they can cause problems and should be used sparingly

Use of plug-ins for viewing and printing content is unavoidable. To illustrate, here are the plug-ins that currently must be installed to use all online products available to University of Nevada, Reno, affiliates:

- Adobe Acrobat 5.0 (for viewing pdf files)
- IBM techexplorer v3.1 (for viewing TeX, LaTeX, and MathML documents)
- HarpWeek print client
- JPRINT (optimized print client for JSTOR)
- Citrix ICA client (allows users to run a variety of Windows-based applications on library MetaFrame servers using a Web browser)
- LUNA In*sight* (image viewer)
- Quick View Plus (viewer that supports over 200 file types)
- RealPage Reader (view proprietary format used by CatchWord)
- CPC Lite (Cartesian Document Image Viewer)
- ArcExplorer (for viewing and manipulating spatial data)

STRATEGIES FOR USER SUPPORT

From the discussion of authenticating, authorizing, and enabling access for remote users, it becomes clear that making a commitment to adequately supporting off-site users is essential to their success, and therefore to yours. You will need to continually seek new strategies and fresh perspectives in your quest to serve users well.

TEST IT

Nothing is more important than continuous and rigorous testing as a strategy for finding ways to improve services. Consider recruiting both library staff and library users to serve as testers for every conceivable environment in which a constituent could attempt to use licensed resources from a remote location. You want testers to explore every aspect of your library's Web pages, your access management system, and your licensed resources in order to understand what a user will see and experience.

To the extent possible, set up models to test permutations of the following:

- connecting from off-site via:
  o telephone dial-up to the institution's modem pool (at various modem speeds)
  o telephone dial-up through a local commercial Internet Service Provider
  o cable modem, DSL, ISDN, and satellite broadband
- recent versions of standard Web browsers. We are committed to supporting three generations of Netscape and Internet Explorer (all versions), insofar as possible. There are occasions when a browser version simply does not work with the library's access management system; this is always explained in the Web instructions
- recent versions of non-standard Web browsers such as America Online's default Web browser and Opera
- text browser such as Lynx
- Computers with older and newer operating systems
  o DOS, Windows
  o Macintosh
  o Unix

Ask your testers to stretch the boundaries of their online research behavior. Have them try printing and e-mailing documents. Ask that they print or write down any unexpected results, describe situations where they had trouble, and alert you to instructions that are insufficient or difficult to interpret. Encourage them to download and install the plug-ins that are required for viewing and printing specialized resources.

Test the permutations of your authentication system. Ask the circulation staff to set your patron record to "expired" and see what happens when you try to authenticate. You get the idea.

There is a strategy you can use from your library office to determine what non-authenticated off-site users will see when visiting your library's Web pages. View the pages from a privacy service such as Anonymizer.com (www.anonymizer.com). Although usability testing is not the intended purpose of a privacy site, it works well for replicating non-IP-authenticated sessions, since your workstation's IP address is masked.

Also consider the security of your system. Consult with sophisticated computer users to ensure that the methods of security you chose for your authentication system really do stand up to the standards required by the resource provider.

THE LIBRARY'S WEB SITE

The greatest thing about a Web site is that it is available 24 hours a day. The library's Web site, with its links to online resources and user instructions, may be all the contact many users will have with the library. If all goes well and they find what they want, then that's all the contact they need.

So, the Web site had better be good. There are many sources of information on Web page design and usability. Be prepared to use them. Of course, you should test the pages with real users. We had the disheartening experience of hearing uncensored opinions of our site from students in an upper-level journalism class. The class was assigned to share examples of their most favorite and least favorite Web sites. To our dismay, our library's Web site was brought to the class as a "least favorite" site. Follow-up conversations with those students were enlightening.

STAFF TRAINING

The secret of successfully supporting off-site users is to thoroughly train the library's public service staff. Frustrated remote users usually call the library, although occasionally they send questions or complaints via e-mail. Any member of the public service staff may get a question about remote access and should be prepared to answer it.

The best way to learn about remote access is to do it. Staff should be encouraged to use licensed library resources from home. Release time can be given, if necessary, so that adequate time will be spent. As remote resources are added and changed, all public service staff should take a turn as testers.

COLLABORATIVE PLANNING

Ultimately, users will benefit most from online resource services that are well conceived, carefully planned, and thoughtfully implemented. The best approach to planning requires collaboration at various levels of the organization: within the library, within the institution, and external to the institution.

Within the library, staff from public services, materials processing units, and systems support should work together to determine the best approaches for solving the problems of remote access to information.

Network access management at the institution level is usually handled by information systems personnel, who may be motivated by policy imperatives and priorities that are very different from those of the library. Because authentication and access management need to come together in a common infrastructure that will ultimately support many purposes, libraries and IS groups must establish a dialog to ensure that the systems that are ultimately deployed work for everyone.

Ongoing conversations with resource providers will inform them about the library's needs and should result in improved vendor products.

REFERENCES

Arms, Caroline. 1999. "Enabling Access in Digital Libraries: A Report on a Workshop on Access Management" [Online]. Available: www.clir.org/pubs/reports/arms–79/contents.html [2001, August 8].

Bishop, Ann Peterson. 1998. "Measuring Access, Use, and Success in Digital Libraries." *Journal of Electronic Publishing* 4 no. 2 (December) [Online]. Available: www.press.umich.edu/jep/04–02/bishop.html [2001, November 13].

Cearley, Kent, and Lindsay Winsor. 1997. "Securing IT Resources with Digital Certificates and LDAP" [Online]. Available: www.educause.edu/ir/library/html/cnc9707/cnc9707.html [2001, August 8].

Flecker, Dale. 2000. "Harvard's Library Digital Initiative: Building a First Generation Digital Library Infrastructure." *D-Lib Magazine* 6 no.11 (November) [Online]. Available: www.dlib.org/dlib/november00/flecker/11flecker.html [2001, August 8].

Lynch, Clifford, editor. 1998. "A White Paper on Authentication and Access Management Issues in Cross-Organizational Use of Networked Information Resources." Coalition for Networked Information. Revised Discussion Draft of April 14, 1998 [Online]. Available: www.cni.org/projects/authentication/authentication-wp.html [2001, August 8].

Tillett, Scott, and Rutrell Yasin. 2000. "Feds Build ID Model for E-Biz." *InternetWeek* 821 (July 17): 1.

Tung, Brian. 1999. *Kerberos: A Network Authentication System.* Reading, Mass.: Addison-Wesley.

University of California Office of the President. 2000. *Why UC Must Invest in a Public Key Infrastructure (PKI): The Case for Digital Certificates* [Online]. Available: www.ucop.edu/irc/auth/whypki.pdf [2001, December 19].

9 FUNDRAISING AND PUBLIC RELATIONS IN AN ELECTRONIC ENVIRONMENT

by Betty J. Glass and Vicki L. Toy Smith

CHAPTER OVERVIEW

- Identifying and Tracking Current and Potential Donors and Advocates
- Different Strokes: Niche Marketing
- Some Things Are for Everyone: Promote What You Have
- Maintaining Your E-Presence
- Fundraising on the Web

The last two decades of breakthroughs in information technology have not merely transformed library resources and services, they have helped create the current climate of hyperchange in which libraries exist. The good news for libraries is that, in spite of the radical changes in education brought forth by the information revolution, donations to educational institutions continued to increase through the late 1990s. The Internet is a powerful tool that libraries can use to state their cases to remote patrons for private support. Once attracted and nurtured, these patrons form a strong potential donor pool. A library's Web site must provide the opportunity for relationship building. "It must provide communication. It must be entertainingly interactive, and it must provide an opportunity to give" (Johnston, 1999: xii). The challenge for today's librarians is to understand how to utilize the radically changing world of online access to attract and cultivate future donors and advocates. If she were available for consultation, the Delphic oracle might cryptically observe that the solution lies within the challenge.

IDENTIFYING AND TRACKING CURRENT AND POTENTIAL DONORS AND ADVOCATES

Twenty-first century library fundraisers must first make sure that there is a system in place to identify and track the giving history of current donors. Then the challenge becomes identifying potential donors and advocates from among huge pools of individuals and groups that qualify as neighborhood, campus, community, state, and even national and international constituents. Most fundraisers know how to gather lists of political heavyweights, community activists, wealthy philanthropists, successful businesses, and alumni (in the case of academic libraries) for cultivation purposes. Successful fundraisers will also be guided by demographic changes occurring in the library's constituencies and consciously seek to diversify their cultivation list to ensure it resembles the diversity of its users. As death erodes the ranks of the Great Depression and World War II generations, libraries must attract and engage a younger and more diverse segment of donors.

Because the younger generations of donors tend to be "wired" and busy, it makes perfect sense to connect with them through the Internet, to customize special services for them through the Web, communicate with them through e-mail, and provide a virtual community to help library friends stay in touch with the library and with each other.

Identifying your current donors and your potential donors and advocates will serve a myriad of purposes. First, you can use these lists for personal contact (solicitation), newsletter mailings, etc. Second, you can invite selected individuals and groups to events and functions that suit their range of interests. The University of Nevada, Reno Library, for example, maintains a database of over 4,000 names of potential donors and advocates who receive the Friends of the Library newsletter and invitations to events. But more to the point of this book, you can use the lists to create targeted information services that will ultimately pay off by transforming users into donors.

Put some thought into which individuals, foundations, businesses, and corporations have the potential of helping your library politically or monetarily. Every library must do its own homework in this area. For example, who are your political representatives at the local, state, regional, and national levels? Libraries with government information departments have a head start in gathering such information and may already have a relevant Web page listing such individuals. Who are your community leaders and philanthropists? Assign staff responsibility for routine monitoring of local and regional newspapers, including minority publications. Gather newsletters of other nonprofits in your area and add names of board members and donors. Gather lists of Chamber of Commerce officials, corporate officers in your community, service organization leaders. Any civic leader or philanthropist who is not already involved with your organization is a potential advocate or donor. If yours is an academic library, your campus development office may already have this sort of information available to you or can supply addresses and phone numbers for names you choose to target.

Public and academic libraries may be dependent upon bond elections or special appropriations for financial support. It is important to have politicians and local community administrators on your side and aware of the projects your library has undertaken well in advance of major initiatives to gain financial support. When lobbying local decision makers on behalf of your library, you might be able to impress them with Web sites sporting resources especially selected to appeal to them.

One benefit of identifying the political players, civic leaders, and philanthropists in your library's region is the concurrent development of an important pool of influential people to draw upon for service on advisory boards for capital campaigns and/or to serve as board members for Friends of the Library organizations. Take advantage of the expertise of political leaders in working with the various levels of government that interact with your library. Networking with the policymakers can reap benefits for your library in unexpected and valuable ways.

CREATING DATABASES TO TRACK DONORS, POTENTIAL DONORS, AND ADVOCATES

The first step is to assess your current ability to track donor and potential donor data. Begin with your current pool of donors. What do you know about them? How is the information gathered and by whom, not just in the library but across your campus, multi-site public library system, or within a county or state library system?

At the simplest level, a small community library could develop a spreadsheet for relevant data about its donors and potential donors, including:

- name
- mailing and e-mail address

- phone
- age
- gender
- income bracket
- education level
- profession
- ethnic background
- lifestyle (single, college-age children, elder parent care, etc.) (Brondmo, 2000: 79–82)

Add additional information as you build relationships, perhaps noting birthdays, names of children, preferences for reading, research, or music for future gift ideas, and types of events attended. The University of Nevada, Reno Library Development Office, for example, uses Microsoft Access to track its donors and potential donors. Access allows a great deal of data to be stored with a minimum of effort. Additional fields, such as a notes column, can be added to store any information considered important.

The more data you can gather about a patron, the easier it becomes to personalize follow-up contacts with them and to identify services and resources relevant to them. Donor/advocate profiles are the foundation for developing quality service relationships, but they become especially important when reaching out to virtual users.

For larger systems, a commercial software package is a wise investment to help fundraisers maintain efficient records for large in-house donor databases. Academic libraries should investigate opportunities for resource sharing with their campus development office. The Development Officer of the University of Nevada, Reno, Libraries, for example, has online access to The Raiser's Edge software from Blackbaud, which is used across the campus for tracking data about UNR alumni and friends (www.blackbaud.com). This resource complements the library's in-house Access database, and, because it tracks all alumni and donors to the University, it is much more comprehensive. Public and school libraries should determine whether fundraising software is already available in city, county, or state government offices. If so, does it fit their needs for gathering patron/donor data? Does the license allow multiple users throughout a public library or school library system? Standardized software usage throughout a system facilitates communication between different groups and simplifies work for everyone involved.

Plan on long-term use of your in-house database for the lifetime of your organization's relationship with its donors and potential donors. Keep personal data private and secure, and make it easy for donors to provide more data as your relationship with them matures. When creating interactive Web forms to gather user information, however, make most of the data fields optional. This is a way of maintaining the trust of your virtual patrons. "The most effective subscription forms . . . tie every question directly to the value delivered and make it clear which fields are required and which are optional" (Brondmo, 2000: 83).

ATTRACTING DONORS, PROSPECTIVE DONORS, AND ADVOCATES THROUGH WEB SITES

A subsidiary company of Procter & Gamble has a position entitled "Director of Customer Delight," whose goal is to reinforce customer loyalty (Rapp and Martin, 2001). Pleasing the donor and prospective donor is as crucial for nonprofit organizations as customer satisfaction is in the for-profit arena. Satisfied users reward a library with their loyalty and support. To compete with other Internet attractions, libraries must create an ongoing bond with their virtual users and find ways to transform them into donors and advocates. Such bonds form when one-of-a-kind quality relationships are developed, the kind of quality service that stands above and apart from the snazzier bells and whistles of commercial Web sites. The appeal of the Internet is its potential in helping blur the line between a library's product and service for the virtual patron (Rapp and Martin, 2001).

"The best way to get a customer is to serve them a product they're interested in," notes Steve Lacy, President of the Integrated and Interactive Media Group for Meredith Corporation, which publishes *Better Homes and Gardens* and *Ladies' Home Journal* (Rapp and Martin, 2001: 30).

POTENTIAL DONORS AND DEMOGRAPHICS

Once you have a database to identify prospects, you can strategize about how to provide the most appealing information and services for them. Fundraising experts specialize in conducting demographic analyses to identify different philanthropic psychographics for various population groups. Librarians should take advantage of such analyses when planning Web sites. Careful attention to demographic variations can help transform potential donors and advocates into active donors and advocates. Generation and ethnic differences in financial support for nonprofit causes exist at the national level in the USA. An understanding of predictable characteristics drawn from demographic data is invaluable when planning donor strategy. Happily, determining which demographic and philanthropic trends are relevant is easier than interpreting tea leaves. *Transforming Fundraising* provides very useful demographic insights for libraries (Nichols, 1999).

Generational Differences

- The children of the Great Depression, those born before 1939, tend to be fiscally conservative. They are civic-minded and believe they have a duty to help make society better. Loyalty and duty particularly motivate men to make donations. They tend to prefer cash transactions and distrust newer finance technologies, especially electronic transfer of funds and Web-based purchases or donations.

- World War II babies, born from 1940–1945, entered an uncertain world of rationing and global turmoil. They were taught to support the will of the group and to be selfless. Those in retirement are finally reaping the rewards of a lifetime of hard work and are learning to indulge themselves. They also tend to prefer cash transactions and distrust newer financial technologies. Concerns about longer lifespans and health needs are causing this group to rethink their retirement and philanthropic strategies. Like the Depression Generation, however, they remember hard times and are motivated by loyalty and duty to pay back to society for the benefits they've enjoyed.

- The news-making baby boomers, born from 1946–1964, now comprise 42 percent of the adult USA population. They had the luxury of idealism during their formative years and believe in changing the world. They are comfortable with a credit card balance lifestyle and are generous in their philanthropy. However, they do not like workplace giving programs and prefer to support causes that are linked to their personal lives. For example, they are more likely to support a research fund for a disease that has affected someone in their immediate family. While boomers have a track record of active participation in nonprofit causes, time conflicts are lowering their attendance at special fundraising events. Their comfort level with newer technologies is often driven by what they've had to adapt to in their work environment.

- The baby busters, generation x, are the numerically smaller group born from 1965–1977. They distrust the American Dream and doubt they'll be better off than their parents. They'll still be working when the boomers retire. X'ers tend to be pragmatic, wanting to fix the world instead of change it. They are highly computer literate and prefer the cashless society. Like boomers, however, they dislike workplace giving and prefer personal charities and personal involvement in them. They often have high discretionary incomes, but they may still be living with their parents.

- The baby boomlets, born from 1978–1994, are the internet generation. They are civic-minded children of idealistic parents and can influence the philanthropic decisions of their parents and grandparents. They are growing up in a world with fewer boundaries than previous generations, and they expect global connectivity. They are very comfortable with interactive technology. Like the boomers and generation x, they prefer personal charities, oftentimes as volunteers. This is an early indicator that they may eventually be generous financial donors, but they are years away from being in such a position.

Gender Considerations

A traditional patriarchal approach to identifying potential donors is a very retro twentieth century attitude. Women today

- are more highly educated than previous generations
- have fewer children
- are more likely to be in the workforce
- enjoy higher salaries than did their predecessors
- may have no children and live alone
- tend to live seven years longer than men do
- outnumber men three-to-one after age 85

During the first quarter of the twenty-first century, the elderly in the USA will be predominantly female. Thus, 86 percent of wealth in this country passes through the hands of women.

Women tend to have different philanthropic priorities than men. While they make three times as many philanthropic gifts as men, they tend to be more financially cautious. Generally, men respond well to the competition in some fundraising campaigns, but women don't. Women are potentially good prospects for planned giving, but they want convenience and respect for their achievements. Some campuses actually have separate funding campaigns targeting only women (Nichols, 1999). As Faith Popcorn has noted in *EVEolution* (2001), her in-depth analysis of the best marketing approaches for women, these days everyone is wearing multiple hats and attempting to juggle various demands on their time. Since many of today's female college students are nontraditional, often with full-time employment and family responsibilities, it makes sense for libraries to try to simplify their lives. Popcorn's summary of her marketing insights about women at www.faithpopcorn.com/trends/eveolution.htm may provide libraries with many ideas for customizing Web pages for women patrons.

Sexual Orientation

Another nontraditional angle for fundraisers to consider is to segment current and potential patrons and donors by sexual orientation. Ongoing civic challenges for economic equity and tolerance still undermine the ability to obtain reliable demographics for this population. The emergence of positive portrayals of gay, lesbian, bisexual, and transgendered (GLBT) people in popular culture, however, along with the establishment of professional groups such as the American Library Association's Gay, Lesbian, Bisexual, and Transgendered Round Table, indicate that old prejudices and fears are slowly being replaced with tolerance and understanding.

Like the ethnic minorities who endured the civil rights struggles of a generation ago, GLBT people demand acceptance by mainstream society and equal, not special, consideration. Libraries, with their tradition of freedom of information, are strong contenders for the philanthropic response of the GLBT population. Library resources, services, and programming-supporting GLBT interests speak louder than any promotional words, however. Information posted on a library Internet site affords anonymity, confidentiality, and discretion for people researching sensitive topics. Libraries are in a position to provide current, relevant information to the GLBT population in a neutral, safe virtual setting, thus earning their loyalty and support (Davis, 2000).

Disabled Supporters

Other groups that fundraisers shouldn't overlook are the disabled. In 1993, almost 43 million USA citizens had recognized disabilities. The National Organization on Disability (www.nod.org) personalizes that number: "One out of five Americans has a disability." A quick glance at the age clusters of our population shows that more and more of us will enter the ranks of the disabled, in one form or another, as age and accidents take their toll. The disabled represent a niche outreach opportunity for fundraisers, however. It makes sense to support the information interests of 20 percent of the USA's population. Nonprofit organizations that actively cultivate the disabled and strive to meet their needs will simultaneously impress their spouses, family, friends, and business associates (Reedy, 1993). That is the kind of return on effort investment that libraries cannot afford to ignore.

DIFFERENT STROKES: NICHE MARKETING

Many fundraising books are available on how to market to potential donors using traditional offline methods. The challenge we face now is to develop innovative ways to use new online methods to supplement traditional fundraising activities and, more importantly, harness them to reach a new generation of traditional and nontraditional donors.

The way to approach this daunting task is niche marketing, based on your in-house database of donor information. Systematically acquire new donors by targeting a previously identified demographic segment and cultivating people in that category with relevant services and information. What interests do the individuals in the segment have in common? What characteristics naturally group them as candidates for specific outreach efforts or services? Does the group's size or strategic importance justify developing a "virtual community" for them via your Web site? Content-rich, high-quality virtual communities are especially appreciated by those who, for whatever reason, do not come to a traditional library for their information needs. Linking to regional resources, such as a local little theatre's forthcoming plays calendar, is beneficial for many virtual communities. Such goodwill gestures foster a spirit of cooperation between the library and the larger community without requiring much staff time.

Once you've caught a potential donor's attention, the goal is to convince them that they want regular contact with your organization. E-mail and interactive Web forms are the easiest way to establish communication with distant users. Listen to their input and solicit responses to a few questions for a basic profile in your in-house database. After the first substantive contact by a new donor, you may begin your library's service relationship with them by delivering tangible value. Use what you know about their interests to provide relevant information, news, entertainment and targeted promotions.

As the relationship matures through successive satisfactory interactions, the potential donor will develop a committed relationship to your library and become an ally. "Community On Line" (html.miningco.com/cs/communityonline/index.htm) is a useful Web site for assisting librarians charged with developing virtual communities. It provides how-to articles, Web design tips, forums, chat rooms, and links to relevant Web design tools. Another site that provides support for developing virtual communities is available at www.benton.org/Practice/Toolkit/community.html. Sponsored by the Benton Foundation, the site is information rich with practical applications and advice for creating high-quality Web resources for your library's virtual visitors. Web appeal will vary according to the group you are focusing on.

UNIVERSITY ALUMNI AND LIBRARY TRUSTEES

In 1996, 81 percent of Internet users were university graduates. A "Multimedia Audiences" sampling conducted by Mediamark Research, Inc. in the spring of 2000 found that 76.5 percent of people who'd used the Internet in the previous month were college graduates (Mediamark, 2000). This means most of the online community is preselected to be somewhat receptive to fundraising for higher education. Academic libraries should form an online partnership with their campus alumni association. Create an area within the library's Web pages for library-related news that would be of interest to alumni and link to existing alumni association Web pages for added value. If there is a master campus Web calendar for forthcoming cultural and sports events, link to that, too. Make sure your reference staff knows about alumni-targeted Web pages so that they'll take advantage of them during alumni encounters when campus offices are closed.

Value-Added Services Provided and Promoted Through the Web

Think of ways the library can add value to alumni's lives. The University of Nevada, Reno (UNR), provides a free lifetime library card to its alumni. Since any family member can use the card, we often have children of our local alumni coming in to do research for their school projects. Consider arranging a mini-reunion for engineering or social work graduates along with faculty from their academic departments. You can provide informational content on new resources for practitioners in their field and provide participants with an opportunity to network with their peers while strengthening their interest in their alma mater. Take advantage of such events to alert attendees to current fundraising campaigns, recent library achievements, and the library's vision for its future. Capture the event through photos and text on your Web site.

Consider compiling a list of books by alumni authors for display on the Web site. To get such a list started takes some detective work, but librarians certainly have the skills to track down published works. Once the list is begun, you can publicize its URL in your university's alumni newsletters and arrange for links to it from the university's alumni Web space. This might be the resource that first attracts alumni to the library's site. The list will grow as alumni send you the names of additional alumni authors and their books. An alumni authors list compiled at the New Mexico State University Library (lib.nmsu.edu/depts/specol/authors.html) attracted a great deal of attention in the local press and some sizable donations from authors who appreciated the recognition.

Consider having different Web areas by clusters of graduation years. Not only would this Web design direct alumni to Web pages specifically designed for them, but it could facilitate their networking with their former classmates.

Mississippi State University has created a four-star ranked Web site for its alumni and development programs (msuinfo.ur. msstate.edu/friends/). Besides online order forms for fundraising merchandise, their site offers entertaining informational content such as lyrics to school songs and audio links for the songs' melodies. Useful links for alumni planning a trip back to your campus might include a local weather-travel advisory site (including road construction alerts) and a calendar of forthcoming campus and community events.

Communication and Information Exchange

Providing sites for interactive information exchange is a way of ensuring dynamic library-centered conversation among potential donors and advocates. The more a library is viewed as "with it," the more attractive it becomes to potential donors and advocates. Set aside a portion of the alumni Web area to explain how your library's fundraising goals will solve problems for current students, faculty, and the region. Provide an interactive form and ask a few questions for a basic "potential donor" profile for your in-house database. Let alumni "opt in" to receive a free copy of the Friends of the Library newsletter if it is not yet available online. Would your alumni like to receive occasional e-mail alerts from the library about relevant new resources and services? Let them identify specific areas of interest and opt into an e-mail alert service. Coordinate this effort with your subject specialists, who often are already providing similar alerts to faculty and students in their assigned academic areas. Creating a list of interested alumni to copy on such e-mail alerts is not labor intensive.

Access to Valuable Information Resources

Harvard University has developed a way to provide access to licensed online databases for alumni of its Business School. The eBaker Library program provides alumni off-campus access to four business databases: ABI Inform (ProQuest), Career Search, Hoover's Online, and OneSource Global Business Browser. MBS graduates, graduates of programs in Executive Education, and doctoral recipients are eligible for this fee-based service. The Harvard Business School Working Knowledge Web site and the Baker Library at Harvard are co-sponsoring alumni access to the databases. The eBaker project (www.hbsworkingknowledge.hbs.edu/ebaker/) links to the portal of information and activities of the Harvard Business School. The portal was designed to help Harvard business alumni stay current with the rapid changes in business and management. Currently, 1,355 alumni are customers of this service. The cost of the service is partially underwritten by Harvard University, which hopes to see a return in its investment in the form of greater alumni satisfaction and long-term support for the Harvard Business Library by alumni and Friends (Michalak, 2000).

The University of Pennsylvania entered a partnership with Northern Light Technology to enable virtual users to download articles via their portal. Northern Light provides the "Research Engine" that enables virtual users to search a full-text database of over 7,100 periodicals. More than 80 percent of the full-text search results are freely available, and the rest are available for $3-$5 each. The UP Alumni and Friends portal may be viewed at www.library.upenn.edu/portal. The service for article purchases from Northern Light may be viewed at www.library.upenn.edu/portal/nl/search.html.

Develop a special Web area for your library's alumni or trustees. This is an occasion when rank should have some privileges. Provide informational/educational marketing as well as interactivity to this group:

- update them on the library's achievements and new resources
- share anecdotal glimpses of how the campus and/or region are benefiting from the library's programs
- describe the library's disabled access resources
- prepare a Web page sequence of the library's history, from its beginnings (however humble) to its visionary hopes for the future
- give trustees and administrators the opportunity to list their e-mail addresses for networking among themselves
- make it easy for them to communicate with the library. Provide a link to your e-mail reference service and an e-mail link to your library director or dean
- display photos of the director and the trustees
- provide a link to the campus online calendar for forthcoming events and develop an interactive registration form

for special library-sponsored events at which they'd be honored guests

- appeal to trustees to set a good example with early donations during major fundraising campaigns. The goal for your trustees is always 100 percent participation at a meaningful level
- provide an interactive form for them to update their profile data. Remind them to alert you if they've moved or gotten a new e-mail address

COMMUNITY ACTIVISTS

Community activists are sometimes overlooked, but they are potential supporters for libraries, academic or public. They have networks that can be tapped on the library's behalf. Host special events to cultivate new audiences from this sector. Use your database to create a mailing list and spotlight the event on your Web site. In conjunction with this effort, examine your region's demographics and develop appropriate outreach efforts for various ethnic groups.

What are the main environmental and social concerns in your region? Provide information on how your library recycles resources and is otherwise earth-friendly. Find ways to increase public-private partnerships for delivery of educational and social services to the broader community.

Provide an interactive data-gathering Web form, allowing online visitors to identify their areas of interest. Let them submit their e-mail addresses if they want to receive periodic alerts about relevant new resources or forthcoming library/campus events. Make use of the expertise in your region. What films or books would they recommend for the library to acquire to raise public awareness about their social causes or cultural avocations?

Invite community volunteers to serve on an ongoing listserv advisory group for the library. This will enable them to participate in dialogue about the library's future course of service. Make sure it is easy for everyone to "opt out" of such a virtual group whenever they wish.

THE LOCAL BUSINESS COMMUNITY

The for-profit arena operates on a quid pro quo basis. For this affluent and influential group, develop a Web area providing information of value to corporate executives. Provide an educational page on cross-cultural etiquette for business travelers and companies hosting international business associates. Academic libraries might recruit their business librarian to write new resource alerts for regional company newsletters. Provide an online events calendar for forthcoming business school public lectures and evening courses. Borrow from the dot.com arena to provide fee-based advertising opportunities on your Web pages for businesses. Maxymuk (2001) discusses successful partnerships libraries are experiencing with companies by entering affiliate programs. An international list of libraries experimenting with corporate affiliations is available at (www.lights.com/webcats/support/libs.html). Some useful Web-based strategies to use with this group are to

- seek community partnerships for grant opportunities that could increase the delivery of educational and social services to your region
- use this Web area for opinion testing and sampling of your regional business niche. Solicit a cross-section of volunteers for an ongoing e-mail focus group
- encourage feedback on what services and resources would be of greatest interest to them. It would be best if your business librarian could serve as moderator for them
- provide opportunities for businesspeople to opt in for occasional e-mail alerts concerning relevant new resources, online products, and campus events. The support of your business librarian is crucial for the success of such an outreach effort

MAJOR DONORS

How is the Internet changing outreach to major donors? For those of the Great Depression and World War II generations, informational screens explaining why donations are needed can supplement direct-mail campaigns and printed brochures. Recruit a few of your most loyal donors from these demographic segments to showcase on your development Web pages. Use photographs and quotations to convey the results of their donations and why they chose to support the library. Mention the Web address in print newsletters and press releases.

Use your Web site to educate your constituents concerning your organization's needs in the nonprofit political arena. Provide information about legal matters that will impact philanthropists. Mississippi State University's Foundation, for example, uses its Web site to provide coverage of recent gift law (msuinfo.ur.msstate.edu/devweb/giftlaw.html). In 2001, the National Council of Nonprofit Associations and Independent Sector launched a Web site that serves as a portal for those interested in public policy issues affecting nonprofit organizations (www.givevoice.org).

FRIENDS OF THE LIBRARY AND VOLUNTEERS

Friends of the Library organizations are important because their membership often includes many of the library's major gift donors. Often, too, the annual giving program for the library is linked to Friends memberships. Moreover, Friends are often leaders of their alumni reunion classes. Alumni classes frequently decide to make a large gift to their alma mater's library. In addition to monetary gifts, Friends may donate books or manuscripts to the library or they may generously volunteer their time to help the library with special events or short-term projects. Library Friends are a link to the library's regional community and population. Therefore, Friends can provide libraries with invaluable feedback on how the library is meeting the community's information needs.

Think about ways to use the Web to enhance support for your Friends of the Library organization. How can you strengthen your Friends board via your Web site? What online benefits can you offer to library Friends? Membership dues result in higher expectations about online content and benefits. What types of full-text publications can be added to the Friends' Web site? Corson-Finnerty and Blanchard (1998) note that your Friends Web site can serve as a method of showcasing past events, announcing forthcoming events, and attracting new Friends for your library.

At the University of Nevada, Reno, we have created an "Events and Tours" link (Figure 9–1) that provides pictures of past successful Friends events, such as cultural trips to France, Greece, California, and Virginia. Photographs from our recent "Palates and Palettes: Food and Art of France" expedition will eventually give way to virtual memories of more recent events. Our Friends site is kept current, with information about older events eventually being "un-linked" (see more information at www.library.unr.edu/friends/).

The Web Portal for community users at the University of Pennsylvania (UP) was designed for those who cannot come to the library in person, for whatever reason. UP's Alumni and Friends portal (www.library.upenn.edu/portal/) includes buttons that provide access to e-news and e-journals, quality Web sites, a library book club, the library's online catalog, and alerts about new library resources.

Your Friends Web site should be responsive to the needs of your particular Friends group. The number of services you offer your Friends is limited only by your available staff resources:

- investigate the feasibility of offering e-mail accounts to Friends who join at a specific level. Yale University and the University of Michigan provide e-mail to their alumni.

Figure 9–1. Friends "Events" Page

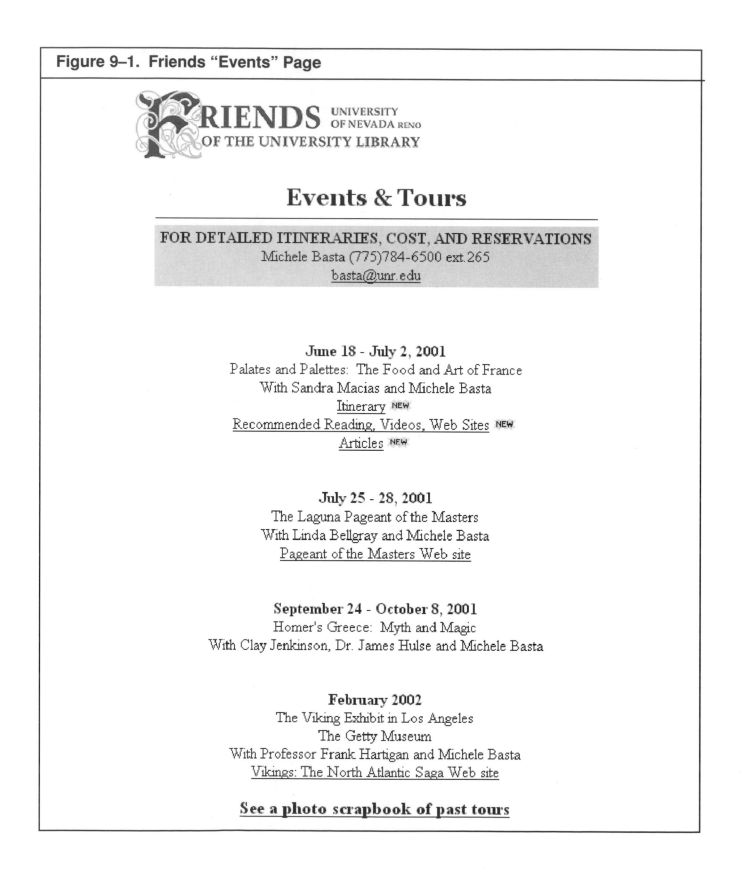

Network security concerns must be addressed when contemplating widening the pool of people served by your e-mail system, however

- provide updates on library achievements via an online edition of the print Friends newsletter
- provide an online membership and membership renewal form for your Friends group. Link to a site offering library and/or campus merchandise for sale online. Negotiate for a discount for Friends members
- post book reviews written by Friends members and offer the book through on-line purchase from your campus or a community bookstore
- consider creating a new category of "E-Friends," who don't pay membership dues and only receive e-mail alerts about relevant free online resources and/or forthcoming volunteer opportunities
- solicit volunteers for current and forthcoming Friends projects. Volunteers usually welcome the opportunity to provide meaningful service for a specific period of time. Let your volunteers help nurture projects to success, and they'll commit to a long-term relationship with your organization
- provide a way for Friends and volunteers to update their profile data for your in-house database, such as a new e-mail or snail mail address. Provide an e-mail link or Web form that enables them to suggest areas in which they're interested in volunteering. Just as for your other supporters, find as many ways as possible to give public credit to your Friends and volunteers for their contributions of time. Explain how their efforts make a difference in your library's achieving its goals.

SOME THINGS ARE FOR EVERYONE: PROMOTE WHAT YOU HAVE

Corson-Finnerty and Blanchard (1998) state that libraries can use the Web to create a new library image that can be changed periodically to match the interests of a large, diverse group of virtual users and supporters. What are your library's areas of specialization? Draw upon them to provide unique information to a cross-section of patrons and supporters. A unique component of the UNR Libraries, for example, is our Basque Studies Library. Its Web site (www.library.unr.edu/depts/basqlib/) is designed to attract and reach out to many constituencies besides its primary user group, the Basque Studies researchers and students affiliated with the university.

ONLINE EXHIBITS AND SHOWCASES

When designing a Web portal for your library's virtual community, don't forget to include an area for exhibitions of the unique and special resources that constitute your library's treasures. Online exhibitions may be used as a "front door" to lead prospective patrons and donors further into your library's Web pages. Advances in the quality of digital photography have made it worthwhile to mount online exhibitions of materials for distant users. The Web has become a showcase for many libraries' Special Collections holdings. Not only are Web-based exhibits a secure way to share priceless resources with the public, but such Web sites are powerful public relations tools for libraries. For examples of online exhibition sites, take a virtual visit to the:

- Library of Congress (memory.loc.gov/ammem/ amhome.html)
- University of Nevada, Reno (www.library.unr.edu/specoll/ artwork/)
- University of Pennsylvania (www.library.upenn.edu/ special/events.html#virtual)
- University of Virginia (www.lib.virginia.edu/speccol)

Some libraries have links from their Special Collections Department to their Friends Web site, and the links can go both ways. Special Collections departments have interesting materials that can be shared with your Friends members. Since some Special Collections departments are responsible for managing the library's Friends organization, finding their common interests is a natural avenue to pursue.

SATISFY YOUR SECONDARY USERS

Many academic libraries serve the general public in their region, supplementing the resources of public libraries. The demand for online information is growing in direct proportion to the Internet's permeation of the general population. How can a library meet the increasing expectations of virtual users who do not meet the criteria of the library's primary clientele?

Licensing restrictions prohibit libraries from allowing everyone access to online databases. However, some online databases are open to the general public. Sandy Lewis (2001) writes about ways to share public URLs with non-affiliated patrons and donors. Analysis of your in-house database of patron/donor profiles should help you identify relevant databases for virtual users who are not entitled to direct connection to all of your library's online resources. Examples of free bibliographic databases are *ingenta* (formerly *Carl UnCover*), *ERIC*, *Agricola*, and *Medline*. The interdisciplinary scope of these resources makes them relevant to a large cross-section of people.

EVENTS AND HUMAN RESOURCES

You might also consider developing a Web page that underscores areas of expertise of the library dean or director and other information specialists available for presentations to service and educational organizations in the community. Patrons can fill out e-forms to receive information about scheduling a talk or presentation. Sharing your staff's expertise with other segments of your community is a way to break down perceived barriers between "town and gown" and a way to share information that might otherwise be unavailable to the community-at-large. Try to attain a schedule of at least one speaking engagement per month in the region (Nichols, 2001). The Web is ideally suited for the organization of information about speakers and events. Use it to provide

- a calendar of forthcoming library and/or campus events of interest to different age groups
- an interactive registration form for those who plan on attending an open house, participating in a cultural tour sponsored by the library or University or other outreach event
- visual Web memories of past donor/Friends events, explaining what they accomplished for the library's mission

If you are in an academic library, work with your campus development office to identify a group of financial planning specialists who are willing to provide advice via e-mail to prospective donors in all categories. Perhaps you can enlist specialists from the ranks of your alumni, enabling them to volunteer their time and expertise to support their alma mater.

MAINTAINING YOUR E-PRESENCE

Designing informative Web sites and providing interactive Web forms to gather profile data from your potential supporters is only half the job. You must consider various factors when planning on how your library will support informative and interactive Web sites. As Web sites become more information rich, more staff time is required for checking links and adding, modifying, and deleting material. It is important to develop a systematic schedule for regular feedback to your niche marketing groups. Someone must be assigned the duty of monitoring all patron/donor feedback, quantifying what is important to patrons/donors, getting the relevant data to the most appropriate people in the library for action, and reporting back to the niche groups on how their ideas are making a difference. Moreover, to assess the success of a fundraising program, libraries need to audit their public image. Steele and Elder (1991) write about library staff and fundraising officers taking a self-image test to see if the library is meeting the needs of its community. Although it is difficult to gauge whether the library is adequately serving its constituency, measurement of service is important.

If you are accepting online donations or pledges, you should enact an "after-marketing matrix" program to maximize donor retention. This is a formal, multi-step effort for following up on first-time donors. Because there is always a degree of uncertainty about whether a Web transaction has gone through, you should respond instantly through e-mail that the donation was received, and then follow up with more traditional responses. Prepare a new donor welcome packet. Have envelopes printed with "Thank you!" on the outside to use for follow-up contacts with all donors. Include a copy of your Friends' newsletter and a fact sheet or general brochure, along with the business card of your development officer. Personalize each letter of thanks as much as possible. Similarly, if Web forms offer registration for forthcoming events, opt-ins for e-mail alert service, or virtual membership in a book discussion listserv, it is crucial to provide prompt, regular follow-through by designated members of your staff.

In a time of downsized staff and dwindling newcomers to librarianship, libraries are challenged by the 24/7 presence of the Internet. The for-profit model for adequate staffing for successful Internet marketing is rare in the nonprofit arena (Brondmo, 2000). The challenge for libraries is to determine how existing staff positions can be redefined to take on the new kinds of work required to support virtual libraries. One possibility is to match the interest areas of your donors/patrons with assigned subject areas of your collection development librarians. This is an equitable way to distribute the virtual support work. The hard decisions involve identifying which traditional services and resources should be phased out in order to reallocate staff and financial resources for development of the virtual library. What software and hardware expertise exists among your staff? How can those skills be enhanced? Is there funding for new hires to cover some of this work so that your librarians can continue providing their own expertise to support the library's mission? Could an academic library use interns from a public relations or marketing program? The impact on staff time cannot be ignored. Tailor the number of Web sites and the amount of material and services offered accordingly. Keep your organization honest. Follow through and do what you say you'll do. This is the foundation of integrity, and it is often unavailable via the Internet.

ASSURING PRIVACY

American libraries have a long tradition of providing confidentiality for their patrons. The reference interview and circulation records are areas in which USA patrons can expect respect for their privacy. The frequent news stories about hacker attacks against high-profile targets do not persuade the financially cautious that it is safe to trade their credit card information for a Friends membership, a donation, or an online purchase. You will reassure your potential donors if you follow these guidelines:

- develop a clear and unambiguous privacy statement and display it on each Web page that solicits information from online visitors
- advise them of what data you collect about them and how you intend to use it
- let them know that they can request removal from your organization's users' profile database
- never share a patron's personal profile information with other organizations without express permission from the individual
- make sure your system has adequate data protection
- as a community service, provide informational alerts to online users concerning ways they should protect their home and/or office computers, too (Brondmo, 2000)

FUNDRAISING ON THE WEB

The goal of fundraising is the same, whether it is pursued on or offline: to raise funds. It is imperative to find as many opportunities as possible to ask for money from your donor pool. The Internet provides a new medium for one-to-one solicitation, whether by e-mail, desktop monitor, or Palm device. Fundraising with the Web is still in its infancy, but the Web can be a very effective tool for the development officer. However, it would be a mistake to completely abandon traditional fundraising methodologies and place all of your library's capital campaign hopes in the Web basket. A personal, human connection is vital for a successful fundraising effort, and the Web can be a rather passive, impersonal place.

Traditional fundraising strategy is to allocate the largest percentage of your efforts in the stewardship of your best donors. Translating this for an online campaign, Corson-Finnerty and Blanchard (1998) suggest that the highest priority for a fundraising Web site is to support your organization's major gifts program.

The design of your Web site has a direct impact on its effectiveness as a fundraising tool. The last thing you want is to provide a Web encounter that potential donors find slow to load, confusing, boring, or out of date. *The Fund Raiser's Guide to the Internet* (Johnston, 1999) suggests using a quick-loading home page that fits onto a single, nonscrolling screen. This design saves time for a Web visitor and spares them the annoying necessity of manually scrolling down to see the entire page. Other principles to keep in mind when developing a fundraising site are to

- be concise and precise
- follow the general standards for effective writing
- avoid cliches and trite terminology. You do not want to use overly formal language, but you should maintain dignity and sophistication. Think about the impression your Web message conveys to virtual visitors
- avoid redundancies, such as "online" or "here is"
- avoid the "under construction" note, so prevalent on the Web—it has no place on your fundraising pages. You do not want to give potential donors the impression that your campaign isn't ready for prime time (Johnston, 1999)

The hitdonate.net site provides a wealth of information for designing Web sites for fundraising (www.hitdonate.net).

HIGHLIGHT YOUR NEEDS AND OFFER RECOGNITION

The Web expands a fundraiser's palette and provides exposure to an ever-widening audience. Make your Web pages catchy but not cutesy. Your first-priority funding needs should be clearly stated, along with the requested amounts, naming opportunities, and contact information. Each donation opportunity page should include a method of making a contribution by snail mail, as well as via a Web form, and should supply a telephone number to enable a prospective donor to talk to a real person about donation options. Other information about current donors and past successes should be easy to find.

Work with your technical staff to explore the feasibility of using *CUseeMe Videoware* (www.fvc.com/products/videoware.htm) that, with accompanying voice software, transmits live images via the Internet. Thus equipped, your development officer can provide a "virtual visit" for prospective major donors who cannot or do not want to come to the library. The use of such equipment makes solicitation contacts more convenient for wealthy and affluent baby boomers and generation x'ers and increases the outreach capabilities of your development staff. However, don't forget to use television and space ads to duplicate your message to your audience across various media formats.

Moreover, provide noninteractive informational elements to your fundraising Web pages, including easily understandable charts or graphs that explain how donated funds are or will be used. Mal Warwick is a veteran author of fundraising books. The Web site for Mal Warwick & Associates, Inc., provides many useful how-to ideas for libraries grappling with Internet fundraising (www.malwarwick.com).

Tier donors by amount of donation and develop a scaled system of rewards for them. The value of the benefits should correspond to the level of support, but it should be easy for all donors to receive some sort of reward. Find ways to thank all of your donors, supporters, and volunteers, both online and offline, within the library and in regional media outlets. Surprise your best donors with creative and unexpected benefits. Thoughtful gestures such as these will keep their interest in the library alive, because you find innovative ways to make their support fun and rewarding.

OFFER OPTIONS AND LEVELS OF INFORMATION

Yale University's Office of Development uses its Web site to explain the many donation options available to its supporters. Categories of giving are defined, along with explanations of how donations are used to improve Yale's service to its students. There are links to information pages designed to assist in the selection of the most appropriate donation option for an individual's personal financial situation. Explore this site at www.yale.edu/development/.

Mississippi State University takes advantage of streaming video software to inform its virtual visitors about

- the university's areas of research specialization
- the history of the university
- testimonials from students about the value of their educational experience at MSU (msuinfo.ur.msstate.edu/video/)

The University of Rhode Island's Fund Raising site has a pull-down menu that allows virtual donors to direct their gift to different areas of the university. The menu provides links to a variety of funding options, including:

- an annual program
- a parent's fund
- a capital campaign
- the graduate fund
- special campaigns

Note the site's privacy and security statement and the subtle encouragement embedded in the phrase, "all online donations are tax-deductible" (advance.uri.edu/fundraising/default.htm).

BUILD A USER-FRIENDLY SITE

Proponents of the Internet stress its convenience. Take time to assess your fundraising campaign from the potential donor's point of view. Do you provide a choice of response methods, enabling the donor to use the contact method most convenient to them? A virtual visitor who is not provided an 800 number or who doesn't get a prompt response to their e-mail query may decide against supporting your organization.

If you sell merchandise via your Web site as a fundraising gimmick, do you make ordering hassle-free? (Rapp and Martin, 2001) If you are exploring the feasibility of merchandising as a component of your campaign, visit www.fundraising.com/. It claims the title of "the #1 Internet Fundraising Company" and specializes in merchandising products. A megasite for library fundraisers is Helping.org, which is sponsored by the AOL Time-Warner Foundation. Its "Nonprofit Resources" section provides links to high quality sites that assist nonprofit organizations in getting the most out of the Internet as a funding tool (helping.org/nonprofit/index.adp).

When your fundraising site is ready for the world, systematically visit the major Web search engines and use their "submit URL" or "submit new site" features. On a more practical level, make sure your fundraising site is generously linked throughout the library's Web pages and/or those of your parent organization. What other cross-connections make marketing sense for your library's virtual fundraising efforts? Keep track of all such links, however. They'll need prompt maintenance whenever a URL changes.

FINANCIAL TRANSACTIONS

Once you've developed a creative, informative, and inspirational fundraising Web site, don't forget to include ways for potential donors to make their donations! Provide a hypertext link that displays a preaddressed e-mail form. Provide contact information for your library's development officer: e-mail, telephone, and snail mail. Remember that you want to make giving easy, so accommodate as many different methods of communication and donation as possible.

Corson-Finnerty and Blanchard (1998) discuss a variety of Web-based financial transactions suitable for fundraising sites. These include online pledging, credit card donations, and entertainment vehicles such as auctions, games, and gambling.

ONLINE PLEDGING

Your Web area should devote a page to pledging options. Display the possible levels of support on an interactive form. Provide the potential donor with choices for both the amount of their financial support and the frequency with which they wish to participate. Some people are interested in monthly or quarterly donation schedules, while others only want to give once a year.

Carefully select designations for donation categories that support the self-esteem of donors. On the UNR Friends of the Library site, for example, those who join with a contribution of $1,000 or more are named "President's Associate for the Library." See Figure 9–2.

Online pledging should be confirmed with an actual signature or some other type of official written confirmation. Work with your Systems and/or Web staff to develop an automatic e-mail response message for preliminary feedback to virtual donors. After receiving an online pledge, follow through with a telephone call and arrange an in-person visit with the donor, if it is desired. The follow-up contact is an opportunity to gather more informa-

Figure 9–2. Categorizing Friends

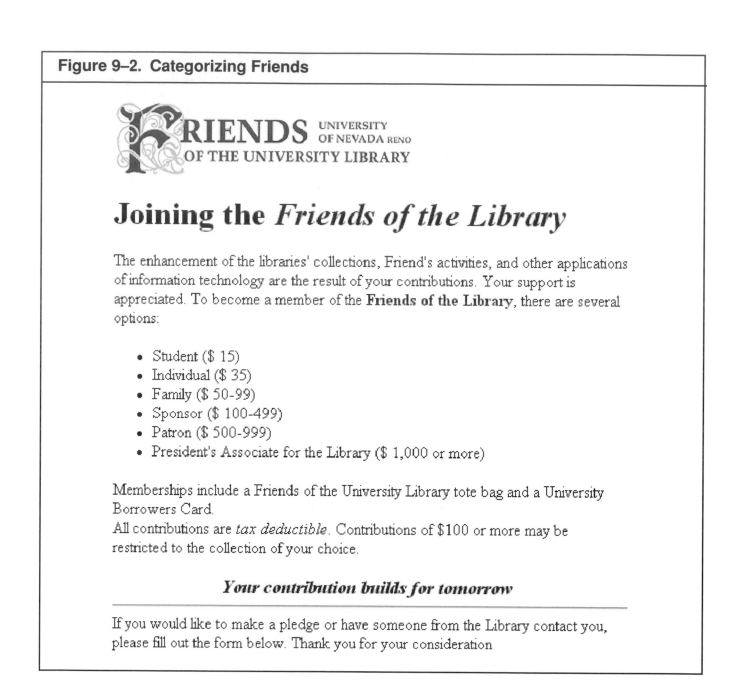

RIENDS UNIVERSITY OF NEVADA RENO
OF THE UNIVERSITY LIBRARY

Joining the *Friends of the Library*

The enhancement of the libraries' collections, Friend's activities, and other applications of information technology are the result of your contributions. Your support is appreciated. To become a member of the **Friends of the Library**, there are several options:

- Student ($ 15)
- Individual ($ 35)
- Family ($ 50-99)
- Sponsor ($ 100-499)
- Patron ($ 500-999)
- President's Associate for the Library ($ 1,000 or more)

Memberships include a Friends of the University Library tote bag and a University Borrowers Card.
All contributions are *tax deductible*. Contributions of $100 or more may be restricted to the collection of your choice.

Your contribution builds for tomorrow

If you would like to make a pledge or have someone from the Library contact you, please fill out the form below. Thank you for your consideration

tion for the donor's profile in your in-house database. Moreover, it provides the development officer an opening to discuss other support options with the donor and to learn whether they're interested in perhaps serving as a volunteer or participating in a forthcoming Friends event.

CREDIT CARD TRANSACTIONS

Privacy and security are paramount concerns for Internet users. Work with your technical staff first to determine whether your Web site is a safe place for solicitation of credit card donations. Do not offer this option to your virtual donors if you cannot guarantee the security of their personal credit information.

Some libraries enjoy a privileged corporate sponsorship with a credit card company. All other libraries should cater to the diverse virtual community and make it easy for donors to use one of several major credit cards: American Express, Master Card, or Visa.

Research done by American Express has found that 81 percent of cardmembers who used their American Express card for a charitable donation agreed that credit and charge acceptance makes donations via the Internet easier. In May 2001, on the occasion of recognizing a donor for his record-setting online credit card donation of $100,000, Glenda McNeal, Vice President for New Industries at American Express, observed, "Consumers are increasingly comfortable using the Internet for e-commerce, and charities are in a unique position to capitalize on this trend. By welcoming 'e-donations,' nonprofit groups have the opportunity to improve their fundraising efforts and enhance donor satisfaction" (McNeal, 2001).

A four-step process is recommended for credit card donations:

1) Ask for a specific amount of money for a specific cause
2) Do not ask for unneeded information about donors to avoid seeming intrusive
3) Present all of the information that you have gathered from a donor on a single screen for review by the donor. Place a single "YES" button nearby for easy confirmation of the data. Give donors the convenience of making any desired corrections to their information on the same screen
4) Thank the donor three times. Have an automatic e-mail message thank the donor when s/he clicks the "YES" button. An instant display provides immediate reassurance to the donor that the software donation worked. A traditional snail mail thank you should be sent out in less than three business days after receipt of a virtual donation. Then, follow up with a telephone call to thank the donor again and to suggest forthcoming Friends or alumni events they may want to attend (Lee, 2001).

Remember, whenever you obtain new information relevant to a donor's profile, be sure to update your in-house database.

DONOR RECOGNITION

Use your Web site to showcase naming opportunities for major donors, offering tangible and public recognition for major investments, such as naming a physical facility or establishing an acquisition endowment fund for a specific subject area. Mississippi State University's Web site includes photographs of its campus "Walk of Honor" and Eternal Flame Monument, providing public recognition for its supporters.

Similarly, the Office of Development for UNR's College of Education raises money for its new building by offering memorial engravings on its foyer mural and personalized bricks in its outdoor patios (www.unr.edu/educ/ood/indexcoe.html).

Recently, Pehong Chen, founder and CEO of BroadVision, and his wife, Adele, offered a $15 million donation to Stanford to establish a new institute for the study of particle astrophysics and cosmology. The Web page acknowledging their donation is an online press release, with photographs of the donor and various university officials. There is a link to a "quicktime" video of the donor and his wife. The page provides links to other parts of the Stanford Web site and relevant "current events" sites (givingtostanford.stanford.edu/press/index.html).

The University of Pennsylvania offers another example of a high-quality Web recognition site that it developed in honor of Marian Anderson. The development staff at the Penn Library created a Web exhibition based on the material that Marian Anderson donated to the library. The Web site was used to raise $300,000 to create a Music Study Center in honor of Anderson and to promote a 100th birthday celebration for the singer. The site features Anderson's biography, photographs from her career, and audio excerpts from an interview and a few of her songs. For further details, see her site at: www.library.upenn.edu/special/gallery/anderson/. As the University of Pennsylvania has proven, a personalized Web page designed for a supporter may lead to further donations.

The Web site for UNR's Friends of the University Library provides an example of a simple but effective promotional technique. Figure 9–3 shows pictures of a new study area in the main campus library, along with the donor who provided funding for the area. We deliberately included a digitized photo of the donor with our Dean of Libraries, because the library director plays a crucial role in the fundraising process. Without the director's enthusiastic involvement and support, a fundraising effort cannot achieve its best potential. Prospective donors need to have positive contact with the power players in your library. Donors want to believe their contributions are influential and significant. It is the

Figure 9–3. Recognizing Donors on the Web

responsibility of the library director and development officer to ensure donor satisfaction in that regard.

Your fund raising Web site should include recognition of major donors' contributions. Prepare an honor roll of donors, with appropriate graphics to make it attractive and impressive. A new word, "cyber-plaquing," is emerging to describe methods of designing Web recognition for donors, volunteers, and other supporters. Virtual donor plates that identify who have given books, films, or other resources to the library are an example of cyber-plaquing. Not only does Web recognition honor current donors, but the global availability of such recognition will be attractive to future Internet-savvy donors. A few caveats need to be expressed: always get permission to use a donor's photo and name on the Internet and don't reveal the dollar amount of any donation unless the donor clearly understands that you are posting it on the Internet.

TAKE A CHANCE: ONLINE AUCTIONS, GAMES, AND GAMBLING

Auctions and Web games are clever approaches to attracting donors to online giving. The Riddler.com site, an entertainment portal for the 24/7 Media dot.com, provides examples of scavenger hunts, word games, and trivia contests that may or may not be appropriate to use with your donor community (www.riddler.com/marketers/index.html).

Corson-Finnerty and Blanchard point to a Web portal for the virtual auction community (www.usaweb.com/auction.html). Its menu directs visitors to a calendar of forthcoming auctions, an auctioneer referral service, and a free newsletter. The home page includes a link to the eBay home page.

Bidding on a Chance to Sponsor a Treasure

One idea is to conduct online auctions of sponsorships for rare items in the library's Special Collections Department. While the rare materials remain secure in their atmosphere-controlled environment, donors may bid for recognition as the sponsor for a particular treasure in the collection. A photo gallery of sponsored items could be mounted in both the Special Collections and Friends Web areas to recognize the sponsors and help make a library's unique resources more visible to patrons.

REFERENCES

Brondmo, Hans Peter. 2000. *The Eng@ged Customer: The New Rules of Internet Direct Marketing*. New York: HarperBusiness.

Corson-Finnerty, Adam, and Laura Blanchard. 1998. *Fundraising and Friend-Raising on the Web*. Chicago: American Library Association.

Davis, Judy. 2000. *A Guide to Web Marketing: Successful Promotion on the Net*. Dover, N.H.: Kogan.

Johnston, Michael. 1999. *The Fund Raiser's Guide to the Internet*. New York: John Wiley & Sons.

Lee, Marc. 2001. "The Four Step Process for Online Donations by Credit Card." Affinity Resources [Online]. Available: www.affinityresources.com/pgs/awz55donationprocess.html [2001, July 23].

Lewis, Nicole. 2000. "You've Got a Charity Solution." *Chronicle of Philanthropy* (November 30) [Online]. Available: philanthropy.com/free/articles/v13/i04/04002501.htm [2001, April 24].

Lewis, Sandy. 2001. "There is Such a Thing as a Free Lunch: Freely Accessible Databases for the Public." *Issues in Sciences and Technology Librarianship* (Winter) [Online]. Available: www.library.ucsb.edu/istl/01-winter/internet.html [2001, August 1].

Maxymuk, John. 2001. "The Green Pastures of Library Fundraising on the Internet." *The Bottom Line* 14, no. 2: 90–93.

McNeal, Glenda. 2001. "Multi-million Dollar Online Credit Card Donation Ushers in New Era of e-Philanthropy." News Release, American Express Company (May 15) [Online]. Available: home3.americanexpress.com/corp/latestnews/e-philanthropy.asp [2001, August 1].

Mediamark Research Inc. 2000. "Multimedia Audiences—Summary: 2000." in *Statistical Abstract of the United States*. Washington, D.C., U.S. Census Bureau: 567. [Online]. Available: www.census.gov/prod/2001pubs/statab/sec18.pdf (p. 5) [2001, November 13].

Michalak, Thomas J. 2000. "HBS Baker Library Takes the Lead in New Web Site Launch." *Harvard University Library Notes* 1292 (February) [Online]. Available: hul.harvard.edu/publications/library_notes/pdfs/HULN1292.pdf [2001, October 6].

Nichols, Judith E. 1999. *Transforming Fundraising: A Practical Guide to Evaluating and Strengthening Fundraising to Grow with Change*. San Francisco: Jossey-Bass.

"People with Disabilities and Specific Community Activities." 2001. National Organization on Disability (July 24) [Online]. Available: www.nod.org/cont/dsp_cont_item_view.cfm?viewType=itemView&contentId=145 [2001, August 4].

Popcorn, Faith, and Lys Marigold. 2000. *EVEolution: The Eight Truths of Marketing to Women*. New York: Hyperion.

Prince, Russ Alan. 1994. *Seven Faces of Philanthropy*. San Francisco: Jossey-Bass.

Rapp, Stan, and Chuck Martin. 2001. *Max-e-Marketing in the Net Future*. New York: McGraw-Hill.

Reedy, Joel. 1993. *Marketing to Consumers with Disabilities*. Chicago: Probus Publishing Company.

Steele, Victoria, and Stephen D. Elder. 1991. *Becoming a Fundraiser: The Principles and Practice of Library Development*. Chicago: American Library Association.

INDEX

ABOUT THE CONTRIBUTORS

RICK ANDERSON is the Director of Resource Acquisition at the University of Nevada, Reno Library. He has previously worked as Head Acquisitions Librarian at the University of North Carolina, Greensboro and as a bibliographer for Yankee Book Peddler, Inc. He has written on acquisitions, vendor relations, copyright/licensing, and the economics of information production for *Against the Grain, Serials Review* and *Library Acquisitions, Practice and Theory*, among other publications. He is editor of *CD HotList: New Releases for Libraries*.

DONNELYN CURTIS is the Director of Research Services at the University of Nevada, Reno Library. She was formerly Head of Collection Services at the New Mexico State University Library. She is a co-author of the Neal-Schuman book *Developing and Managing Electronic Journal Collections: A How-To-Do-It Manual for Librarians* and has published articles and book chapters on technical communication, information literacy training, and children's and young adult literature.

BETTY J. GLASS is the Grants Developer and Humanities Subject Specialist at the University of Nevada, Reno, Library. She is a past chair of ACRL's Women's Studies Section and writes the "Women's Studies: Feminist and Special Interest" section for *Magazines for Libraries* (Bowker). She is a co-editor of *Women in Nevada History: An Annotated Bibliography of Published Sources*. She writes the column "Intersections: New Information Resources and You" for the UNR faculty and staff paper, *Nevada News*.

ARABY Y. GREENE has been the Web Development Librarian at the University of Nevada, Reno Library since June 2000. She was formerly the Coordinator of Electronic Resources and Government Information at the University of North Carolina at Asheville, where she established a UNCA Library Web site in 1996, and chaired the Library Web Team. She taught a credit course in Library Research for 12 years, and contributed chapters to the course textbook. She also designed the interface for the Western Carolina Library Network WebPAC and was a member of the WNCLN Web team.

TERRY A. HENNER is the Head of Information and Education Services at the Savitt Medical Library, University of Nevada School of Medicine. He has previously worked as Education Services Librarian at Wright State University School of Medicine and Assistant Director of Public Services, Temple Medical School. He has written on bibliographic instruction in distance education, evaluation of online database interfaces, and videoconferencing technologies for *Medical Reference Services Quarterly* and *Bibliotheca Medica Canadiana* among other publications.

CAROL A. PARKHURST is the Director of Library Systems at the University of Nevada, Reno. For four years, until very recently, she served as the Director of Computing and Telecommunications at UNR. She is currently the library's Coordinator of Planning for a new library building. She has worked for the Multnomah County Library and for CLSI. She has been active in LITA and in developing Nevada statewide networks. She edited *Library Perspectives on NREN, the National Research and Education Network* and the *ASIS '85* conference proceedings, and she has written articles on systems and cataloging issues.

MARGRET J. RESSEL is currently a Reference Librarian and the Distance Education Librarian at the University of Nevada, Reno. She originated and coordinates Electronic Reserves within the Libraries and instructs teaching faculty on incorporating library resources into their courses. She was previously the Physical Sciences Librarian at the University of Nevada, Reno.

AMY W. SHANNON is the Head of the Life and Health Sciences Library at the University of Nevada, Reno. She has previously worked as a Science Librarian at the University of Oklahoma and Texas A&M University. She is active in the Science and Technology Section of ACRL. She has written on the development of online college courses, managing selection and acquisition of online materials, and science reference resources.

MILLIE L. SYRING has been the head of Document Delivery Services at the University of Nevada, Reno since 1995. Previously she was head of Interlibrary Loan at the Nevada State Library and Archives for six years. She has written about collection development and document delivery.

VICKI L. TOY SMITH is a Catalog Librarian at the University of Nevada, Reno. She has previously worked at the University of California, Berkeley, the University of Michigan, and University

Microfilms International. Vicki has written articles on special formats cataloging, cooperative cataloging projects, and local cataloging procedures for *Cataloging & Classification Quarterly*, *Journal of Media and Information Sciences*, and *College and Undergraduate Libraries*. She is Book Review Editor for the *OLAC Newsletter*.